# Outcomes-Focused Regulation

Other titles available from Law Society Publishing:

**Alternative Business Structures: The Compliance of Law Firms**
Iain Miller

**Solicitors' Accounts Manual, 12th edn**
Solicitors Regulation Authority

**Solicitors and the Accounts Rules: A Compliance Handbook, 3rd edn**
Peter Camp

**SRA Handbook**
Solicitors Regulation Authority

**The Solicitor's Handbook 2011**
Andrew Hopper QC and Gregory Treverton-Jones QC

Titles from Law Society Publishing can be ordered from all good bookshops or direct (telephone 0870 850 1422, email **lawsociety@prolog.uk.com** or visit our online shop at **www.lawsociety.org.uk/bookshop**).

# OUTCOMES-FOCUSED REGULATION

Andrew Hopper QC and Gregory Treverton-Jones QC

The Law Society

Crown copyright material is reproduced with the permission of the Controller of Her Majesty's Stationery Office

ISBN-13: 978-1-907698-09-5

Published in 2011 by the Law Society
113 Chancery Lane, London WC2A 1PL

Typeset by Columns Design XML Ltd, Reading
Printed by TJ International Ltd, Padstow, Cornwall

The paper used for the text pages of this book is FSC certified. FSC (the Forest Stewardship Council) is an international network to promote responsible management of the world's forests.

MIX
Paper from
responsible sources
FSC      FSC® C013056
www.fsc.org

# Contents

# Foreword

Since at least the thirteenth century, lawyers, in one form or another, have been required to observe a code of professional ethics. The new Code of Conduct is one more link in that chain. In stark contrast to its immediate predecessors, it is not a prescriptive, rule-based Code, but one which is more focused on ethical principles, and their practical application and consequences. Greater weight is placed on the duty of individual solicitors to exercise their judgment, and to put into practice their commitment to professional ethics consistently with the principles articulated in the Code. With that greater weight comes greater responsibility, both on the part of individual solicitors and on the part of the Solicitors Regulation Authority, to ensure that the profession remains one which commands public confidence and carries out the practice of law not just in the consumer interest, but crucially, in the public interest.

The publication of this book will provide invaluable help to every solicitor, and to the Solicitors Regulation Authority, as it will assist them in understanding and implementing the new outcome-focused regulatory regime. It will, I am sure, play a crucial role in ensuring that the new Code of Conduct does not become a mere 'parchment barrier' against improper conduct. On the contrary, this Guide will no doubt help to render the principles which underpin the new Code, and its new regulatory approach, even more familiar to practitioners than was its predecessor, and consequently even more effective.

I commend this book to you.

The Right Honourable Lord Neuberger of Abbotsbury
The Master of the Rolls

# Preface

On 6 October 2011, solicitors and other legal practitioners will wake up to a brand new rule book. The new Code of Conduct will come into force that day, and the short-lived 2007 Code will be consigned to the history books. The new Code is the most visible part of an entirely transformed style of regulation, outcomes-focused regulation, to be adopted by the Solicitors Regulation Authority (SRA). Instead of rules and guidance, solicitors will have to become used to principles, outcomes and indicative behaviours. Indeed, it is the abandonment of written guidance that has prompted us to write this book. Although the reforms are to be welcomed, practitioners will nevertheless need assistance in identifying what changes have been made, and how their own conduct and procedures may have to alter in the light of the new Code. We intend that this book will provide that assistance: we have sought to show how the new Code differs from the old, how solicitors can be confident of complying with it, and how the SRA is likely to alter its own approach to regulating the profession in the light of the reforms.

We are very grateful to Professor Julia Black for her analysis of the history of and philosophy behind outcomes-focused regulation, and to Vanessa Shenton of The Compliance Partner for her substantial contribution to the chapter on future SRA visits to firms and other regulated entities. The responsibility for any errors and omissions is ours alone, and we have stated the law as at 30 April 2011.

Andrew Hopper QC
Gregory Treverton-Jones QC

# Table of cases

# Table of statutes

# Table of statutory instruments

# Abbreviations

| | |
|---|---|
| ABS | alternative business structure |
| CAC | command and control |
| CCBE | Council of the Bars and Law Societies of Europe |
| CFA | conditional fee agreement |
| CLC | Council for Licensed Conveyancers |
| COFA | compliance officer for finance and administration |
| COLP | compliance officer for legal practice |
| FSA | Financial Services Authority |
| HFEA | Human Fertilisation and Embryology Authority |
| HOFA | head of finance and administration |
| HOLP | head of legal practice |
| HSE | Health and Safety Executive |
| LeO | Legal Ombudsman |
| LLP | limited liability partnership |
| LSB | Legal Services Board |
| MDP | multi-disciplinary practice |
| OFR | outcomes-focused regulation |
| PBR | principles-based regulation |
| PSU | Practice Standards Unit |
| RADC | Risk Assessment and Designation Centre |
| RBR | risk-based regulation |
| REL | registered European lawyer |
| RFL | registered foreign lawyer |
| SDT | Solicitors Disciplinary Tribunal |
| SIRC 1990 | Solicitors' Introduction and Referral Code 1990 |
| SRA | Solicitors Regulation Authority |

# CHAPTER 1

# Introduction

Before the creation of the Solicitors Regulation Authority (SRA) as the fully independent regulatory arm of the Law Society in 2007, the regulation of the solicitors' profession had been administered with a comparatively light touch. The Solicitors Complaints Bureau, and its successor the Office for Supervision of Solicitors, trusted the profession to conduct itself to the high ethical standards required of solicitors, and concentrated on protecting the public (and the profession) from those whose conduct fell far below what was required.

Sir David Clementi's report *Review of the Regulatory Framework for Legal Services in England and Wales*, published in December 2004, made clear that in the modern world, where the interests of the customer/consumer had become paramount, the legal profession's representative and regulatory arms had to be separated in order to maintain public confidence. Though remaining part of the Law Society, the SRA achieved independence in 2007 and, perhaps inevitably, it wished to prove that it was truly independent. The light touch was replaced by a heavier hand. The SRA saw itself as a policeman rather than a supervisor. The Law Society's Ethics Helpline, previously renowned as a vital resource for solicitors in doubt as to which course of action to take, became less helpful. In February 2007, the SRA's Referral Arrangements Compliance Project was launched with a warning to all solicitors that the SRA was 'cracking down on solicitors'.

The mighty Solicitors' Code of Conduct 2007 (which throughout we will refer to as the 2007 Code) made its bow on 1 July 2007. Running to well over 200 pages, it represented an attempt to set out a prescriptive set of rules for solicitors that would tell them the answer to every regulatory problem. It replaced a series of Solicitors' Practice Rules which had steadily grown in size over the years. The dangers of creating such an all-encompassing Code rapidly became apparent: precisely one month after it came into force, and after the printed version of it had gone on sale to the profession, the Code was amended because the regulations concerning the provision of home information packs had come into force, making it necessary to change rule 18 to record the additional obligations that those regulations imposed.

The 2007 Code was not successful. It was too long, too detailed, and too prescriptive. Because of its all-encompassing nature, the Code and the guidance associated with each rule had to be amended regularly, which caused problems for solicitors who found it difficult to pinpoint what rule or guidance was in force at a given time. This was accompanied by an approach to regulation by the SRA which appeared to concentrate on minutiae – for example, precisely what needed to be said to clients about referral arrangements, and when it had to be said, about which it was not difficult to make mistakes, even when solicitors were doing what they thought was entirely proper.

The passing of the Legal Services Act 2007, the inevitable need to create a regulatory environment which would work for both traditional law firms and alternative business structures (ABSs) and strong guidance from the Legal Services Board, created the need to move to a different basis and style of regulation. Principles-based regulation had been pioneered by the financial services industry. Instead of professionals being bound, and often hamstrung, by a prescriptive set of rules, the onus shifts to the regulated individual or entity to deliver satisfactory outcomes for consumers, based upon an over-arching set of ethical principles. Thus, more than 200 pages of rules are reduced to little more than 50, and the regulated individual, the solicitor, is trusted to think for himself in order to achieve satisfactory outcomes for clients.

## 1.1 A CHANGE OF CULTURE

It is a well-recognised fact in the solicitors' profession that the relationship between the regulator and the regulated has soured in recent years. Among the causes of this is the perception among many solicitors who have found themselves on the SRA's radar, that the regulator has been unsympathetic to the realities and pressures of everyday practice as a solicitor. They found that it was often very difficult to have a constructive dialogue with the SRA, by which regulatory shortcomings could be discussed and corrected, without the need for formal disciplinary action.

If outcomes-focused regulation (OFR) is to be successful, this perception will have to change, and the relationship between the regulator and those it regulates will have to improve. As we wrote at p.32 of the *Solicitor's Handbook 2011*, OFR:

> ... is designed to move away, both in the form of rules and the way in which they are policed, from the tick-box, strict liability, 'every breach is a breach' approach ... which has seriously damaged the relationship between the profession and the regulator. The problem with that approach has been that it has been too easy to hit the wrong target: the solicitor trying to get it right but making mistakes, as opposed to the one who does not care, or deliberately breaks the rules.
>
> In an open and healthy manner the SRA has announced that [in 'Freedom in Practice: Better outcomes for consumers: A passport to regulatory reform']:
>
> 'We know that the current rule book is too prescriptive. OFR will give firms the flexibility to do new and better things for consumers. It will lead to a more grown-up relationship between the SRA and the regulated community.'
>
> and:

'The introduction of OFR will give a simplified rulebook and freedom to practise innovatively, which will be good for consumers and providers of legal services alike. OFR is risk-based regulation; firms will have to comply with broad principles rather than detailed rules. Firms will be able to comply with the principles in the ways which best suit their businesses. Formal rules will still apply in important areas including accounts and indemnity, where they are necessary. …

The SRA's enforcement of OFR will be effective, fair and proportionate. We will focus on the things which really matter to consumers; for example risks which may lead to a loss of their money, justice, or social or economic wellbeing.'

This is profoundly welcome as it turns the clock back to a time when the consequence of something going wrong – whether there was in fact any mischief or prejudice caused, as opposed to being a 'bare breach' – was an important if not determinative factor in how the regulator treated the solicitor concerned.

## 1.2 THE PRINCIPAL CHANGES

The new Code is built around 10 core Principles – four more than the core duties set out in rule 1 of the 2007 Code. It is divided into five sections comprising 15 chapters in all:

- 1st Section – You and your client (Chapters 1 to 6) contains client care, equality and diversity, conflicts, confidentiality and disclosure, the client and the court, and introductions of clients to third parties.
- 2nd Section – You and your business (Chapters 7 to 9) contains business management, publicity, and fee sharing and referrals.
- 3rd Section – You and your regulator (Chapter 10) covers co-operation with regulators and ombudsmen.
- 4th Section – You and others (Chapters 11 and 12) covers relations with third parties and separate businesses.
- 5th Section – Application, waivers and interpretation (Chapters 13 to 15) deals with the application of the rules, waivers, interpretation, commencement and repeals.

Each chapter contains mandatory 'outcomes' rather than prescriptive rules, and non-mandatory 'indicative behaviours', which are both positive (consistent with compliance) and negative (indicative of non-compliance). There are some, very limited, notes and no published guidance at all. This is a deliberate policy by the SRA: there is always a danger that non-mandatory guidance becomes seen as a rule, and that the solicitor stops thinking for himself or herself.

As for the detail in the first 12 chapters of the new Code, in the broadest terms, and except in two important respects (acting for buyer and seller in conveyancing transactions and a change in focus in the regulatory approach to business management) and several less crucial respects, solicitors who were compliant with the 2007 Code will be compliant with the new Code. The introduction of the new Code is designed to make compliance more, rather than less, straightforward. However, there are significant changes. These are set out and explained in the pages that follow, and can be summarised thus:

- Chapter 1 – Client care

  - There is no longer any reference to contingency fees, and rule 9.01(4) of the 2007 Code, which outlawed arrangements with introducers in personal injury cases who charged contingency fees has been removed (see **5.2.1** and **5.2.5**).
  - There are new requirements concerning information to clients about complaints procedures (see **5.2.1**).
  - The rule on solicitors receiving commissions has been simplified, although as we explain, the illogicality of the old rules has not been removed (see **5.2.1** and **5.2.6**). The £20 *de minimis* exception to the general rule about accounting to clients for commissions has been abolished.

- Chapter 2 – Equality and diversity

  - There is a new emphasis upon 'encouraging' equality of opportunity and respect for diversity (see **5.3**).

- Chapter 3 – Conflicts of interests

  - Although it is not specifically stated in any of the outcomes, the SRA now takes the view that the circumstances in which there is no conflict of interest nor a significant risk of such a conflict between buyer and seller in conveyancing transactions are extremely limited, and it will become the exception, and not the rule, for solicitors to act for both parties in such transactions (see **5.4**).

- Chapter 4 – Confidentiality and disclosure

  - For the first time, there is specific reference to the importance of the protection of confidentiality by those to whom solicitors outsource work (see **5.5**).
  - The rules and guidance relevant to information barriers have been simplified (see **5.5.3**).

- Chapter 5 – Your client and the court

  - Little change but some alteration in phraseology which is helpful.

- Chapter 6 – Your client and introductions to third parties

  - The referral provisions in Chapter 6 now apply to referrals between lawyers; previously, such referrals were exempted from the rules (see **5.7.4**).

- Chapter 7 – Management of your business

  - There is a substantial shift in emphasis in terms of the management of risk.

Firms are required to identify, monitor and manage 'risks to compliance' and to take steps to address issues identified, and also to monitor risks to financial stability (see **5.8** and **5.8.3**).

- A standard question in future might be: 'What are the major risks to compliance and the financial viability of your firm that you have identified, and what steps have you taken to address them?'
- Outsourcing has now become a specific regulatory issue (**5.8.4**).

- Chapter 8 – Publicity

  - Letterheads must be changed again; the new requirement is that it should be announced that firms are: 'Authorised and regulated by the Solicitors Regulation Authority'.
  - There are some new provisions appropriate for ABSs providing both regulated and unregulated services (see **5.9.3**).

- Chapter 9 – Fee sharing and referrals

  - Much of the information that had to be provided to clients no longer has to be so provided, and the prescriptive set of rules in rule 9 of the 2007 Code is much simplified and reduced (see **5.10.4**).
  - Rule 9.01(4) of the 2007 Code, which outlawed arrangements with introducers in personal injury cases who charged contingency fees, has been swept away (see **5.10.4**).
  - The rule against fee sharing has been abolished (see **5.10.5**).
  - As noted above, the new Code applies to referrals between lawyers.

- Chapter 10 – You and your regulator

  - There is now an unambiguous duty on a solicitor to self-report to the SRA where he or she has committed serious misconduct (see **5.11.4**).

- Chapter 11 – Relations with third parties

  - The rules concerning undertakings and multiple buyers have been simplified and reduced (see **5.12.4**).

- Chapter 12 – Separate businesses

  - There is simplification and reduction of the safeguards that had to be in place under the 2007 Code for solicitors undertaking a separate business (see **5.13.4**).

## 1.3  AN EXPLANATORY NOTE

The new Principles and Code apply, as did their predecessors, to every person and body regulated by the SRA: solicitors of course, but also registered European lawyers (RELs), registered foreign lawyers (RFLs), the business entities them-selves, partnerships, limited liability partnerships (LLPs), limited liability com-panies, recognised sole practitioners, legal disciplinary practices, ABSs and ABSs in the form of multi-disciplinary practices, and everyone employed by a regulated entity. In this book, for simplicity we will generally refer to 'solicitors', 'practition-ers' and 'firms', but the reach of regulation should not be overlooked.

As well as dealing with the Principles and Code, we will point to the other major changes for which the profession must prepare by virtue of the SRA Authorisation Rules, and will provide a comprehensive list of the various obligations to report and provide information to the SRA, many of which are new.

# CHAPTER 2

# OFR: the historical context

*Professor Julia Black*

## 2.1 WHAT IS IT, WHERE DID IT COME FROM, AND DO WE NEED IT?

To a newcomer to regulation debates, the language of regulators can be bewildering, serving more to confuse than to clarify. Not only do regulators (and governments) talk about 'better' regulation, or more recently 'smart' regulation, regulation can come in many different guises. Regulation, it seems, can be 'outcomes focused', 'principles based', 'risk based', 'evidence based': the list goes on.

Furthermore, rather than getting on with the job, regulators seemed to be trapped in a quasi-existential crisis, worrying about what their 'approach' or 'philosophy' should be. Surely regulation is quite straightforward? Write a rule, make sure people are complying with it, and if they are not, punish them. To an extent, that is what regulation entails. Unfortunately, actually 'doing' regulation can be harder than it seems. Some firms may be willing to comply, others will quietly ignore a rule or escape through loopholes if they disagree with it or it impedes their ability to make a profit. Some (be they large or small) may be well organised and have systems and frameworks in place to ensure compliance, others may have spent less time and resources on the matter, or have less to spend. Regulators may in some cases be able to identify what conduct should be prohibited, but the range of possible circumstances in which a rule will apply is usually so great that they cannot specify in advance exactly what conduct is necessary in every case.

Moreover, when regulators are charged with managing risks (including risks of non-compliance), they have to decide in particular instances whether they prefer to err on the side of assuming something is safe when it is risky (the 'light touch' approach which runs the risk of criticism that they failed in their duties when risks crystallise), or whether they prefer to err on the side of assuming something is risky when it is safe (in which case they are likely to be accused of 'over-regulation' when risks don't materialise).

Further, regulators are usually operating in a complex institutional framework, where they may be reliant on others to set their rules, budgets and personnel policies, and in some cases to perform inspections for them. Finally, they are often operating in a political context which is demanding but fickle, and in which there are tensions and contradictions in the demands made of regulators by firms, consumers and politicians. Whilst government expands regulatory remits, it also requires regulators to 'reduce burdens on business'. Complaints about 'regulatory creep', the 'nanny state' or 'health and safety gone mad' sit alongside criticisms that regulators 'were asleep on the job' and demands that 'something must be done' whenever accidents or losses occur.

So should we feel sorry for the regulators? Not necessarily – no one is forced to be a regulator, after all. This is not an apology for regulators, it is rather to provide some indication of the context in which regulators operate, and why they embark on what, to outsiders, may seem to be odd and largely pointless debates about 'approach' or 'philosophy'. The reasons they do engage in these debates, however, come partly from the edicts of central government or other overseers, or their governing statutes, that demand it of them, partly from a desire to be at the forefront of whatever form the 'better regulation' movement is currently advocating, and partly from a genuine desire to do a better job, often with less resources.

The aim of this chapter is to try to shed some light on some of the most recent trends in regulatory approach, notably outcomes-focused regulation (OFR), and its close cousins, principles-based regulation (PBR) and risk-based regulation (RBR). It will set these in a broader historical and academic context, and provide examples of other regulators which have also adopted these approaches, often quite recently. It has to be remembered, however, that these terms are terms of art, not science. What lies under the labels is an agglomeration of regulatory styles and approaches, some of which are exhibited by some regulators, but not all of which are exhibited by all. What follows is therefore a rough guide to a roughly drawn regulatory world and how it has evolved.

## 2.2 A BRIEF GUIDE TO THE EVOLUTION OF 'PHILOSOPHIES' OF REGULATION

The trends are depicted here in overly generalised terms, but broadly the evolution of regulatory philosophy, in the UK and many other OECD countries, has been thus. Initially, almost all regulation took the 'command and control' (CAC) model of laws backed by criminal sanctions imposed by the courts. In the UK, the Health and Safety Executive (HSE) was a notable exception, as it introduced the notion of 'enforced self-regulation' of firms, an invention of Robens which was decades ahead of its time.[1] Firms were charged with developing their own plans for achieving health and safety in the workplace, which were then approved by the HSE.

The 1980s saw the advent of privatisation accompanied by economic regulation, which opened up debate on whether the way regulation was conducted in other sectors could also adopt a more market-based form. Through the 1990s–2000s there has been increasing political and academic discussion of the limits of CAC regulation, and governmental and academic publications appeared both in the UK

---

[1] A previous version of these Rules (the Qualified Lawyers Transfer Regulations 2009) remain in force and will form part of the Handbook.

and overseas on 'alternatives to regulation', such as self-regulation and 'co-regulation'. Ofcom, for example, was a great proponent of co-regulation, outsourcing some of its functions to the Advertising Standards Agency.[2] In financial services, 'co-regulation' was attempted in the model of the Securities and Investments Board's supervision of approved self-regulatory organisations, though from its inception and through the 1990s that model was certainly creaking.[3] Notwithstanding its faults, it was that model which formed the basis of Clementi's recommendations[4] and for the system of regulation introduced for legal services under the Legal Services Act 2007.

Also throughout the 1990s–2000s, the 'de-regulation' rhetoric of the 1980s moved to the rhetoric of 'better regulation'. It is through the 'better regulation' agenda that we have seen a marked re-centring of government control over regulatory bodies. After the dispersal of regulatory functions out to the independent regulatory agencies, and the increasing political salience of regulation, central government realised it wanted to exercise control over the manner in which regulators regulated; not over the substance necessarily, though that has also happened, but over how they went about their task.

So we began to see the introduction of principles of 'good' or 'better' regulation emanating from central government. This phenomenon was not confined just to the UK. Australia, Canada and the USA all saw central governments seeking to exert greater control. On a transnational level, the OECD issued its initial principles of good regulation in 1995, updating them a decade later.[5] In the UK, the 'PACTT' principles of proportionality, accountability, consistency, transparency and targeting were adopted in 1998 by central government's then Better Regulation Unit as exhortations for regulators to follow.[6] They are now enshrined in the statutory mandates of many modern regulatory bodies, including the Legal Services Board, as principles to which they have to have regard.[7] This is part of a broader trend to give legal force to principles of better regulation (and, incidentally to provide potential statutory grounds for judicial review), manifested both in the individual statutes creating regulators and in cross-cutting regulatory instruments such as the Compliance Code, introduced under the Legislative and Regulatory Reform Act 2006.

The 'better regulation' model has evolved to contain a number of more specific components. At first it was associated with the use of cost benefit analysis and

---

[2]   A previous version of these Rules (the Higher Courts Qualification Regulations 2000) remain in force and will form part of the Handbook.

[3]   Published on SRA website as a draft – correct at 19 August 2011.

[4]   Standard mortgage definition- a mortgage which is provided in the normal course of the lender's activities which forms a significant part of the lender's activities and the mortgage is on standard terms

[5]   Individual mortgage definition-any other mortgage

[6]   Report of the Robens Committee on Safety and Health at Work, Cmnd 5034 (HMSO, 1972).

[7]   Ofcom, *Identifying Appropriate Regulatory Solutions: Principles for Analysing Self- and Co-regulation – Statement* (December 2010).

regulatory impact assessment.[8] These have now become central to all 'better regulation' agendas in those countries that have one and have been adopted by the EU Commission.[9] In addition, within the UK, independent regulators have been required since 2007 to implement RBR, under the statutory Compliance Code noted above. From the early 2000s, a small group of regulators had been independently developing RBR, but the movement was given considerable impetus by the Hampton Review of Inspection and Enforcement which led to the Code.[10] RBR is now used in a number of regulators in the UK, including the Food Standards Authority, the Environment Agency, the Financial Services Authority (FSA), the Pensions Regulator and the HSE, and by a number of their counterparts in the US, Australia, Canada and elsewhere.[11] In legal services, regulators in New South Wales and Victoria in Australia have recently moved to adopting a risk-based approach.[12]

That brings us to PBR, and in turn to outcomes-based or outcomes-focused regulation (OFR). Of the various regulatory approaches, PBR has played the strongest role in political rhetoric, particularly in the context of financial regulation. Before the global financial crisis, PBR was seen as the solution that firms and regulators were looking for to deliver an effective and responsive regulatory regime and was feted by politicians as one of the reasons for London's attractiveness as a financial centre. Post-crisis, PBR is seen as being the source of the problem: light touch regulation that placed too much reliance on firms themselves to behave responsibly. PBR is a multi-faceted strategy which was always more complex than being 'light touch' regulation. But PBR was oversold by the government as 'light touch', and the FSA itself arguably 'over-bought' into this interpretation of the notion, at least in its regulation of the wholesale markets. Unfortunately, the FSA invested so much reputational capital in PBR, particularly from 2006–7, that after the financial crisis it had no choice but to withdraw the brand from the market and to re-launch a different regulatory model under a different strapline: 'outcomes-based regulation'.

The FSA was not the only regulator adopting a principles-based or outcomes-focused approach, however. Regulators as diverse as the Human Fertilisation and Embryology Authority (HFEA), the Financial Reporting Council, the Tenant Services Authority, the Local Better Regulation Office and the Care Quality Commission have all moved recently to adopt such approaches, albeit in slightly

---

[8]  For a contemporaneous assessment see A. Large, *Financial Services Regulation: Making the Two Tier System Work* (Securities and Investments Board, 1993).

[9]  D. Clementi, *Review of the Regulatory Framework for Legal Services in England and Wales* (December 2004).

[10]  OECD, *Recommendation on Improving the Quality of Government Regulation* (Paris, 1995); and OECD, *Guiding Principles for Regulatory Quality and Performance* (Paris, 2005). At the EU level, the Mandelkern report articulated its own set of principles: necessity, proportionality, subsidiarity, transparency, accountability, accessibility and simplicity: Mandelkern Group, *Better Regulation Final Report* (Brussels, 2001).

[11]  Better Regulation Task Force, *Principles of Better Regulation* (London, 1998).

[12]  Legal Services Act 2007, s.28.

different ways.[13] More pertinently for lawyers, the Legal Services Board has issued Guidance requiring all approved regulators to adopt an approach which is outcomes focused and principles based. But just what is PBR, what is its relationship to RBR, and how do they in turn relate to OFR? It is to these questions that we now turn.

## 2.3   WHAT IS PRINCIPLES-BASED REGULATION?

Briefly, PBR can take one or both of two forms: rule book PBR, which is how the rules in a rule book or code of conduct are written, and operational PBR, which is how the regulator performs its regulatory tasks. Odd though it might seem, one can have one without the other. Normally, the principles are addressed to firms or individuals who are being directly regulated. However, where there are a number of different regulators involved, principles can be addressed to other regulators within the regime in an attempt to set standards for regulation and to manage the regime.

### 2.3.1   Rule book PBR

Rule book PBR involves formulating rules which are broad, general and purposive, i.e. principles, for example, 'you shall act with integrity', or 'firms shall act in the best interests of their clients'. These are in contrast to 'bright line rules', which contain specific, often quantitative provisions, and detailed, often prescriptive rules, which contain a number of preconditions or exceptions.[14]

Thus a rule focused on how people drive could be expressed as a principle: 'you must drive safely'. Or it can be expressed as a bright line rule: 'you shall drive at 30 miles per hour'. Or it can be expressed as a detailed rule: 'you must drive at the following speeds in the following circumstances: (a) 30 miles per hour in built-up areas [separately defined] except in the following circumstances where you must drive at 20 miles per hour: outside schools or hospitals, when the road is wet, when the road is less than $x$ metres in width; (b) 40 miles per hour where . . .' and so on.

How the rule is expressed makes a difference to how it is understood and applied, and as to whether it achieves its purpose. Generally, those subject to a rule want three things from it: to be straightforward to apply, to be certain and to achieve its purpose (be congruent with its objective). From the regulator's point of view, a fourth aim of the way a rule is expressed is to reduce the scope for 'gaming' the rule, in other words, the scope for complying with its letter but not its spirit. Unfortunately, no one type of rule can achieve all four aims, as the table below illustrates.

---

[13]   For discussion see C. Radaelli, 'Diffusion without convergence: how political context shapes the adoption of regulatory impact assessment' (2005) 12(5) *Journal of European Public Policy* 924–43.

[14]   In the EU context see Mandelkern Group, *Better Regulation Final Report* (Brussels, 2001); EU Commission, *European Governance – White Paper* COM/2001/0428 final (Brussels, 2001).

**Table 2.1** Trade-offs in using rules

| Rule type | Ease of application | Congruence | Certainty | Scope for gaming |
|---|---|---|---|---|
| *Principle: 'drive safely'* | Depends | High | Depends | Low |
| *Bright line rule: 'drive at 30 mph'* | High | Low | High | High |
| *Complex and detailed rule: 'drive at the following speeds in the following circumstances'* | Medium/Low | Medium/Low | Medium/Low | Medium/High |

Bright line rules, such as speed limits, are easy to apply and clear, but they can be over-inclusive (apply in circumstances where they are not necessary) or under-inclusive (not apply where they are necessary). Driving at 30 mph may be unnecessarily slow to achieve the goal of safe driving in some circumstances, but too fast to be safe in others. They are also easy to 'game'. Under the capital rules for banks, for example, loans to related companies had to be reported if they were for a term of more than a year, therefore many banks issued rolling 364 day loans.

Detailed, complex rules, subject to their drafting, can be reasonably easy to apply and reasonably clear, and in their fine tuning they can try to achieve the purpose of the rule. But all too often, the level of detail is such that they become difficult to apply, and consequently lack certainty. Contrary to lawyers' dearly held beliefs, there is not necessarily a correlation between precision and certainty, or at least not after a certain point. The more precise the rules, the more complex they become. Moreover, the greater the number of 'gaps' that are created, the greater the potential for internal inconsistencies in their application, and the more uncertain their application becomes in any particular circumstance. They can also fail to achieve their purpose, either because they have become outdated or do not deal adequately with particular situations, or because they are 'gamed' around.

Principles, on the other hand, are highly congruent with their purpose and provide almost no scope for gaming. However, the most contested elements of principles, their ease of application and the degree to which principles are clear or opaque cannot be read off the face of the principle. Certainty comes not from the structure of the rule or principle *per se*, but from the interpretation it receives. Whether a rule, principle, or any written norm is certain depends on the extent to which there is a shared understanding as to their meaning and application within and between the regulator, regulated and the final interpretive authority, i.e. any organisation (regulatory decisions committee, court or tribunal) called upon to make a determination.[15]

Developing that shared understanding can be facilitated in a number of ways, and by a number of different actors. It can be facilitated by the regulator or others supplementing the principle with further rules or guidance. Such guidance can take many forms. It may create 'safe harbours' or can be merely indicative and non-binding. It can be produced by regulators or other rule intermediaries such as trade associations and professional bodies. In some cases, the regulator may encourage or be involved in the formation of that guidance or indeed may endorse it; in others, guidance may be developed quite separately from the regulator.

There are several advantages to using principles. For the regulated, PBR can provide flexibility and facilitate innovation, and so enhance competitiveness. For the regulators, PBR can provide flexibility, facilitate regulatory innovation in the methods of supervision adopted, and enable the regulatory regime to have some durability in a rapidly changing market environment. Other stakeholders, such as consumers, can benefit from the improved conduct of firms as they focus more on improving substantive compliance and achieving outcomes and less on simply following procedures (box ticking) or on working out how to avoid the rule in substance whilst complying with its form (gaming the rule or 'creative compliance').

However, in practice, very few regulators rely on principles alone. Most supplement principles with guidance or more detailed rules. Such a strategy is supported in academic literature which has explored the issue of rules and their interpretation. The presence of such fundamental trade-offs in using rules means that the optimal strategy is to have a tiered rule structure, with principles supported in particular instances by detailed rules or guidance.[16] Furthermore, regulators may be implementing rules from a number of sources in their rules or codes of conduct. Rules may derive, for example, from EU directives, national legislation, regulators' own codes or professional bodies' rules. Some regulators, such as the FSA and the HFEA, annotate their rule books by using symbols to denote the different source and status of individual provisions.[17]

Nonetheless, simply in terms of defining PBR as rule book PBR, we can say that a regulatory regime is principle based if it contains norms which use broad, general and often evaluative terms (e.g. fair, reasonable, best interests) and which express the purpose of the rule, and which may or may not be elaborated in further rules or guidance. However, the principle forms the 'backstop' to those more detailed provisions, and acts as a guide to their interpretation and application in particular instances.

---

[15] P. Hampton, *Reducing Administrative Burdens* (London, 2005).

[16] For review see J. Black, 'Risk-based regulation: choices, practices and lessons being learned' in OECD, *Risk and Regulatory Policy* (Paris, 2010); J. Black, 'The emergence of risk-based regulation and the new public risk management in the United Kingdom' [2005] *Public Law* 512.

[17] Office of Legal Services Commissioner of New South Wales, *Annual Report 2009-10* (New South Wales, 2010); Legal Services Board of Victoria, *Annual Report 2009-10* (Victoria, 2010).

## 2.3.2 Rule book PBR and OFR

OFR can be a natural concomitant to PBR. Principles express the purpose of the rule, and either in themselves express the outcomes to be achieved or can be easily related to particular types of outcomes. For many regulators, PBR and OFR go together and, rhetoric aside, can be largely interchangeable. The FSA sees OFR as one part of its overall approach, together with PBR. Outcomes can be achieved by compliance with principles.[18] The Council for Licensed Conveyancers, for example, argues that OFR and PBR together mean that 'legal services providers must be encouraged to focus upon the positive outcomes they can generate for consumers of those services. Outcomes will be delivered by acting in accordance with high-level principles – these require you to act in a principled, professional manner – rather than concentrating on complying with prescriptive rules.'[19]

Others eschew the language of PBR, but in practice the differences can be slight. OFR can also be expressed in a tiered approach to rules, or more broadly, regulatory requirements. The Financial Reporting Council, for example, has articulated six high-level strategic outcomes, which are further specified in 'supporting outcomes', which in turn are supported by a series of 'major components'.[20] In each case, a series of increasingly specified outcomes and means to achieving those outcomes flows from the broader, strategic outcome. For other regulators such as the HFEA or the FSA, more detailed requirements need not flow from just one principle but can be linked to two or three principles. Rule books can be designed in different ways. But in rule book PBR, principles or outcomes play a key role in how regulatory requirements are articulated and interpreted.

---

[18]  Financial Reporting Council, *Strategic Framework* (London, 2007); Tenant Services Authority, *The Regulatory Framework for Social Housing from April 2010* (London, 2010); Local Better Regulation Office, *Priority Regulatory Outcomes: A New Approach to Refreshing the National Enforcement Priorities for Local Authority Regulatory Services* (Birmingham, 2011); Care Quality Commission, *CQC Strategy 2010–2015* (London, 2010).

[19]  There is a considerable academic literature on the different types of rules and their implications. See F. Schauer, 'The tyranny of choice and the rulification of standards' (2005) 14 *Journal of Contemporary Legal Issues* 803; R. Korobkin, 'Behavioural analysis and legal form: rules vs. principles revisited' (2000) 79 *Oregon Law Review* 23; F. Schauer, 'The convergence of rules and standards' [2003] *New Zealand Law Review* 303; R. Baldwin, 'Why rules don't work' (1990) 53 *Modern Law Review* 321; J. Black, *Rules and Regulators* (OUP, 1997); J. Braithwaite, 'A theory of legal certainty' (2002) 27 *Australian Journal of Legal Philosophy* 38; J. Black, M. Hopper, and C. Band, 'Making a success of principles based regulation' (2007) 1(3) *Law and Financial Markets Review* 191; J. Black, 'Forms and paradoxes of principles based regulation' (2008) 3(4) *Capital Markets Law Journal* 425; R. Baldwin, *Rules and Government* (Clarendon Press, 1995); C.S. Diver, 'Regulatory precision', in K. Hawkins and J.M. Thomas (eds), *Making Regulatory Policy* (Pittsburgh, 1989); C.S. Diver, 'The optimal precision of administrative rules' (1983) 93 *Yale Law Journal* 65; C. Ford, 'New governance, compliance and principles-based securities regulation' (2008) 45(1) *American Business Law Journal* 1. Regulators also stress these points. See for example FSA, *Principles-based Regulation: Focusing on the Outcomes that Matter* (April 2007), p.6; Council for Licensed Conveyancers, *Draft CLC Code of Conduct Consultation Paper* (July 2010), p.4.

[20]  J. Black, 'Talking about regulation' [1998] *Public Law* 77.

### 2.3.3 Operational PBR

In operational or substantive PBR, regulators adopt particular approaches to regulation. In debates on rules-based versus principle-based regimes, the focus is often on these substantive aspects, even if only implicitly, as each type of rule is asserted to be associated with particular forms of regulatory practice. However, it is important to note that regulatory practices can be quite divorced from the nature of the rules being implemented. Operational PBR can be achieved through the flexible implementation and enforcement of a highly detailed set of rules. Conversely, rule book PBR may in practice end up as no better than detailed box ticking if the principles are given particularly 'hard edges' in the way they are interpreted by regulators or courts, or are coupled with a highly deterrence-based and unpredictable enforcement regime which prompts very conservative behaviour by firms.

Given the variety of regimes that are styled, or style themselves, as PBR regimes, this discussion creates an 'ideal type' in the Weberian sense, i.e. a set of generalised abstractions about a social practice. The construction of an ideal type necessarily means that some regimes will accord more strongly with certain features than others. However, operational PBR has at least one of the following five characteristics.

First, interpretation and application of the rules involves considerable discussion and negotiation within the firm and between the firm and the regulator. In practice, others can play a key role in these conversations, in particular consultants and other external advisers, perhaps even consumers. In these conversations, it is not the case that any interpretation that the parties can agree upon will suffice; the interpretation is always structured by the goal the principle is trying to achieve or the value that it is expressing: to act fairly, or with integrity, or with due care and diligence, for example. Disputes over the application of principles are thus resolved not through detailed linguistic (legal) interpretive approaches but through purposive interpretations and consequentialist reasoning.

A second characteristic of substantive PBR is a focus on outcomes throughout the whole regulatory process. There is no analytical correlation between using rules of a particular type (principles) and OFR, however. Targets are outcomes, and they can be extremely precisely defined, and as such be as open to gaming and 'creative compliance' as detailed rules. Studies of how hospitals and other public service providers 'game' the performance targets set for them by central government illustrate this very clearly.[21] However, in operational PBR, outcomes are defined in qualitative and/or behavioural terms, for example, to act 'with integrity', 'fairly', 'in the best interests of the client'.[22] As noted above, it is hard to game purposive provisions of this nature.

---

[21] J. Black, 'Using rules effectively' in C. McCrudden (ed), *Regulation and De-regulation* (Oxford University Press, 1999), p.95; J. Braithwaite, 'A theory of legal certainty' (2002) 27 *Australian Journal of Legal Philosophy* 47.

[22] *FSA Handbook* (FSA, 2011); HFEA, *Code of Practice*, 8th edition (London, 2010).

A third characteristic of operational PBR is that the responsibility for ensuring that the objectives of the principles are met is shifted, in part, from the regulator to the regulated. More general rules (principles) allow firms greater discretion as to what to do. With that discretion comes the need, and responsibility, for working out what they should do. Where the balance should be struck between firms thinking for themselves and the regulators providing guidance is endlessly contested; each thinks the other should be doing more. Firms want more specific guidance; regulators think firms should work it out for themselves. Firms do not want to do the regulators' job for them; regulators do not want to become unpaid consultants. This tension in their relationship, as to what the regulatory compact entails, is not unique to PBR regimes. Regulators implementing detailed rules face the same tension, as the National Audit Office's review of the five largest regulators in the UK confirms.[23] But PBR involves a significant shift in responsibility to firms, and requires a substantially different set of skills on the part of inspectors and compliance staff to engage in the negotiations and qualitative judgements that are entailed.

A fourth characteristic of operational PBR is a conscious and deliberate focus by the regulator on the firms' internal systems of management and controls.[24] Given that any regulatory regime requires firms to internalise the regulatory requirements into their own systems and processes for it to be complied with, this could be argued to be not so much a radical new strategy of regulation but as regulators making a virtue out of a necessity, or at least recognising that necessity. In management-based or meta-regulatory regimes, the regulator focuses its attention on ensuring that the firms' own internal rules, systems and processes are such that they will ensure compliance. As Power comments, internal management systems become the critical interface between regulatory and business values, and hence between society's and the organisation's goals and operations.[25] Again the emphasis is on substance not form. Regulators and firms should be focused on the outcomes those systems and processes deliver, not just on the form they take.

Finally, and this is not so much a characteristic as a requirement of successful PBR, regulators need to be clear about the circumstances in which they will enforce regulation. Under PBR, firms are required to think through the application of the provisions to particular situations to a far greater degree than they are with respect to a detailed rule. There is thus a greater exposure to interpretative risk – the risk that they will make the wrong assessment. A wrong assessment is here simply judged in pragmatic terms: it is one with which the ultimate arbiter of interpretation (regulator, tribunal or court) does not agree.[26] Those subject to the principles (or rules) will seek to minimise this risk by calling for greater clarification or even prescription from the regulator. In the absence of that clarification, the enforcement approach is

---

[23] FSA, *Principles-based Regulation: Focusing on the Outcomes that Matter* (April, 2007).

[24] Council for Licensed Conveyancers, *Draft CLC Code of Conduct Consultation Paper* (July 2010), p.4.

[25] Financial Reporting Council, *Strategic Framework* (London, 2007).

[26] C. Hood, 'Gaming in targetworld: the targets approach to managing British public services' (2006) 66(4) *Public Administration Review* 515.

critical. Regulators can manage firms' interpretive risk in two ways: by minimising its probability through issuing guidance or other aides to interpretation, or by minimising its impact through its enforcement approach or, for example, through due diligence defences. In a regime with a tough, punitive approach in which every minor infraction is met with a sanction, PBR will not survive. It will transform into a system of detailed requirements, as that is what firms will need. They will demand rules to provide them and the regulator with clear boundaries. In order to maintain the central role of principles in a PBR regime, enforcement therefore has to be responsive to the firm's own attitude and behaviour.

PBR is thus more than just a reframing of the rule books; it is a reframing of the regulator's relationship with those it is regulating. For that reframing to work, there needs to be trust on both sides. PBR cannot create that trust, however; it has to be forged in other ways.

### 2.3.4 Risk-based regulation

Both PBR and OFR can be linked in practice to RBR. RBR is another newcomer to the regulatory lexicon. It means that regulators will focus their inspection, and often their enforcement, resources on those activities which pose the greatest risks to their statutory objectives or other key aims that they have identified. As such, the approach is predicated on outcomes and thus has a natural affinity with OFR: where conduct breaches a rule but does not have a substantive impact on, for example, consumer protection, the regulator will not act, or at least will not treat the issue as a matter of priority.

As noted above, RBR has been adopted by a wide range of regulators in a number of countries, and the number is increasing. The reasons for its adoption vary but include the need to develop a systematic and defensible framework for allocating scarce resources, a desire to improve the targeting and effectiveness of regulation, a wish to introduce a system of internal management and control, and a way to create a common language and understanding across the regulatory organisation about risk and the relative importance of different aspects of the regulator's remit and activities in achieving its overall objectives.[27]

The frameworks vary considerably in their complexity. However, all have a common starting point, which is a focus on risks not rules. Risk-based frameworks require regulators to begin by identifying the risks that they are seeking to manage, not the rules they have to enforce. Regulators are usually over-burdened by rules. They cannot enforce every one of these rules in every firm at every point in time. Selections therefore have to be made. These selections have always been made, but risk-based frameworks both render the fact of selection explicit and provide a framework of analysis in which selections can be made.

---

[27] Outcomes are usually distinguished from outputs in performance evaluations: outputs are easier to game than outcomes.

Although the frameworks themselves very considerably, they share six common core elements. First, they require a determination by the organisation of its objectives, or framed differently, the outcomes it wishes to achieve. These are the risks that a risk-based regulator is concerned to address.

Second, they require a determination of the regulator's own risk appetite – what type of risks is it prepared to tolerate and at what level. This can be an extremely challenging task for a regulator. In practice, a regulator's risk tolerance is often ultimately driven by political considerations. All regulators face political risk, the risk that what they consider to be an acceptable level of risk will be higher than that tolerated by politicians, the media and the public, and that the uncertainties that they face will be unrecognised and/or will not be tolerated. However, the political context is often fickle, as noted above, and in practice regulators can find that it is politicians, not themselves, who set their risk tolerances for them.

Third, risk-based frameworks involve an assessment of the hazard or adverse event and the likelihood of it occurring. Terminology varies: food and environmental regulators tend to talk in terms of hazards and risks; financial regulators talk in terms of impact and probability. But in general, two broad categories of risk are identified: the *inherent risks* arising from the nature of the business's activities and in environmental regulation, its location; and *management and control risks*, including compliance record. The methods by which management and control risks are combined with or offset against inherent risk scores vary but, broadly speaking, the regulators are concerned with the effect of management and controls in either exacerbating the inherent risk or mitigating it.

Risk assessments may be highly quantitative (as in environmental regulation) or mainly qualitative (as in food safety regulation in the UK, or financial supervision more generally). Quantitative assessments involve less individual judgement and in environmental regulation are often performed by the firm itself or can be contracted out by the regulator to a third party. Qualitative assessments allow for more flexibility and judgement, but critically rely on the skill and experience of regulatory officials who are making the subjective judgements. Although the terminology of risk is used throughout, in practice, regulators will operate in quite differing conditions of uncertainty. In some scenarios, there will be high numbers of incidents from which data on their probabilities of occurrence in different situations can be assessed but, in other circumstances, the regulators will be dealing with low frequency events, from which reliable probabilistic calculations cannot easily be drawn or with conditions of uncertainty, where the risk is inherently insusceptible to probabilistic assessment.

Fourth, regulators assign scores to and/or rank firms or activities on the basis of these assessments. These scores may be broadly framed into three categories or traffic lights (high, medium or low) or there may be a more granular scoring system, with 10 or more categories. Where numerical scores are used, these will often operate as shorthand for more complex underlying judgements and they may conceal hesitancies and qualifications in the confident exposition of the number itself. (The expression of subjective judgements as series of numbers can also lead observers to misconstrue all risk-based systems as purely quantitative, whereas in practice their character can vary quite considerably between regulators.)

Finally, regulators assign supervisory, inspection and often inspection resources to firms or issues on the basis of their risk scores. In practice, resources do not always follow the risks in the way that the frameworks would suggest, but resource allocation remains a key element of risk-based frameworks.

RBR is a challenging approach for regulators to adopt, and most have found that it can take some time to get the calibration of regulation right. Each aspect of a risk-based framework involves a complex set of choices. They require decisions by the regulator regarding matters such as the risks it will identify as requiring attention; the indicators and methods it will use to assess those risks; where it will prioritise its attention and where it will not; and, ultimately, political risk: what level of risk or failure the regulator is prepared to accept – or at least thinks it can withstand. Despite these challenges, RBR is regarded by its proponents as a systematic way of making difficult choices. Regulators always have to prioritise; RBR can give them a systematic and defensible way to make those choices.

### 2.3.5    Principles-based, risk-based and outcomes-focused regulation

PBR, RBR and OFR can coexist. Principles express the purposes of the regulatory requirements. Those requirements can additionally or alternatively be framed as broad outcomes to be achieved. RBR is a system the regulator uses to determine how much regulatory effort it will put in to ensuring that the principles are being upheld or the outcomes are being achieved by those being regulated, based on its assessment of the relative risks that exist that the outcomes will not be or are not being achieved. RBR thus has a narrower focus, being directed primarily at how a regulator prioritises and organises its supervision and enforcement activities. But as noted above, these are all terms of art, not science. For the SRA, OFR is comprised of all three. Others may use the terms distinctly. There is no right or wrong in this, but it is important to understand how these terms are being used.

However, what PBR, RBR and OFR all have in common is a focus on outcomes not systems and processes. Under risk-based systems, the focus is on what risks are posed to the achievement of those outcomes. In rule book PBR, the outcomes are expressed in the rulebooks themselves, either as principles or outcomes. In operational PBR, the focus is on achieving those outcomes, with responsibility for identifying how to achieve them placed as much on the regulated firm or individual as the regulator. However, each has to identify measures which demonstrate when those outcomes have been achieved, and here some regulators are more advanced than others. The Care Quality Commission, the Local Better Regulation Office and the Financial Reporting Council, for example, have begun to develop a range of outcome measures that those they regulate have to achieve.[28]

---

[28]    National Audit Office, *Regulatory Quality: How Regulators are Implementing the Hampton Vision* (London, 2008), para 4.5, notes that 'Regulators with direct inspection responsibilities face

In moving to OFR, therefore, the SRA is not acting alone. Such a move does require a profound shift in the way both regulators and those they regulate approach the task of regulation, however, and indeed approach their relationship to one another. PBR, OFR and RBR all mark a significant shift in the terms of the regulatory contract between the regulator and the regulated. Those being regulated have to take more responsibility for ensuring that they are achieving the right outcomes, and not just going through the right processes. Regulators have to take more responsibility for articulating what those outcomes are, and assessing when going through the processes is simply not enough. It is a challenging new approach for both but one which, hopefully, will produce better outcomes in the end.

---

[the] challenge of determining where to draw the line between their preferred stance of neutral guidance provider and educator of business and the more hands on consultant-cum-management role many businesses seem to want.'

# CHAPTER 3

# The SRA's approach to OFR

The SRA recognises that the uncertainty which necessarily flows from OFR can be expected to be disconcerting to the regulated community. In 'Delivering Outcomes-focused Regulation – Policy Statement' (November 2010) it also recognises its own contribution to that discomfort:

> 28 ... rules are seen as not simply providing clarity for individual solicitors and firms but also as a 'protective barrier' against the actions of a regulator whose approach and response to particular circumstances has not in the past been trusted. We recognise this and are committed to addressing the underlying causes for these concerns ... our future approach will be one where we will constructively engage with firms who seek to achieve the necessary outcomes for clients and take responsibility for addressing any weaknesses or failures in approach, or underlying systems and processes.
>
> 29 We do not aim to 'catch firms out' but to ensure that compliance is achieved, risks managed and any weaknesses addressed. The corollary of this is that where firms knowingly or recklessly fail in their responsibilities or show no commitment to achieving compliance, we will take swift and appropriate action to protect individual consumers and the public.

This is welcome, both as a recognition of past mistakes and as an expectation of a better future. But firms will have to change their culture too:

> 30 ... For firms, we expect to see a strong focus on the identification of risk and to see them take responsibility for managing those risks effectively. We expect firms to be forward-looking, so that they try to identify emerging risks before they occur. This will also be the SRA's focus, including a greater interaction with firms about risks. We will, for example, be publishing a Risk Outlook on a periodic basis. The Risk Outlook will inform firms about the particular risks we are concerned about. The Outlook will *not* be a set of rules: firms will be able to see what behaviours and outcomes we are concerned about and will be able to act on them. We will also be proactive in discussing with firms what risks they foresee. Working in this way with firms will help firms in meeting their responsibilities to achieve the required outcomes.

Future regulation will also be increasingly risk based:

> 34 This approach will extend to us dealing in a risk-based way with regulatory breaches, whether by individual solicitors or by regulated firms, that have already taken place. Identifying and investigating breaches of regulatory requirements will

continue to be a part of our work but our approach and response to any particular breach will be informed by the relative risk that any breach presents and we will take proportionate responses.

This will lead to a very different way of allocating resources:

45      . . . Under the historic approach, resources were largely deployed in reacting to crystallised risks, events which had already happened. In addition, those risks were primarily defined as breaches of rules (non compliance), rather than their effect on desired outcomes. This is a very reactive way of working and the result of that approach in the case of the SRA and many other regulators was an insufficient focus on tight authorisation processes (to reduce scope for unacceptable risks), and the deployment of disproportionate resources in responding to breaches, some of them very minor, rather than in pre-empting unacceptable risks.

46      The historic approach has also been to direct much resource reactively to dealing with individual complaints about solicitors rather than robustly treating complaints against solicitors as evidence to assess whether an entity, individual or group of entities poses an unacceptable risk to achieving our public interest and consumer protection objectives . . .

48      We will remove a large amount of regulatory activity from issues that matter little and target our resources on both prospective and realised higher-level risks. We will make intelligent decisions about the intensity of supervision of categories of firms and individuals.

49      In order to focus our efforts on the risks that matter, we will exclude lower level risks from substantive action. We will deal sensitively and courteously with people who wish action to be taken against firms or individuals, but where we have concluded that the information they have provided does not justify the use of our finite resources we will explain why our approach is appropriate. We will, in other words, become equally good at deciding what not to do as we will be in deciding what we should do.

This promises what many commentators have perceived the 'old SRA' to lack – a sense of and commitment to proportionality: 'cracking down' on matters which, on mature reflection, did not appear to matter very much or to have any adverse consequences.

The SRA will also use a Risk Centre to consider 'thematic' risks. These are risks caused by the behaviour of groups of firms or firms delivering a particular category of service, or emerging external risks, such as possibly a new kind of fraud.

This will involve much more information gathering from firms to enable risks to be assessed. The information demands on firms can be expected to become significantly more burdensome.

The organisational focus of the SRA will change so that there will be three regulatory functions: authorisation, supervision and enforcement.

●      *Authorisation* will assess the risks that applicant firms and individuals present, with the intention of minimising the extent to which unsuitable firms and individuals are able to enter the regulated community.

There can be little doubt that far greater resources will be committed in future to ensuring that those intending to offer regulated legal services are positively vetted:

60 . . . Our objective is to identify risks accurately at the point of entry to inform both the initial authorisation decision and the supervision required for those who are approved. This is in contrast to the historic process, in which identity and qualification checks were insufficiently rigorous, and in which firms were allowed to enter the market with little, if any, assessment of the risks which they might pose.

- *Supervision* will monitor, and seek to anticipate and manage, the risks that firms and individuals represent.
- *Enforcement* will be employed where a deterrent is needed, or where firms are unable or unwilling to deal appropriately with risks; ultimately by removal from the regulated community if necessary.

An extensive quotation from the SRA's November 2010 policy statement is justified in relation to the regulator's intentions as to supervision, as this is the clearest available guidance as to how the profession can expect to encounter the SRA in future:

72 The Supervision function is the risk-based oversight of the entire regulated community. For most firms, their main continuing relationship with the SRA will be with supervision teams. Supervision will encourage and support firms to deal with their own risks, help improve standards, and provide the required outcomes for clients. We will achieve this by means of risk-based supervision and constructive engagement with all regulated firms. In particular, we will not be seeking to 'catch firms out' or undertake 'fishing expeditions' to seek any breaches. Referrals for enforcement action will only be taken where a firm is unwilling or incapable of making the necessary improvements, or where the issue is so grave that formal sanctions are required to maintain public confidence or to act as a deterrent.

73 Supervision will:

- undertake desk based firm supervision or visits, maintain close and continuous involvement, or any combination of these, depending on events, themes and the risk rating of firms;
- conduct detailed assessments of firms' systems, controls and governance arrangements; and
- deliver constructive engagement to encourage firms to find and implement their own solutions to problems.

74 All firms will be supervised according to a risk assessment. There will be a variety of supervisory approaches, tailored to the nature of the firm and its work. So for example, we might take a closer supervisory interest in a large firm that has many vulnerable clients and holds a substantial amount of client money, even if the controls in place in the firm mean that it is well-managed. This would make it sensible for us to use some of our limited resources to understand the nature of the firm, its business and the challenges it faces. The fact that the SRA considers that a firm requires higher intensity supervision is not therefore an indication that the SRA has concerns about the firm's viability or its motives. We are considering the following three main approaches to supervision:

- *Low intensity supervision of firms* – The SRA will contact the firm as required. For example, we may contact or visit a firm as a result of an event, such as a partner leaving, or as part of a thematic review designed to examine or improve standards in a particular area. At this point, we do not envisage low risk firms being subject to periodic inspections.
- *Medium intensity supervision of firms* – The SRA will supervise using desk

based or visit based supervision. We are exploring the use of a periodic inspection regime on a frequency of around three to seven years . . .

- *High intensity supervision of firms* – The firm will have a closer and in some cases continuous experience of supervision. Firms may be subject to regular periodic inspection.

75    Firms may receive a visit as a result of:

- The periodic visit programme;
- Event driven reports; or
- Thematic reviews.

76    We will also conduct random visits to provide us with a 'control' group which may help us refine our supervisory approach. Visits will be tailored to the circumstances of each firm.

77    Firms under close and continuous supervision will require specific work because of the higher level of risk they present. To address these points effectively we will produce a tailored supervisory strategy. This is a detailed plan setting out the matters to be addressed and the method of engagement with the firm.

78    We are likely to consider the following as standard on each visit to a firm under close and continuous supervision:

- The *environmental risks* affecting the firm, for example, the economic environment for conveyancing firms.
- The firm's *business model*, for example the spread of the firm's business, how is it financed, and what services it offers.
- The firm's *business processes*, for example:
    - the firm's structure and ownership
    - the extent of any risks posed by staff, including owners or managers
    - controls over its financial position
    - IT systems
    - exposure to legal/litigation risk
    - conflict and client care procedures
    - quality control and management of client matters;
- The firm's *control functions*, for example the work done by the COLP and COFA, together with internal audit (if the firm has an internal audit function – many smaller firms will not need one). We will consider the firm's governance arrangements, the strength of the relationship with the SRA (and its other regulators, if any), together with the strength of its management and its internal culture.

In relation to enforcement, the SRA has published the SRA Enforcement Strategy (January 2011). These are relevant extracts:

2.    The outcomes we seek to achieve by enforcement include

(a)    credible deterrence of behaviours that breach the core principles,

(b)    the encouragement and facilitation of compliance with the core principles and other regulatory requirements,

(c)    control of firms that represent a risk to the public or the core principles,

(d)    removal of those who represent a serious risk to the public ...

5.    Our methods of constructive engagement will be flexible and develop over time but are likely to include

- relationship management,
- supervision,
- advice and firm-specific guidance,
- agreed compliance plans, and
- regulatory settlement agreements ...

7. Dedicated supervisory staff will have regular contact with the firm including face to face or by telephone. Continuing dialogue between the SRA and the firm will concentrate on the firm's internal systems and its exercise of judgement. There may be periodic assessment of the firm's processes to achieve required outcomes. The form and scale of relationship management will depend on the risk posed by the firm. We may use permanent relationship for some and others may be in relationship management for a period of time ...

8. Supervision will involve both supportive and robust challenge and will include, where necessary collaborative and intensive supervision. Supervision will involve a variety of methods, such as desk-based supervision based primarily on documentation and correspondence, meetings and visits, assessments, telephone and written contact. The form and scale of supervision engagement will vary for each firm based on the risk that they pose ...

9. Where we find issues, we may choose to address these via 'Dear Managing Partner' letters that go out to an individual firm or, where appropriate, a number of firms who may be affected by a specific issue. We may also choose to provide specific guidance to firms that are or have been engaged in relationship management or the supervision process ...

10. When we identify specific issues within a firm that requires corrective action, we will consider whether agreeing a compliance plan with the firm provides proportionate outcome. This would not prevent further action being taken in some cases where necessary, but may often enable firms to engage constructively with us, limit the impact of the non-compliance, and satisfy us that they are committed to compliance with the core principles ...

13. When a firm has failed to comply with its regulatory duties, we may be able to deal with it without formal enforcement action. Properly received guidance, supervision and monitoring of firms, coupled with an open, cooperative and constructive approach by firms, may lead us to decide against taking formal action. In those cases, we will expect the firm to take prompt remedial action, agreed with us where necessary. The firm must also demonstrate an understanding and acceptance of applicable principles and the outcomes we seek. If the firm does not do this, we may at any time take disciplinary or other enforcement action in respect of the original behaviours. Failure to take prompt remedial action will be an aggravating factor.

14. While we will offer support and guidance when appropriate, we do not expect firms to try to argue that such support provides them with some sort of amnesty. Supportive and constructive engagement is of a different nature to detailed factual investigation and we are sure that firms would prefer that constructive engagements are frank and open rather than defensive on either side ...

15. In deciding on an appropriate outcome after the identification of possible misconduct, all the circumstances will be taken into account. Examples of relevant factors include:

15.1 The number of clients or others affected and the impact on them;

15.2 The impact or risk to public confidence in the administration of justice arising from the firm's conduct;

15.3 Whether the firm accepts promptly and genuinely that it has acted incorrectly, including whether it has reported the circumstances to us itself;

15.4 Whether the firm genuinely accepts the underlying principles applicable to its behaviour and that it will apply them in future in other, perhaps factually different, situations;

15.5 What the firm has done and is going to do to correct the situation;

15.6 Whether the behaviour:

15.6.1 formed or forms part of a pattern of, or repeated, misconduct or other regulatory failure;

15.6.2 continued for an unreasonable period taking into account its seriousness;

15.6.3 persisted after the regulated person realised or should have realised that it was improper;

15.6.4 affected or had the potential to affect a vulnerable person or child;

15.6.5 affected or had the potential to affect a substantial, high-value or high-profile matter;

15.7 The usual factors relevant to regulatory decisions – such as previous regulatory history, evidence of deliberate intent, recklessness or dishonesty, and personal mitigation …

20. We may focus on priority areas by thematic work. Themes are likely to be selected because there appears to be a particular risk that we need to understand better or to tackle directly. Thematic work will not start with the presumption that it will lead to enforcement outcomes, but it clearly might. Also, the fact that thematic work is likely to relate to areas that are of concern to us means that they are proportionately more likely to result in enforcement action than issues in lower priority areas …

22. The combination of the priority given to certain types of misconduct over others and our risk-based approach to enforcement means that some cases will be subject to enforcement and others not, even when they may be similar in nature or impact. Our choice as to the use of enforcement is therefore a question of how we use our resources effectively and efficiently and how we ensure that the public is protected.

Perhaps this further extract is the most informative in terms of the promised change of culture:

6. Unless we consider that a firm is a serious risk to the objectives and outcomes set out in this strategy, we will aim to encourage compliance, change the firm's behaviour where appropriate, and to deter future non-compliance. We will expect firms to correct harm caused by their non-compliance. If a firm represents a serious or persistent risk, we will seek to remove it from practice or control its form of and ability to operate.

# CHAPTER 4

# SRA Principles

There are 10 mandatory Principles which apply to all those regulated by the SRA.

You must:

1.    uphold the rule of law and the proper administration of justice;
2.    act with integrity;
3.    not allow your independence to be compromised;
4.    act in the best interests of each client;
5.    provide a proper standard of service to your clients;
6.    behave in a way that maintains the trust the public places in you and in the provision of legal services;
7.    comply with your legal and regulatory obligations and deal with your regulators and ombudsmen in an open, timely and co-operative manner;
8.    run your business or carry out your role in the business effectively and in accordance with proper governance and sound financial and risk management principles;
9.    run your business or carry out your role in the business in a way that encourages equality of opportunity and respect for diversity;
10.   protect client money and assets.

Solicitors, RELs and RFLs must comply with Principles 1, 2 and 6 even in relation to activities which fall outside their legal practices, including activities conducted in a private, as well as a business, capacity.

A regulated person must comply with the Principles at all times, but the extent to which they are expected to implement the requirements of the Principles will depend on their role in the firm, or their way of practising. For example, someone who is managing a business will be expected to have more influence on how the business is run than someone practising in-house but not managing a legal department, or someone practising as an employee of a firm.

General guidance on the application of the principles is set out within the Code, but is reproduced here for convenience:

They define the fundamental ethical and professional standards that we expect of all firms and individuals (including owners who may not be lawyers) when providing legal services. You should always have regard to the Principles and use them as your starting point when faced with an ethical dilemma.

Where two or more Principles come into conflict the one which takes precedence is the one which best serves the public interest in the particular circumstances, especially the public interest in the proper administration of justice. Compliance with the Principles is also subject to any overriding legal obligations.

## 4.1  WHAT IS NEW?

Principles 1 to 6 repeat the core duties set out in rule 1 of the 2007 Code, with virtually no change. In relation to the standard of service, the word 'good' in the 2007 Code is replaced with 'proper', which is sensible in setting the standard at what is reasonably required, in place of phraseology which implied that something better than reasonable was necessary. However, this is not to be taken as a relaxation in standards, as opposed to a better choice of language. Solicitors have always been liable to disciplinary action in respect of work carried out to a poor standard.

Principle 6 is rephrased to create a positive obligation to maintain the public trust rather than to avoid behaviour which would tend to diminish that trust, but this is again simply a change of language rather than a change in the nature of the professional obligation. It will remain a 'catch all' upon which to base allegations of professional fault which may not be the subject of an express prohibition or requirement.

Principles 7 and 8 are imported from the former rules 20 and 5 of the 2007 Code, without material change. Principle 10 reflects the obligations imposed by the Solicitors Accounts Rules (to be renamed the SRA Accounts Rules), but extends to other assets such as documents and anything else entrusted to the solicitor. ('Assets' are defined in Chapter 14 of the Code as including 'money, documents, wills, deeds, investments and other property'.) It is questionable whether this adds anything substantive to the duty to act in the client's interests.

The one principle which changes the comparable obligation imposed by the 2007 Code is Principle 9 on equality and diversity. This is also the subject of a specific set of outcomes in Chapter 2 of the Code. While the explanatory notes to Chapter 2 (see **5.3**) assert that the professional duties 'mirror' legal obligations, this is not strictly true. The legal obligation is negative – not to discriminate by reference to any 'protected characteristic' (see generally Chapter 2 of the Equality Act 2010). Principle 9 and Chapter 2 of the Code go further in imposing a positive obligation to encourage equality of opportunity and respect for diversity, as well as a negative obligation to avoid discrimination, and to adopt policies for these purposes.

The SRA's policy statement on 'The Architecture of Change Part 2 – The New SRA Handbook – Analysis of Responses' (8 April 2011), in reaffirming the form that Principle 9 now takes, contradicts the explanatory notes. In this statement it is asserted (at para. 49) that the principle '[goes] beyond mere statutory obligations, without imposing a duty to discriminate positively'.

It must follow that the SRA expects firms to go beyond their statutory obligations in a way that currently remains entirely unexplained.

The guidance note to Principle 9 takes this important point no further:

> Whether you are a manager or an employee, you have a role to play in achieving the outcomes in Chapter 2 (Your clients and equality and diversity) of the Code. Note that a finding of unlawful discrimination outside practice could also amount to a breach of Principles 1 and 6.

This will be considered in more detail in the context of a consideration of Chapter 2 of the Code (see **5.3**).

# CHAPTER 5

# SRA Code of Conduct

## 5.1 OVERVIEW OF THE CODE

The SRA Handbook contains an overview of the Code including this:

> Outcomes-focused regulation concentrates on providing positive outcomes which when achieved will benefit and protect clients and the public. The SRA Code of Conduct (the Code) sets out our outcomes-focused conduct requirements so that you can consider how best to achieve the right outcomes for your clients taking into account the way that your firm works and its client base. The Code is underpinned by effective, risk-based supervision and enforcement.
>
> Those involved in providing legal advice and representation have long held the role of trusted adviser. There are fiduciary duties arising from this role and obligations owed to others, especially the court. *No code can foresee or address every issue or ethical dilemma which may arise. You must strive to uphold the intention of the Code as well as its letter.* (emphasis added)

There is nothing new in the second paragraph quoted. The professional rules and codes have never been able to cover every eventuality (though the 2007 Code sought to do so, which was why it has had to be amended so frequently during its relatively short life).

The key to the first paragraph is the SRA itself; freedom to interpret the rules and to apply them proportionately to the needs of your own clients and style of practice has to be accompanied by a style of policing which permits that flexibility and understands it. The SRA must therefore have and if necessary acquire an understanding of the way that, for example, niche practices or those with particularly sophisticated clients work in ways that are different from, say, a bulk claimants' personal injury practice.

The specified outcomes are mandatory; the accompanying indicative behaviours and notes are not mandatory. The indicative behaviours specify, but do not constitute an exhaustive list of, the kind of behaviour which may establish compliance with, or contravention of, the Principles.

However, there is something of a sting in the tail, and unless there is a very substantial change in the attitude of the SRA (which has emphatically been promised) there is a danger that the indicative behaviours and notes may gradually acquire the status of rules, despite an absolute disavowal that they have that force. This is because the SRA states that the indicative behaviours:

> … may help us to decide whether an outcome has been achieved in compliance with the Principles.
>
> We recognise that there may be other ways of achieving the outcomes. *Where you have chosen a different method from those we have described as indicative behaviours, we might require you to demonstrate how you have nevertheless achieved the outcome.* We encourage firms to consider how they can best achieve the outcomes, taking into account the nature of the firm, the particular circumstances of the matter and, crucially, the needs of their particular clients. (emphasis added)

This is capable of being interpreted to mean: 'Comply with the outcomes *and* the indicative behaviours or the onus will be on you to prove, if you have chosen an innovative approach, how you comply with the outcomes.' If that does happen, it will be contrary to the principles of OFR and will undermine the slogan that the SRA has used to promote its vision of OFR: 'Freedom in Practice'.

### 5.1.1  Private lives

Before considering the Code chapter by chapter, it may be convenient to note those parts of it that apply to solicitors and RELs outside practice, that is, those that apply to practitioners in their private lives.

Paragraph 7 of Chapter 13 (Application and waivers provisions) of the Code specifies that in relation to activities which fall outside practice, whether undertaken as a lawyer or in some other business or private capacity, outcome 11.1 (O(11.1)) and O(11.2) apply to solicitors and RELs. These are the obligations not to take advantage of third parties when acting either in a professional or personal capacity, and to comply with undertakings.

## 5.2  CHAPTER 1 – CLIENT CARE

The introduction is instructive:

> This chapter is about providing a proper standard of service, *which takes into account the individual needs and circumstances of each client.* This includes providing clients with the information they need to make informed decisions about the services they need, how these will be delivered and how much they will cost. This will enable you and your client to understand each other's expectations and responsibilities. This chapter is also about ensuring that if clients are not happy with the service they have received they know how to make a complaint and that all complaints are dealt with promptly and fairly.
>
> Your relationship with your client is a contractual one which carries with it legal, as well as conduct, obligations. This chapter focuses on your obligations in conduct.
>
> You are generally free to decide whether or not to accept instructions in any matter, provided you do not discriminate unlawfully … (emphasis added)

The italicised words enable and encourage an approach which takes account of different kinds of practice and client, from the vulnerable to the powerful, from the ignorant to the sophisticated. This could and probably should result in firms refraining from adopting a 'one size fits all' approach to client care, and particularly to client care letters, depending on the nature of the practice.

### 5.2.1 Chapter 1 outcomes

You must achieve these outcomes:

O(1.1)    you treat your clients fairly;

O(1.2)    you provide services to your clients in a manner which protects their interests in their matter, subject to the proper administration of justice;

O(1.3)    when deciding whether to act, or terminate your instructions, you comply with the law and the Code;

O(1.4)    you have the resources, skills and procedures to carry out your clients' instructions;

O(1.5)    the service you provide to clients is competent, delivered in a timely manner and takes account of your clients' needs and circumstances;

O(1.6)    you only enter into fee agreements with your clients that are legal and which you consider are suitable for the client's needs and take account of the client's best interests;

O(1.7)    you inform clients whether and how the services you provide are regulated, and how this affects the protections available to the client;

O(1.8)    clients have the benefit of your compulsory professional indemnity insurance and you do not exclude or attempt to exclude liability below the minimum level of cover required by the SRA Indemnity Insurance Rules;

O(1.9)    clients are informed in writing at the outset of their matter of their right to complain and how complaints can be made;

O(1.10)   clients are informed in writing, both at the time of engagement and at the conclusion of your complaints procedure, of their right to complain to the Legal Ombudsman, the time frame for doing so and full details of how to contact the Legal Ombudsman;

O(1.11)   clients' complaints are dealt with promptly, fairly, openly and effectively;

O(1.12)   clients are in a position to make informed decisions about the services they need, how their matter will be handled and the options available to them;

O(1.13)   clients receive the best possible information, both at the time of engagement and when appropriate as their matter progresses, about the likely overall cost of their matter;

O(1.14)   clients are informed of their right to challenge or complain about your bill and the circumstances in which they may be liable to pay interest on an unpaid bill;

O(1.15)   you properly account to clients for any financial benefit you receive as a result of your instructions;

O(1.16)   you inform clients if you discover any act or omission which could give rise to a claim by them against you.

### 5.2.2 What is new? Chapter 1 outcomes

There are four material changes. There is no reference to contingency fees; O(1.7) is entirely new; there are new requirements concerning the information to be given to clients about complaints procedures; and there is a simplification of the rules concerning the receipt of commission. In more detail:

## Contingency fees

There is no longer any reference, at all, to contingency fees, either in relation to the solicitor/client retainer (rule 2.04 of the 2007 Code), or in relation to associations with other organisations who charge such fees (rule 9.01(4) of the 2007 Code). The only reference to fee agreements is in O(1.6): 'you only enter into fee agreements with your clients that are legal and which you consider are suitable for the client's needs and take account of the client's best interests'. In other words, to the extent that contingency fees are lawful, they no longer raise any regulatory concern *per se* (but suitability and the best interests of the client need still to be considered). The professional rules follow the law without any additional obligations or constraints.

It will therefore be necessary to have a complete understanding of what the law permits, which is considered below (see **5.2.5**).

## Outcome 1.7

There is a new provision in O(1.7): 'you inform clients whether and how the services you provide are regulated, and how this affects the protections available to the client'. This anticipates the arrival of new business structures – ABSs – which may provide both regulated legal services *and* other services (e.g. funeral services) which will not be regulated by the SRA. Clients will need to be informed which is which, and what the consequences will be.

## Complaints procedures

There are new requirements concerning information for clients about complaints procedures. Outcomes 1.9 and 1.10 impose requirements that all clients are informed at the outset, in writing, of their right to complain and how to do so, and of their right to complain to the Legal Ombudsman and how to do so. This is more burdensome than the equivalent provisions in the 2007 Code. This is also the case in relation to the (otherwise materially unchanged) obligation to provide the best available information about costs, O(1.13). Under rules 2.03(7) and 2.05(2) of the 2007 Code, practitioners could elect not to provide some or all of the information under the general heading of 'client care' if it could be demonstrated that it was inappropriate in the circumstances to do so; in other words, if there were repeat clients or sophisticated clients who evidently knew their rights and did not need to be informed or reminded, it was possible to avoid providing basic client care information. This is no longer the case. It would seem that client care letters will now be required when they were not previously needed. It may not even be possible for the client to waive the requirement.

Note 1 to Chapter 1 of the Code confirms:

> The information you give to clients will vary according to the needs and circumstances of the individual client and the type of work you are doing for them, for example an individual instructing you on a conveyancing matter is unlikely to need the same information as a sophisticated commercial client who instructs you on a regular basis.

This approach is not, however, maintained logically when the Chapter 1 outcomes are considered, in requiring complaints information to be given even where the client plainly does not need it.

Moreover O(1.10) fails altogether to take into account that many clients have no right to complain to the Legal Ombudsman (LeO). In general terms, only individuals and small businesses may do so. Larger corporate clients have no such remedy (see rules 2.1–2.5 of the Legal Ombudsman Scheme Rules 2010 and Chapter 12 of the *Solicitor's Handbook 2011*).

As the outcome requires solicitors to inform clients of 'their right' to complain to the LeO, it follows that initial letters may in appropriate cases need to state that the client does not have that right. It would be inappropriate to use the same formula across the board, thus potentially misleading some clients into believing that there was a further remedy when there is not.

In some cases, it might be that solicitors would not know at the outset, or even at the conclusion of the retainer, whether a business client is able to complain to the LeO, because this is a question determined by the number of staff, turnover, balance sheet value, net asset value or annual income. One could envisage situations in which advice on a specific point might be sought without the need for disclosure of that level of information. In those cases it will be necessary to inform the client of the possibility of the existence of a right to complain to the LeO, with the relevant time limits and contact details, subject to the client being within the LeO Scheme Rules.

Firms will have to adapt their standard documentation to match their client base and the specific needs of clients.

## Commissions

The rule on commissions (O(1.15)) is simplified: 'you properly account to clients for any financial benefit you receive as a result of your instructions'. There is no longer a *de minimis* £20 figure below which the rules do not apply, and the word 'commission' does not appear in the relevant outcome, being replaced with 'financial benefit' which is defined thus: 'includes, for example, any commission, discount or rebate, but does not include your fees or interest earned on any client account'.

This also, on the face of it, brings the professional rules in line with the law, which we will likewise consider in detail (see **5.2.6**).

## 5.2.3   Chapter 1 indicative behaviours

Acting in the following way(s) may tend to show that you have achieved these outcomes and therefore complied with the Principles:

**Dealing with the client's matter**

IB(1.1)   agreeing an appropriate level of service with your client, for example the type and frequency of communications;

IB(1.2)   explaining your responsibilities and those of the client;

IB(1.3)   ensuring that the client is told, in writing, the name and status of the person(s) dealing with the matter and the name and status of the person responsible for its overall supervision;

IB(1.4)   explaining any arrangements, such as fee sharing or referral arrangements, which are relevant to the client's instructions;

IB(1.5)   explaining any limitations or conditions on what you can do for the client, for example, because of the way the client's matter is funded;

IB(1.6)   in taking instructions and during the course of the retainer, having proper regard to your client's mental capacity or other vulnerability, such as incapacity or duress;

IB(1.7)   considering whether you should decline to act or cease to act because you cannot act in the client's best interests;

IB(1.8)   if you seek to limit your liability to your client to a level above the minimum required by the SRA Indemnity Insurance Rules, ensuring that this limitation is in writing and is brought to the client's attention;

IB(1.9)   refusing to act where your client proposes to make a gift of significant value to you or a member of your family, or a member of your firm or their family, unless the client takes independent legal advice;

IB(1.10)  if you have to cease acting for a client, explaining to the client their possible options for pursuing their matter;

IB(1.11)  you inform clients if they are not entitled to the protections of the SRA Compensation Fund;

IB(1.12)  considering whether a conflict of interests has arisen or whether the client should be advised to obtain independent advice where the client notifies you of their intention to make a claim or if you discover an act or omission which might give rise to a claim;

**Fee arrangements with your client**

IB(1.13)  discussing whether the potential outcomes of the client's matter are likely to justify the expense or risk involved, including any risk of having to pay someone else's legal fees;

IB(1.14)  clearly explaining your fees and if and when they are likely to change;

IB(1.15)  warning about any other payments for which the client may be responsible;

IB(1.16)  discussing how the client will pay, including whether public funding may be available, whether the client has insurance that might cover the fees, and whether the fees may be paid by someone else such as a trade union;

IB(1.17)  where you are acting for a client under a fee arrangement governed by statute, such as a conditional fee agreement, giving the client all relevant information relating to that arrangement;

IB(1.18)  where you are acting for a publicly funded client, explaining how their publicly funded status affects the costs;

IB(1.19)   providing the information in a clear and accessible form which is appropriate to the needs and circumstances of the client;

IB(1.20)   where you receive a financial benefit as a result of acting for a client, either:

- paying it to the client;
- offsetting it against your fees; or
- keeping it only where you can justify keeping it, you have told the client the amount of the benefit (or an approximation if you do not know the exact amount) and the client has agreed that you can keep it;

IB(1.21)   ensuring that disbursements included in your bill reflect the actual amount spent or to be spent on behalf of the client;

**Complaints handling**

IB(1.22)   having a written complaints procedure which:

- is brought to clients' attention at the outset of the matter;
- is easy for clients to use and understand, allowing for complaints to be made by any reasonable means;
- is responsive to the needs of individual clients, especially those who are vulnerable;
- enables complaints to be dealt with promptly and fairly, with decisions based on a sufficient investigation of the circumstances;
- provides for appropriate remedies; and
- does not involve any charges to clients for handling their complaints;

IB(1.23)   providing the client with a copy of the firm's complaints procedure on request;

IB(1.24)   in the event that a client makes a complaint, providing them with all necessary information concerning the handling of the complaint.

Acting in the following way(s) may tend to show that you have not achieved these outcomes and therefore not complied with the Principles:

**Accepting and refusing instructions**

IB(1.25)   acting for a client when instructions are given by someone else, or by only one client when you act jointly for others unless you are satisfied that the person providing the instructions has the authority to do so on behalf of all of the clients;

IB(1.26)   ceasing to act for a client without good reason and without providing reasonable notice;

IB(1.27)   entering into unlawful fee arrangements such as an unlawful contingency fee;

IB(1.28)   acting for a client when there are reasonable grounds for believing that the instructions are affected by duress or undue influence without satisfying yourself that they represent the client's wishes.

### 5.2.4   What is new? Chapter 1 indicative behaviours

There is little here that is new; the section on fees, in particular, reproduces very familiar principles (indicative behaviours 1.13 to 1.19). It is not clear why indicative behaviour 1.9 (IB(1.9)) and IB(1.12) appear here rather than in Chapter 3 – Conflicts of interests.

Indicative behaviour 1.21 reflects the widespread problems over the misdescription of telegraphic transfer fees, now likely to be only of historical interest as firms will have reacted to the publicity associated with this issue. The (hopefully past) problem was that firms developed a practice of making a charge for undertaking routine telegraphic transfers in conveyancing. There was nothing wrong with that, but what tended to happen was that if the bank charged the firm, say, £10, the firm would make a charge to the client of £20 – but still describe the fee as a disbursement, as if it had all been paid to the bank. The mischief was neither in passing on the bank's charge, nor in charging a fee for the work entailed, but rather in misdescribing a charge as a disbursement. This misled the client and hid the fact that the firm was making an extra modest profit.

Indicative behaviour 1.11 supports O(1.7) to deal with the situation in which the firm is providing regulated and unregulated services.

Some indicative behaviours look very like rules, rather than unenforceable guidance, for example IB(1.4) on disclosing fee sharing and referral arrangements; IB(1.8) on limitation of liability; IB(1.9) on refusing gifts unless there is independent advice; and IB(1.12) on conflicts of interest.

Indicative behaviour 1.20 dealing with financial benefits – what used to be called commission – is problematic and will be considered in detail below (see **5.2.6**).

### 5.2.5 When are contingency fees lawful?

*The general law*

NON-CONTENTIOUS WORK

It has always been lawful for solicitors to charge contingency fees in non-contentious work. This is currently enshrined in the Solicitors Act 1974, s.57:

(1)     Whether or not any order is in force under section 56, a solicitor and his client may, before or after or in the course of the transaction of any non-contentious business by the solicitor, make an agreement as to his remuneration in respect of that business.

(2)     The agreement may provide for the remuneration of the solicitor by a gross sum or by reference to an hourly rate, or by a commission or percentage, or by a salary, or otherwise ...

Solicitors can (and always have been able to) enter into a retainer in respect of non-contentious business whereby the solicitor can be remunerated by way of a cut of any spoils, or conditional on the result. To be enforceable, a non-contentious business agreement must be in writing and signed by the person to be bound by it 'or his agent in that behalf' (s.57(3)). The Solicitors Act 1974, s.87 defines contentious business:

'contentious business' means business done, whether as solicitor or advocate, in or for the purposes of proceedings begun before a court or before an arbitrator, not being business

37

which falls within the definition of non-contentious or common form probate business contained in section 128 of the Senior Courts Act 1981.

Any business that is not within that definition is non-contentious. In order to fall within the definition, proceedings must actually have been commenced before a court or arbitrator. Thus, work undertaken in relation to a claim which might be litigated, but which is in fact resolved without the issue of proceedings, remains outside the definition of contentious business.

Similarly in 'proceedings' which bear all the attributes of contentious work, such as those in employment tribunals, but which are not proceedings before a court or an arbitrator, solicitors have been able to charge clients on a contingency fee basis. Contingency fee agreements in relation to employment matters are now subject to express regulation (Courts and Legal Services Act 1990, s.58AA (introduced into that Act by the Coroners and Justice Act 2009, s.154) and the Damages-Based Agreements Regulations 2010, SI 2010/1206).

Otherwise there is no statutory or regulatory limit on what a solicitor may charge by way of a contingency fee in non-contentious work. Outcome 1.6, of course, requires that the fee agreement is not only legal, but also suitable for the client's needs and that it takes account of the client's best interests. It has to, in short, be fair.

Outcome 1.14 requires that clients are informed about their right to challenge or complain about bills. Costs due under a non-contentious business agreement are liable to detailed assessment and the costs judge/officer may enquire into the facts and if appropriate certify for the court that the agreement should be set aside or the amount payable reduced, and the court may so order (Solicitors Act 1974, s.57(5)).

Solicitors need also to have one eye on the doctrine of unconscionable bargain (see **5.10.4**), although there is no example of a contingency fee agreement in non-contentious work between solicitor and client being struck down as unconscionable. If such an agreement were found to be an unconscionable bargain, the solicitor would be at risk of a finding that he had breached Principle 6, which requires him to 'behave in a way that maintains the trust the public places in you and in the provision of legal services'.

## CONTENTIOUS WORK – CONDITIONAL FEE AGREEMENTS

For centuries, contingency fees in contentious work were outlawed on public policy grounds as offending the rule against champerty. The scope of the law of champerty has become attenuated in the light of shifting public policy perceptions. The funding revolution of the 1990s brought an end to the absolute prohibition by permitting conditional fee agreements (CFAs), and CFAs are now permitted in all types of proceedings save for family and criminal proceedings, provided that they comply with formalities imposed by delegated legislation. From November 2005, most of the burdensome formalities imposed by the Conditional Fee Agreements Regulations 2000, SI 2000/692 were removed. There is a maximum success fee of 100 per cent of basic costs, and the client is protected by the solicitor/own client assessment procedure. The unsuccessful defendant will have to pay the success fee if reasonable. Different costs rules apply to smaller claims. A detailed consideration of the legal framework for conditional fee agreements is beyond the scope of this book, and it is not affected by changes in the SRA's rules.

The issue of contingency fees and the reach of the modern law on champerty has recently been revisited by the Court of Appeal in *Sibthorpe and Morris* v. *Southwark LBC* [2011] EWCA Civ 25. Two important principles emerge. The first is that the law has developed in relation to CFAs in a way that significantly erodes the relevance of the law of champerty, so that, where the client contracts with a party (such as a litigation funder) which is not a person conducting the litigation or providing advocacy services, the correct approach is now to look at the agreement in the round, and to decide whether it would undermine the purity of justice, or would corrupt public justice, a question to be decided on a case-by-case basis (*Factortame & Ors, R (on the application of)* v. *Secretary of State for Transport (No.8)* [2003] QB 381; *Sibthorpe* at [35] and [36]). However, that approach is not to be adopted where the agreement is with someone having conduct of the litigation or providing advocacy services, because there are particular public interest sensitivities in those cases. Here, the law is unchanged and conditional or contingent fee agreements which do not comply with s.58 or s.58AA of the Courts and Legal Services Act 1990 remain unenforceable.

The second principle is that whereas the common law on champerty may not be further eroded in this specific area other than by the legislature, neither may it be extended. In *Sibthorpe* the solicitors did not stand to gain if the claim was successful (save under a CFA which was otherwise lawful) but they did stand to lose if the claim failed because, in the absence of affordable after the event insurance, the firm offered its clients an indemnity in respect of adverse costs. The solicitors therefore did have a financial interest in the outcome. The court held that there was no public interest offended by this arrangement, and there was much to commend it by the same standard. No decided case on champerty had involved the contracting party suffering only a financial loss in the event of failure, but gaining no share of the spoils in the event of success. The court declined to extend the reach of champerty to such circumstances and held that the agreement was lawful and valid.

INTRODUCERS OPERATING ON A CONTINGENCY FEE BASIS

Subject to the doctrine of unconscionable bargain, there is no inhibition in the general law against introducers charging clients whom they introduce to solicitors on a contingency fee basis.

## *The old rules*

### SOLICITOR/CLIENT RETAINERS FOR CONTENTIOUS WORK

Rule 2.04(1) of the 2007 Code re-enacted rule 8 of the Solicitors' Practice Rules 1990 by providing that:

> You must not enter into an arrangement to receive a contingency fee for work done in prosecuting or defending any contentious proceedings before a court of England and Wales, a British court martial or an arbitrator where the seat of the arbitration is in England and Wales, except as permitted by statute or the common law.

The exception in the last phrase was introduced into rule 8 of the Solicitors' Practice Rules 1990 in January 1999 in response to *Thai Trading (a firm)* v. *Taylor* [1998] QB 781 as it was thought that it might be possible for solicitors to enter into some forms of contingency or conditional fee arrangements at common law, on the basis that public policy no longer required a complete prohibition of such arrangements. However, subsequent cases, including most recently *Sibthorpe* reaffirmed the common law's objection to contingency arrangements in relation to contentious proceedings where the contracting party is responsible for the conduct of the litigation or is supplying advocacy services, and the only arrangement that is permitted as an exception to the rule is one authorised by statute; that is, a lawful CFA or damages-based agreement.

### INTRODUCERS OPERATING ON A CONTINGENCY FEE BASIS

Rule 9.01(4) of the 2007 Code re-enacted rule 9 of the Solicitors' Practice Rules 1990 and controversially provided that:

> You must not, in respect of any claim arising as a result of death or personal injury, either:
>
> (a)    enter into an arrangement for the referral of clients with; or
> (b)    act in association with,
>
> any person whose business, or any part of whose business, is to make, support or prosecute (whether by action or otherwise, and whether by a solicitor or agent or otherwise) claims arising as a result of death or personal injury, and who, in the course of such business, solicits or receives contingency fees in respect of such claims.

Controversy arose from the fact that the 2007 Code, in all its draft forms up to the beginning of 2007, did not contain any such provision. The policy decision had been made to abolish the rule, not least because claims managing companies were to become regulated under the Compensation Act 2006. The late resurrection of the prohibition has never been satisfactorily explained, but it is understood that the Law Society never intended that the rule should operate to prohibit arrangements or associations with regulated claims managers complying with their own regulatory regime.

We have now come full circle, the rule again being abandoned by the omission of any comparable provision in the 2011 Code.

In the meantime, solicitors have found themselves before the Solicitors Disciplinary Tribunal (SDT) as a result of arrangements made with introducers who have charged on a contingency fee basis in both contentious and non-contentious work. Many solicitors handling miners' compensation cases under the claims handling agreements relating to vibration white finger and pulmonary disease claims were disciplined because introducers (whether commercial entities or trades unions) had agreed to take a slice of the miners' compensation. The courts eventually ruled that these were contentious proceedings (*Beresford and Smith* v. *The Solicitors Regulation Authority and The Law Society* [2009] EWHC 3155 (Admin)). There have also been a handful of successful prosecutions arising out of solicitors' arrangements with an organisation known as Justice Direct, which introduced employment tribunal and personal injury claims to solicitors in return for a 'broker's fee' calculated as 25 per cent of any sum recovered plus a percentage of the fees charged by its panel solicitors. Whereas such an arrangement did not breach rule 9.01(4) in employment tribunal cases (because those claims were non-contentious), it undoubtedly did so in personal injury cases where proceedings were commenced (*Tilbury* (App. 9880-2008, SDT); *Kelsall* (App. 10352-2009, SDT)).

## The new rules

The prohibition in rule 9.01(4) of the 2007 Code (introducers charging contingency fees) has been entirely removed. Rule 2.04 of the 2007 Code (prohibition of contingency fees in contentious proceedings) has been replaced with a simple requirement that all fee agreements must be lawful. The focus now will be upon whether the solicitor can properly maintain independence if he has an arrangement with an introducer who operates on a contingency fee basis, and whether the agreement with the introducer is in the client's best interests. The SDT decision in *Tilbury* will remain highly relevant, and solicitors must ask themselves when taking on a new client whether a contingency fee arrangement between the client and the introducer was an unconscionable bargain or otherwise not in the best interests of the new client. This will be considered in more detail in relation to the outcomes required by Chapter 9 of the Code (see **5.10.4**).

In relation to CFAs between solicitor and client, the situation has become pleasingly free from uncertainty: if the agreement is lawful it is permitted as a matter of professional conduct (if it is not otherwise unsuitable or unfair); if it is not lawful it is prohibited as a matter of professional conduct.

## 5.2.6 Accounting for financial benefits

*The general law*

Whereas, as we have just discussed, in relation to contingency fees the regulatory scheme is in lock step with the general law, in relation to accounting for financial benefits the situation remains unfortunately confused.

On the basis that the rules may be intended to reflect the legal position, the principle is well settled; any person who has a fiduciary duty:

> shall not take any secret remuneration or any financial benefit not authorised by the law, or by his contract, or by the trust deed under which he acts, as the case may be. (per Lord Normand in *Dale* v. *Inland Revenue Commissioners* [1954] AC 11 [27])

Also:

> If the person in a fiduciary position does gain or receive any financial benefit arising out of the use of the property of the beneficiary he cannot keep it unless he can show such authority. (per Lord Reid in *Brown* v. *Inland Revenue Commissioners* [1965] AC 244 [256G])

A fiduciary is accordingly under no obligation in law to account for benefits which he is authorised to take under the terms of the agreement under which he acts as a fiduciary.

The principles are therefore for present purposes: (1) a fiduciary may not retain a secret benefit; (2) a fiduciary may retain any benefit if it is authorised by the contractual arrangements between the parties.

The rules about commissions and secret profits are rooted in the duties that are imposed upon a solicitor as a result of the fiduciary relationship with the client (and with each and all of their clients) and by reason of his position as his client's agent. The distinguishing feature of a fiduciary is the obligation of loyalty, resulting from the trust and confidence reposed in him by the other party. A fiduciary must act in good faith; he must not make a secret profit out of his trust; he must not place himself in a position where his duty and his personal interests may conflict; and he may not act for his own benefit or for the benefit of a third party without the informed consent of his principal. When acting for two principals, he must not act with the intention of furthering the interests of one principal to the prejudice of those of the other. All these aspects of the fiduciary relationship are imposed by the law of equity, and are summarised in Millett LJ's judgment in *Mothew* v. *Bristol and West Building Society* [1998] Ch 1.

*The old rules*

Under rule 10 of the Solicitors' Practice Rules 1990, solicitors were obliged to:

> ... account to their clients for any commission received of more than £20 unless, having disclosed to the client in writing the amount or basis of calculation of the commission or

(if the precise amount or basis cannot be ascertained) an approximation thereof, they have the client's agreement to retain it.

This was not materially changed by rule 2.06 of the 2007 Code, which simply modernised the language:

> If you are a recognised body, a manager of a recognised body or a recognised sole practitioner, you must ensure that your firm pays to your client commission received over £20 unless the client, having been told the amount, or if the precise amount is not known, an approximate amount or how the amount is to be calculated, has agreed that your firm may keep it.

The £20 exception was intended to cater for *de minimis* cases, where the time and administrative effort involved in obtaining a client's informed consent were disproportionate to the amount involved. However, for solicitors involved in bulk conveyancing or bulk personal injury work, the £20 exception could be made to work very profitably, and solicitors could make comparatively large sums of money in commission payments, without ever having to inform their clients of the receipt of the money. Moreover, solicitors and service providers became inventive in the commercial arrangements which gave rise to the rewarding of solicitors by service providers. This began to concern the Office for the Supervision of Solicitors, the predecessor of the SRA.

The matter came to a head in *Law Society* v. *Adcock and Mocroft* [2006] EWHC 3212 (Admin), in which a solicitors' firm entered into an arrangement with the Property Search Group (PSG), by which PSG carried out local authority and other searches for the firm in conveyancing matters. Under this arrangement, the lay client of the firm would be charged the nominal full cost of the searches, but after that fee had been paid by Adcocks, the latter invoiced PSG for 'commission', calculated as £20. As the payment was set at the *de minimis* figure there was no disclosure to clients.

The Divisional Court upheld the decision of the Solicitors Disciplinary Tribunal to dismiss the case against the solicitors on a summary basis in view of the obvious confusion which had existed within the Law Society as to the proper interpretation of the rule at that time. While the Divisional Court clarified the rule, the solicitors had acted as many others had in good faith, those other solicitors having been informed by the Law Society that their actions were entirely proper.

The Divisional Court held that the £20 sums paid by PSG to the solicitors were not commission payments, but were in reality a rebate or discount. Crucially, the court did not lay down any general principle that a solicitor could not retain the benefit of a rebate or discount: in para. 7 of the judgment, Waller LJ recorded:

> The Law Society's submission is that the true cost of the searches was only £166.38. The criticism is that [clients] were not told of this.

Unfortunately, when it came to incorporating the *Adcock and Mocroft* decision into the Code of Conduct in 2007, the draftsman appears to have believed that the

Divisional Court had decided that there was a general principle that a solicitor could not retain the benefit of a rebate or discount. Note 59 of the guidance to rule 2.06 (in the final version of the 2007 Code) stated that:

> On the other hand, a discount on a product or a rebate on, for example, a search fee would not amount to a commission because it does not arise in the context of referring your client to a third party. Such payments are disbursements and the client must get the benefit of any discount or rebate.

The last sentence of note 59 was most unfortunately worded. It was not justified by the judgment in *Adcock and Mocroft*. It vividly illustrated the danger of providing a set of rules that was too prescriptive, and trying to fit every conceivable factual situation into those regulatory rules. There was no justification for a regulatory scheme that permitted solicitors to retain *commission* provided that they had the informed consent of their clients, but did not permit solicitors to retain a *discount or rebate* even though they had the informed consent of their clients. Such a distinction made no sense at all.

A further layer of confusion was added by note 61 of the guidance to rule 2.06 of the 2007 Code in the following terms:

> Commission received may be retained only if the conditions within 2.06 are complied with and the arrangement is in your client's best interests – either:
> (a)   it is used to offset a bill of costs; or
> (b)   you must be able to justify its retention – for example, the commission is retained in lieu of costs which you could have billed for work done in placing the business, but were not so billed.

This guidance was as vulnerable to attack as was guidance note 59. On a literal reading, it appeared to provide that the benefit of the commission could never be retained by the solicitor, as it would either be offset against costs, or retained in lieu of costs that would otherwise have been payable. Such a provision would have undermined the specific provision in rule 2.06 that the solicitor could retain the commission provided that the client had given informed consent. Moreover, there is no general requirement upon an agent or a fiduciary to have to 'justify' retention of commission. The obligation is simply not to make a *secret* profit. If an agent obtains the informed consent of his or her principal to retention of commission, that, in law, is an end to the matter. Quite why a solicitor should have to 'justify' such retention was a mystery in terms of the application of well-established legal principles. It was also relevant that in guidance note 56 it was expressly stated that rule 2.06 'reflects the legal position'.

In writing the successive editions of the *Solicitor's Handbook* we have been consistently informed by the SRA that this guidance was mistaken, and we have reflected that advice to us in our commentary on rule 2.06. Indeed, as it was explained to us, the SRA was not able to say exactly how the guidance had come to be written in that form, because although the words of the rule had changed, by modernising the language, there had been no intention to change the substance of rule 10 of the Solicitors' Practice Rules 1990. Tragically, the person who had been responsible for this piece of drafting had been taken seriously ill and subsequently died, and no-one else was able to explain the logic which underlay it.

## The new rules

As noted at **5.2.2**, under the new Code, by O(1.15) in Chapter 1, solicitors must properly account to clients for any financial benefit received as a result of their instructions, and financial benefit is defined so as to include any commission, discount or rebate. Chapter 6 makes clear that the solicitor must retain his or her independence and act in the best interests of clients when recommending that the client uses a third party, and that clients must be fully informed of any financial or other interest the solicitor has in referring the client to a third party (O(6.1) and O(6.2)).

So, as before under the 2007 Code, there is now a clear rule to account properly (that is, in accordance with the law) for any financial benefit.

Under the general law, a solicitor as a fiduciary must not make a secret profit, and must inform his or her client of all relevant matters concerning the client's matter. The general law is satisfied if the fiduciary obtains the informed consent of the client at the outset of the retainer to retention of a financial benefit. The £20 *de minimis* exception has not been reproduced in the rules, and no longer exists; a secret profit is a secret profit, whether of £20 or £20 million, and it is arguable as a matter of legal principle that the Law Society should never have created the *de minimis* exception in the first place.

So far so good: the general law and O(1.15) appear to be entirely consistent. Regrettably, however, confusing non-mandatory guidance accompanying the stated outcome repeats the contradictory guidance to old rule 2.06 – but crucially still without any explanation.

Indicative behaviour 1.20 refers to 'keeping [a financial benefit] only where you can justify keeping it, you have told the client the amount of the benefit … and the client has agreed that you can keep it.'

Indicative behaviours are not mandatory. There is no explanation as to how a solicitor may 'justify' retaining the benefit. This cannot be because, for example, he or she could charge an amount equal to it by way of fees. If that were the case, the solicitor would not be receiving, or retaining, any benefit – the client would be receiving it as a reduction in the charges they would otherwise be liable to pay. This was the essence of the error in the 2007 guidance notes. On the one hand, the SRA was saying (in the rule) that solicitors could retain commission if the client gave informed consent; but on the other, the SRA was also saying, in the non-binding guidance, that consent was not enough and the client had to receive some benefit, one way or the other (so that the solicitor could not really benefit at all).

This error has been carried through into IB(1.20). If the SRA intends to prevent solicitors receiving income from any source but their legal costs, and intends that solicitors should pay all financial benefits received as a result of acting for clients to those clients, it has the power to so decide. But it should make this both explicit and mandatory. Such an important restriction on a solicitor's freedom to obtain commission income should not be imposed by way of a non-mandatory indicative behaviour.

If, on the other hand, solicitors are simply subject to the law on fiduciaries and secret profits, solicitors can 'justify' keeping a financial benefit including commission whenever they have been transparent from the outset about receipt of that sum, and the client has provided informed consent to its retention.

Commissions and payments for introductions are a normal part of business life. There is no reason or justification for taking a puritanical stance inimical to the receipt of secondary sources of income by solicitors – or if that is intended, it needs, in our view, to be expressed. Clients are generally, in our experience, unconcerned with the business arrangements solicitors make with third parties provided that they are transparent and cause no prejudice to the clients. The fact that solicitors may take a commission raises no eyebrows.

No explanation has ever been given as to what the SRA would perceive as appropriate justification – indeed, our enquiries at a high level indicated an acceptance that the guidance was wrong.

If, nevertheless, 'justification' is needed, it could be provided by demonstrating the administrative responsibility that may fall on the firm in their dealings, for example, with an after the event insurer, but may also be justified by the firm's business model – that it relies on certain income streams in planning its business and the services it is able to give to clients.

## A PRACTICAL EXAMPLE

If a solicitor is carrying out personal injury work in bulk on the basis of CFAs, they are likely to have commission arrangements with service providers, such as medical agencies. The solicitor should obtain the informed consent of his or her clients at the outset to retention of the commission. In the absence of any better explanation or guidance from the SRA as to what can 'justify' retention of commission, something along the following lines should be satisfactory:

> If you need to obtain a medical report, we shall put you in touch with an appropriately qualified and experienced medical practitioner through a medical agency. We have an arrangement with X Agency, by which they pay us a commission of £xx for every introduction of one of our clients to the agency. Under the general law and our professional rules, this money belongs to you unless you agree that we may retain it. If we are able to retain it, this assists our cash flow and improves our ability to continue to offer a 'no win no fee' service to our clients. We invite you to agree that we may retain it. By signing and returning the copy of this letter and continuing to instruct us, you agree that we may retain this commission. If you do not agree that we should retain it, we will pay it to you.

## 5.3  CHAPTER 2 – EQUALITY AND DIVERSITY

The introduction to Chapter 2 states it 'is about encouraging equality of opportunity and respect for diversity, and preventing unlawful discrimination'. The requirements apply in relation to age, disability, gender reassignment, marriage and civil partnership, pregnancy and maternity, race, religion or belief, sex and sexual orientation. The SRA intends that everyone should contribute to compliance with these requirements by embedding appropriate values in the workplace and by challenging inappropriate behaviour and processes. The individual's responsibility for embedding these values will vary depending on their role in the organisation. It is plainly intended that the rules of conduct should supplement rather than merely restate the general law.

As noted at **4.1** in the context of Principle 9, the SRA's policy statement on 'The Architecture of Change Part 2 – The New SRA Handbook – Analysis of Responses' (8 April 2011), in reaffirming the form that Principle 9 now takes, asserts (at para. 49) that the principle '[goes] beyond mere statutory obligations, without imposing a duty to discriminate positively', and it follows that the SRA expects firms to go beyond their statutory obligations in a way that currently remains entirely unexplained. Thus:

- Principle 9 requires you to run your business or carry out your role in the business in a way that *encourages* equality of opportunity and respect for diversity;
- The introduction to Chapter 2 states that it is about *encouraging* equality of opportunity and respect for diversity;
- The policy statement asserts that professional obligations *go beyond* 'mere statutory obligations';
- Only one outcome (O(2.4), concerned with recruitment and employment) uses the word 'encourages';
- Guidance note 1 to Chapter 2 states that the obligations in this chapter *closely mirror* the relevant legal obligations, and suggests further information be obtained (as a matter of necessary inference about those legal obligations) from the Equality and Human Rights Commission;
- The Law Society's response to the SRA's consultation expressed concern that this requirement appeared to go beyond statutory obligations, and that it was unclear to what extent firms will be required to take positive action to promote equality and diversity. The Law Society asked the SRA to clarify what is to be expected of the regulatory community. This has not been done.

### 5.3.1  Chapter 2 outcomes

You must achieve these outcomes:

O(2.1)  you do not discriminate unlawfully, or victimise or harass anyone, in the course of your professional dealings;

O(2.2)  you provide services to clients in a way that respects diversity;

O(2.3)  you make reasonable adjustments to ensure that disabled clients, employees or managers are not placed at a substantial disadvantage compared to those who are not disabled, and you do not pass on the costs of these adjustments to these disabled clients employees or managers;

O(2.4)  your approach to recruitment and employment encourages equality of opportunity and respect for diversity;

O(2.5)  complaints of discrimination are dealt with promptly, fairly, openly, and effectively.

### 5.3.2  Chapter 2 indicative behaviours

Acting in the following way(s) may tend to show that you have achieved these outcomes and therefore complied with the Principles:

IB(2.1)  having a written equality and diversity policy which is appropriate to the size and nature of the firm and includes the following features:

- a commitment to the principles of equality and diversity and legislative requirements;
- a requirement that all employees and managers comply with the outcomes;
- provisions to encompass your recruitment and interview processes;
- details of how the firm will implement, monitor, evaluate and update the policy;
- details of how the firm will ensure equality in relation to the treatment of employees, managers, clients and third parties instructed in connection with client matters;
- details of how complaints and disciplinary issues are to be dealt with;
- details of the firm's arrangements for workforce diversity monitoring; and
- details of how the firm will communicate the policy to employees, managers and clients.

IB(2.2)  providing employees and managers with training and information about complying with equality and diversity requirements;

IB(2.3)  monitoring and responding to issues identified by your policy and reviewing and updating your policy.

Acting in the following way(s) may tend to show that you have not achieved these outcomes and therefore not complied with the Principles:

IB(2.4)  being subject to any decision of a court or tribunal of the UK, that you have committed, or are to be treated as having committed, an unlawful act of discrimination;

IB(2.5)  discriminating unlawfully when accepting or refusing instructions to act for a client.

### 5.3.3  What is new? Chapter 2

The language has wholly changed from that used in rule 6 of the 2007 Code, which simply imposed an obligation not to discriminate in a way that would be unlawful, and to have a written policy. Nevertheless the outcomes largely restate what would have been necessary to comply with the former rule, with the sole exception of the vexed issue of 'encouraging' equality and respect for diversity in relation to recruitment and employment.

## Practical suggestions

There is nothing in the indicative behaviours which is novel or of assistance in interpreting the one new requirement to encourage behaviour which goes beyond the statutory requirements. Firms will already have a written policy because it is a requirement of rule 6 of the 2007 Code. That should be checked for consistency with IB(2.1). Firms should also ensure that issues of training are addressed in the document.

In the absence of anything more by way of guidance from the SRA, our view is that the word 'encourage' is to be treated as a regulatory obligation to approach issues of equality and diversity in a positive frame of mind; to be alive to opportunities and, in a manner falling short of positive discrimination, to seek to ensure that issues of equality and diversity remain at the forefront when, in particular, decisions are made about employment matters.

In short, in our view, Chapter 2 is about having the right attitude of mind.

Looking at the matter from a defensive perspective – how do you ensure that the SRA will be satisfied – ask yourself the question: 'How do I/does the firm encourage equality of opportunity and respect for diversity?' and, having determined the answer, write it into your policy document.

The SRA has stated that it intends to carry out a 'thematic supervision pilot' to develop its approach to firms in relation to Principle 9 and Chapter 2, and that it will publish, on its website, frequently asked questions about compliance in this area by September 2011. It is to be hoped that the problems in interpretation of these provisions, highlighted above, will be comprehensively addressed. The FAQs have not been published at the time of going to press.

In the meantime, more positive assistance is available from the Law Society, which promotes a Diversity and Inclusion Charter, the signatories to which make a commitment to:

- Strive to achieve best practice in our recruitment, retention and career progression practices as employers.
- Support the development of good diversity practice by collecting and sharing with other signatories examples of practical activities that contribute to progress.
- Assign responsibility for meeting our Charter commitments to a named, senior level individual.
- Work together to develop and adopt future protocols that support the practical implementation of the aims of this Charter.
- Publish annually the diversity profile of our UK employees and details of our work on equality, diversity and inclusion.
- Publish a joint annual report on the basis of a monitoring exercise to measure the impact of this Diversity and Inclusion Charter and its protocols. These reports will form the basis of regular dialogue with stakeholders, employees and clients.

The Law Society makes available, free of charge to those who commit to the Charter, its 'Equality and diversity standards and toolkit', which is:

designed to help the legal profession to successfully promote and implement best practice in equality, diversity and inclusion – as employers, as providers of legal services, as purchasers of goods and services and in its wider role in society.

For further details visit: **www.lawsociety.org.uk/practicesupport/equality diversity/inclusioncharter/equalitystandards.page**.

## 5.4   CHAPTER 3 – CONFLICTS OF INTERESTS

This chapter, which is the successor to rule 3 of the 2007 Code, involves in part a restatement of current principles and rules, and in part fairly radical changes: in emphasis, particularly on the need for systems to avoid conflicts of interests; in brevity and relative simplicity (the former rule was the longest and most complex in the 2007 Code); and in its practical consequences, particularly for conveyancing.

It also gives a more proportionate prominence to conflicts of interests between solicitor and client (defined as 'own interest conflicts'), which was mentioned almost as an afterthought in the former rule.

It is constructive and to be welcomed that conflict of interests is treated not as one subject, but two, separating 'own interest conflicts' from 'client conflicts'.

Rule 3 of the 2007 Code was in many ways exceptional in that it was substantially concerned with the protection of solicitors rather than their regulation, and imposed limitations on the extent of a solicitor's duties when acting for lenders when the firm also acted for the borrower in routine conveyancing transactions. The rule prevented lenders from imposing onerous obligations and strictly limited the scope of the retainer. That protection survives to a limited extent, in that only a certificate of title in the form approved for the time being by the Law Society and the Council of Mortgage Lenders should be given in these circumstances, although this is no longer a rule, but non-binding guidance.

Much of the former rule was concerned with domestic conveyancing, and the circumstances in which a firm could act for both buyer and seller, as well as for lender and borrower. That part of the rule, and its many predecessors, imposed limitations on the ability of a firm to act for both parties, even if no conflict of interests existed. In other words, it was accepted that there was no inherent conflict of interests in acting for buyer and seller, but by regulation going beyond the requirements of the common law, solicitors were prevented from acting for both parties in most circumstances, even when there was no conflict. Solicitors were permitted to act for both parties, by exception to the general rule, in limited circumstances (for example, where both were established clients and gave written consent), but the exceptions did not apply if there was a conflict of interests.

A rule having this effect was first made in 1972, but the earliest commentary on the subject, in the 1960 Guide to the Professional Conduct and Etiquette of Solicitors (at page 114), stated firmly:

> . . . there are a good many conveyancing transactions in which the possibility of a conflict of interest between vendor and purchaser is remote and is rarely experienced in practice. There is thus nothing inherently improper in a solicitor acting for both vendor and purchaser . . . The complete cessation of the practice of acting for both parties would cause hardship and inconvenience to the public, particularly where both parties are already established clients of the same solicitor . . .

The new rule reflects the view of the SRA that this is not, or is no longer, correct. In its policy statement on 'The Architecture of Change Part 2 – The New SRA Handbook – Analysis of Responses' the SRA states its view in diametrically opposite terms:

> 74.      . . . the circumstances in which either there is no conflict of interests nor a significant risk of a conflict of interests as between buyer and seller must be extremely limited . . .
> 75.      . . . There may, of course, be some conveyancing situations where there are no conflicts of interests, although, for example, as between a seller and a buyer we expect that these will be rare. Our intention was not to prohibit acting in such cases, but rather to put the onus on firms to make the assessment as to whether a conflict exists.

It may be noted that the Council for Licensed Conveyancers (CLC) does not take the same view, and those it regulates may act for both parties in circumstances broadly comparable with rule 3 of the 2007 Code, though the CLC rules are somewhat less restrictive.

The SRA has not yet explained why and on what evidential basis it has come to the conclusion that something that has always in the past been thought not to involve an inherent or overwhelmingly likely conflict, now does.

This is likely to have a profound effect on conveyancing practice.

## 5.4.1   Chapter 3 outcomes

You must achieve these outcomes:

**Systems**

O(3.1)    you have effective systems and controls in place to enable you to identify and assess potential conflicts of interests;

O(3.2)    your systems and controls for identifying own interest conflicts are appropriate to the size and complexity of the firm and the nature of the work undertaken, and enable you to assess all the relevant circumstances, including whether your ability as an individual, or that of anyone within your firm, to act in the best interests of the client(s), is impaired by:

- any financial interest;
- a personal relationship;

51

- the appointment of you, or a member of your firm or family, to public office;
- commercial relationships; or
- your employment;

O(3.3)     your systems and controls for identifying client conflicts are appropriate to the size and complexity of the firm and the nature of the work undertaken, and enable you to assess all relevant circumstances, including whether:

- the clients' interests are different;
- your ability to give independent advice to the clients may be fettered;
- there is a need to negotiate between the clients;
- there is an imbalance in bargaining power between the clients; or
- any client is vulnerable;

**Prohibition on acting in conflict situations**

O(3.4)     you do not act if there is an own interest conflict or a significant risk of an own interest conflict;

O(3.5)     you do not act if there is a client conflict, or a significant risk of a client conflict, unless the circumstances set out in Outcomes 3.6 and 3.7 apply;

**Exceptions where you may act, with appropriate safeguards, where there is a client conflict**

O(3.6)     where there is a client conflict and the clients have a substantially common interest in relation to a matter or a particular aspect of it, you only act if:

(a)     you have explained the relevant issues and risks to the clients and you have a reasonable belief that they understand those issues and risks;

(b)     all the clients have given informed consent in writing to you acting;

(c)     you are satisfied that it is reasonable for you to act for all the clients and that it is in their best interests; and

(d)     you are satisfied that that the benefits to the clients of you doing so outweigh the risks;

O(3.7)     where there is a client conflict and the clients are competing for the same objective, you only act if:

(a)     you have explained the relevant issues and risks to the clients and you have a reasonable belief that they understand those issues and risks;

(b)     the clients have confirmed in writing that they want you to act, in the knowledge that you act, or may act, for one or more other clients who are competing for the same objective;

(c)     there is no other client conflict in relation to that matter;

(d)     unless the clients specifically agree, no individual acts for, or is responsible for the supervision of work done for, more than one of the clients in that matter; and

(e)     you are satisfied that it is reasonable for you to act for all the clients and that the benefits to the clients of you doing so outweigh the risks.

### 5.4.2   What is new? Chapter 3 outcomes

The emphasis on systems may be noted, commensurate with the size of firm.

The prohibition on acting in an own interest conflict is absolute. While it could be said that this has always been so, there has also always been an understanding that not every dealing between solicitor and client which has the potential for conflict in fact involves a conflict or a significant risk of one. Examples are an unsecured interest-free loan from solicitor to client, as an act of humanity; bridging finance on standard terms; or a modest gift in a will, as distinct from a gift which is 'significant' in the terms of the former rule 3.04.

Guidance to rule 3 of the 2007 Code (at note 42) made it clear that solicitors could take security for their costs by a charge over the client's property, and that independent legal advice 'would not normally be essential unless the terms of the proposed charge are particularly onerous or would give you some unusual benefit or profit'. So was that not a conflict, or a conflict that was exceptionally permitted? It would be difficult to argue that it was not, strictly speaking, a conflict of interests (what were the terms of the legal charge to be?).

Are these historic indications still valid? In our view they are. Save in respect of conveyancing, on which there is a plain shift in policy, there are no indications that the former regime is intended to be subjected to material change. Much of the former rule, particularly regarding the exceptions enabling the firm to act in client conflict situations, is reproduced without substantive change.

The SRA's position may also be gauged from another quotation from its policy statement:

> 75. The position under OFR is that we now expect firms to exercise their own judgement as to whether it would be proper to act in a particular situation, rather than the Handbook specifying the circumstances where it is appropriate to do so . . .

That suggests not a change in the rules, as such, but a change in the form of regulation, in effect, placing the onus on practitioners to think and make judgements.

That is indeed the OFR approach, and in our view in the situations described above by way of historic example there would be no failure to comply with the new Code.

As to client conflicts, the exceptions enabling firms to act despite a client conflict – particularly when read together with the relevant indicative behaviours (see **5.4.4**) and the reference to sophisticated clients in this context – reflect the provisions of the 2007 Code, expressed rather more economically. The phrase in the former rule: 'substantially common interest' is repeated verbatim, and now helpfully defined in Chapter 14 – Interpretation:

> . . . a situation where there is a clear common purpose in relation to any matter or a particular aspect of it between the clients and a strong consensus on how it is to be achieved and the client conflict is peripheral to this common purpose

The former provision relating to 'competing for the same asset' becomes 'competing for the same objective' and is also defined:

. . . any situation in which one or more clients are competing for an 'objective' which, if attained by one client will make that 'objective' unattainable to the other client or clients and 'objective' means, for the purposes of Chapter 3, an asset, contract or business opportunity which one or more clients are seeking to acquire or recover through a liquidation (or some other form of insolvency process) or by means of an auction or tender process or a bid or offer which is not public

The genuinely wholly new approach to conveyancing and to acting for buyer and seller can be discerned from the lack of any outcomes equivalent to rules 3.07 to 3.22 of the 2007 Code, from the indicative behaviours (see **5.4.4**) and from the policy statement quoted above.

### 5.4.3   Chapter 3 indicative behaviours

Acting in the following way(s) may tend to show that you have achieved these outcomes and therefore complied with the Principles:

IB(3.1)   training employees and managers to identify and assess potential conflicts of interests;

IB(3.2)   declining to act for clients whose interests are in direct conflict, for example claimant and defendant in litigation;

IB(3.3)   declining to act for clients where you may need to negotiate on matters of substance on their behalf, for example negotiating on price between a buyer and seller of a property;

IB(3.4)   declining to act where there is unequal bargaining power between the clients, for example acting for a seller and buyer where a builder is selling to a non-commercial client;

IB(3.5)   declining to act for clients under Outcome 3.6 (substantially common interest) or Outcome 3.7 (competing for the same objective) where the clients cannot be represented even-handedly, or will be prejudiced by lack of separate representation;

IB(3.6)   acting for clients under Outcome 3.7 (competing for the same objective) only where the clients are sophisticated users of legal services;

IB(3.7)   acting for clients who are the lender and borrower on the grant of a mortgage of land only where:

(a)   the mortgage is a standard mortgage (i.e. one provided in the normal course of the lender's activities, where a significant part of the lender's activities consists of lending and the mortgage is on standard terms) of property to be used as the borrower's private residence;

(b)   you are satisfied that it is reasonable and in the clients' best interests for you to act; and

(c)   the certificate of title required by the lender is in the form approved by the Society and the Council of Mortgage Lenders.

Acting in the following way(s) may tend to show that you have not achieved these outcomes and therefore not complied with the Principles:

IB(3.8)   in a personal capacity, selling to or buying from, lending to or borrowing from a client, unless the client has obtained independent legal advice;

IB(3.9)   advising a client to invest in a business, in which you have an interest which affects your ability to provide impartial advice;

IB(3.10)   where you hold a power of attorney for a client, using that power to gain a benefit for yourself which in your professional capacity you would not have been prepared to allow to a third party;

IB(3.11)   acting for two or more clients in a conflict of interests under Outcome 3.6 (substantially common interest) where the clients' interests in the end result are not the same, for example one partner buying out the interest of the other partner in their joint business or a seller transferring a property to a buyer;

IB(3.12)   acting for two or more clients in a conflict of interests under Outcome 3.6 (substantially common interest) where it is unreasonable to act because there is unequal bargaining power;

IB(3.13)   acting for two buyers where there is a conflict of interests under Outcome 3.7 (competing for the same objective), for example where two buyers are competing for a residential property;

IB(3.14)   acting for a buyer (including a lessee) and seller (including a lessor) in a transaction relating to the transfer of land for value, the grant or assignment of a lease or some other interest in land for value.

### 5.4.4   What is new? Chapter 3 indicative behaviours

Indicative behaviour 3.1 provides a helpful emphasis on training. Qualified lawyers have a fairly well-ingrained instinct about conflicts of interests. As new business models develop in an ABS environment, these instincts will not be able to be taken for granted.

It might be thought that IB(3.2) and IB(3.3), on the other hand, did not really need to be said.

Indicative behaviour 3.4 is consistent with the former restrictions on acting for seller and buyer, and no surprise.

Indicative behaviours 3.5 and 3.6, as well as IB(3.11), IB(3.12) and IB(3.13) sit happily with O(3.6) and O(3.7).

IB(3.7) preserves the *status quo* in relation to acting for lender and borrower in domestic conveyancing transactions, save that the reinforcement on the limitations of the retainer and the obligations a lender could impose, expressed in rule 3.19 of the 2007 Code, do not survive, though the requirement to use only the approved form of certificate of title, formerly the annex to rule 3 of the 2007 Code, is maintained, of course not in rule form, but as unenforceable guidance.

Indicative behaviours 3.8, 3.9 and 3.10 provide unexceptionable and unsurprising examples of own interest conflicts.

The potential for upheaval for conveyancing practice is to be found in IB(3.14) whereby acting for seller and buyer 'may tend to show that you have not achieved' the Chapter 3 outcomes.

We can foresee that the reaction to this change will depend on the attitude of firms to regulatory risk. Some will decide that IB(3.14) is in effect a rule against acting for buyer and seller, bearing in mind that it is unqualified in terms. Such firms will also note the assertions in the SRA's policy statement quoted above that:

74.      . . . the circumstances in which either there is no conflict of interests nor a

> significant risk of a conflict of interests as between buyer and seller must be extremely limited . . .
>
> 75. . . . There may, of course, be some conveyancing situations where there are no conflicts of interests, although, for example, as between a seller and a buyer we expect that these will be rare . . .

and may decide that the SRA's use of 'extremely limited' and 'rare' are a pretty broad hint that it will need a great deal of persuading that it is proper for a firm to act, ever, for buyer and seller and that its default position is that it cannot be done.

The rest of the quotation however may also be noted:

> Our intention was not to prohibit acting in such cases, but rather to put the onus on firms to make the assessment as to whether a conflict exists.

It does not help that no-one knows why the SRA has come to the view that there is almost certainly an inherent conflict when there is a considerable body of opinion, historic and current, that thinks otherwise, including the Council for Licensed Conveyancers.

## Practical suggestions

Firms which have conscientiously applied the exceptions in rule 3.02 of the 2007 Code can confidently continue on the basis that there is no material change.

Firms of all sizes must be able to demonstrate appropriate systems and controls to identify and assess potential conflicts, including staff training.

The historic approach to what is now called 'own interest conflict' will still be applicable.

Practice will have to change in relation to acting for buyer and seller in conveyancing transactions. Whether firms take the safest line and simply cease to act, or risk assess each case and choose to be prepared to justify departure from a perceived norm, it is not an option to carry on as before.

One of the former factors relevant to a firm's decision to act for both parties will continue to be relevant to an assessment of risk and the identification of a conflict: that the transaction is not at arm's length. Others will plainly not be relevant at all. The fact that both parties are established clients or that they are represented by two separate offices of the firm cannot be relevant to the presence or the absence of a conflict of interests.

Another problem is that because the SRA's default position is that only rarely will there not be a conflict of interest, a conveyancing practitioner who genuinely believes that in a particular case there is no conflict, but that there is nothing out of the ordinary about the transaction, may struggle to convince the SRA that it is in the narrow category where it is proper to act.

It would be highly desirable to make a note of the decision to act for both parties and the reasoning.

## 5.5 CHAPTER 4 – CONFIDENTIALITY AND DISCLOSURE

This chapter is the natural successor to rule 4 of the 2007 Code and, although it is drafted in a different style so it is consistent with OFR, the underlying philosophy and regulatory requirements are largely unaltered. It is, however, significantly simplified in relation to situations in which client consent and information barriers may be employed to prevent the misuse of confidential information.

The only wholly new matter is a reference to outsourcing and the protection of confidentiality in that context.

Chapter 4 is, and its predecessor was, mainly concerned in practice with situations in which confidential information is held relating to a former client. If a situation arose in relation to two or more current clients, the principles likely to be applicable will be found in Chapter 3 on conflicts of interest. Nevertheless, Chapter 4 refers throughout to 'clients' and makes no reference as one would expect to former clients. This is because the definition of client in Chapter 14 'where the context permits, includes prospective and former clients'. It should be borne in mind that this definition applies to the Code, and when the SRA completes its overall glossary, probably to the rest of the SRA Handbook, but it is not consistent with the statutory definition in s.87 of the Solicitors Act 1974, so it should not be used or taken to be relevant for other purposes.

### 5.5.1 Chapter 4 outcomes

You must achieve these outcomes:

O(4.1)   you keep the affairs of clients confidential unless disclosure is required or permitted by law or the client consents;

O(4.2)   any individual who is advising a client makes that client aware of all information material to that retainer of which the individual has personal knowledge;

O(4.3)   you ensure that where your duty of confidentiality to one client comes into conflict with your duty of disclosure to another client, your duty of confidentiality takes precedence;

O(4.4)   you do not act for A in a matter where A has an interest adverse to B, and B is a client for whom you hold confidential information which is material to A in that matter, unless the confidential information can be protected by the use of safeguards, and:

    (a)   you reasonably believe that A is aware of, and understands, the relevant issues and gives informed consent;

    (b)   either:

        (i)   B gives informed consent and you agree with B the safeguards to protect B's information; or

        (ii)   where this is not possible, you put in place effective safeguards including information barriers which comply with the common law; and

    (c)   it is reasonable in all the circumstances to act for A with such safeguards in place;

O(4.5)    you have effective systems and controls in place to enable you to identify risks to client confidentiality and to mitigate those risks.

### 5.5.2    Chapter 4 indicative behaviours

Acting in the following way(s) may tend to show that you have achieved these outcomes and therefore complied with the Principles:

IB(4.1)    your systems and controls for identifying risks to client confidentiality are appropriate to the size and complexity of the firm or in-house practice and the nature of the work undertaken, and enable you to assess all the relevant circumstances;

IB(4.2)    you comply with the law in respect of your fiduciary duties in relation to confidentiality and disclosure;

IB(4.3)    you only outsource services when you are satisfied that the provider has taken all appropriate steps to ensure that your clients' confidential information will be protected;

IB(4.4)    where you are an individual who has responsibility for acting for a client or supervising a client's matter you disclose to the client all information material to the client's matter of which you are personally aware except when:

- the client gives specific informed consent to non-disclosure or a different standard of disclosure arises;
- there is evidence that serious physical or mental injury will be caused to a person(s) if the information is disclosed to the client;
- legal restrictions effectively prohibit you from passing the information to the *client*, such as the provisions in the money-laundering and anti-terrorism legislation;
- it is obvious that privileged documents have been mistakenly disclosed to you;
- you come into possession of information relating to state security or intelligence matters to which the Official Secrets Act 1989 applies;

IB(4.5)    not acting for A where B is a client for whom you hold confidential information which is material to A unless the confidential information can be protected.

Acting in the following way(s) may tend to show that you have not achieved these outcomes and therefore not complied with the Principles:

IB(4.6)    disclosing the content of a will on the death of a client unless consent has been provided by the personal representatives for the content to be released;

IB(4.7)    disclosing details of bills sent to clients to third parties, such as debt factoring companies in relation to the collection of book debts, unless the client has consented.

### 5.5.3    What is new? Chapter 4

The importance of systems is again emphasised (O(4.5) and IB(4.1)).

As mentioned above, there is a focus on the preservation of confidentiality in the context of outsourcing. Outsourcing is considered in more detail in the discussion of Chapter 7 (see **5.8.4**).

The rules and guidance relevant to information barriers (Chinese walls or ethical walls) have been redrawn and simplified, but, when fully analysed, without material change from the position under rule 4 of the 2007 Code. However, it is necessary to have regard to the explanatory notes to Chapter 4 to get the full picture. In substance: there are exceptional circumstances in which it is possible to act for one client, to whom a duty would be owed to disclose material information, when there is a contemporaneous duty of confidentiality to a second client (or former client) which would prevent such disclosure. It is possible to continue to act, on the basis that confidentiality to the second client is absolutely maintained, subject to various combinations of informed consent, adequate and effective information barriers, and the common law. It is important to recognise that this is an exception to the normal absolute rule that continuing to act in these circumstances would be bound to put a solicitor in breach of one or other duty, and therefore impossible. (See, for example, *Hilton* v. *Barker Booth and Eastwood (a firm)* [2005] UKHL 8.)

In this chapter it can reasonably be said that the guidance notes, which are not binding, are nevertheless important and an aid to interpretation of the outcomes, and an understanding of the law is also required.

It is convenient first to establish the legal position, not least because O(4.4)(b)(ii) and IB(4.2) require compliance with the law.

## The common law

The line of authorities starts relevantly with *Bolkiah* v. *KPMG* [1999] 2 AC 222 and the judgment of Lord Millett. The principles are helpfully extracted and summarised in *Koch Shipping Inc* v. *Richards Butler* [2002] EWCA Civ 1280 [24] in the following terms:

(1)   The court's jurisdiction to intervene is founded on the right of the former client to the protection of his confidential information (per Lord Millett at p.234).

(2)   The only duty to the former client which survives the termination of the client relationship is a continuing duty to preserve the confidentiality of information imparted during its subsistence (per Lord Millett at p.235).

(3)   The duty to preserve confidentiality is unqualified. It is a duty to keep the information confidential, not merely to take all reasonable steps to do so (per Lord Millett at p.235).

(4)   The former client cannot be protected completely from accidental or inadvertent disclosure, but he is entitled to prevent his former solicitor from exposing him to any avoidable risk. This includes the increased risk of the use of the information to his prejudice arising from the acceptance of instructions to act for another client with an adverse interest in a matter to which the information may be relevant (per Lord Millett at pp.235–236).

(5)   The former client must establish that the defendant solicitors possess confidential information which is or might be relevant to the matter and to the disclosure of which he has not consented (per Lord Millett at pp.234–235).

(6)   The burden then passes to the defendant solicitors to show that there is *no risk* of disclosure. The court should intervene unless it is satisfied that there is no risk of disclosure. The risk must be a real one, and not merely fanciful or theoretical, but it need not be substantial (per Lord Millett at p.237).

(7)     It is wrong in principle to conduct a balancing exercise. If the former client establishes the facts in (5) above, the former client is entitled to an injunction unless the defendant solicitors show that there is no risk of disclosure.

(8)     In considering whether the solicitors have shown that there is no risk of disclosure, the starting point must be that, unless special measures are taken, information moves within a firm (per Lord Millett at p.237). However, that is only the starting point. The *Prince Jefri [Bolkiah ]* case does not establish a rule of law that special measures have to be taken to prevent the information passing within a firm: see also *Young* v *Robson Rhodes* [1999] 3 All ER 524, per Laddie J at p.538. On the other hand, the courts should restrain the solicitors from acting unless satisfied on the basis of clear and convincing evidence that all effective measures have been taken to ensure that no disclosure will occur (per Lord Millett at pp.237–238, where he adapted the test identified by Sopinka J in *MacDonald Estate* v *Martin* (1991) 77 DLR (4th) 249 at p.269). This is a heavy burden (per Lord Millett at p.239).

And at [25]:

It is to my mind important to emphasise that each case turns on its own facts.

A useful example of the practical measures necessary to be taken can be seen from the undertakings given by the solicitors in *Gus Consulting GmbH* v. *LeBoeuf Lamb Greene & Macrae* [2006] EWCA Civ 683 [20]:

(1)     By 5pm on Friday 4 November 2005 the Defendant will cause changes to be made to its working arrangements at its London offices so that the Arbitration Team [named] will not occupy office space on the same floor as those who have previously carried out work for CAIB and are still with the Defendant, and who are listed in the table attached to this order ('the relevant partners and staff');

(2)     The Defendant will, as soon as is reasonably practicable, issue an instruction in writing by e-mail to the relevant partners and staff that they are not to discuss that work with any member of the Arbitration Team or amongst themselves;

(3)     None of the Arbitration Team will seek any information about CAIB from any of the relevant partners and staff, nor seek access to any paper or electronic files concerning CAIB;

(4)     None of the relevant partners and staff will discuss CAIB work amongst themselves or with any member of the Arbitration Team;

(5)     The Defendant will until otherwise agreed by the Claimant or approved by the Court;

   (a)     at all times maintain the ethical wall presently in place
   (b)     take reasonable steps to monitor the effectiveness of the ethical wall
   (c)     take reasonable steps to monitor compliance with undertakings (2)–(4) set out above.

(6)     The Defendant will, during the months of April and October of every year during the currency of LCIA Arbitration 2371

   (a)     issue a fresh instruction repeating the instruction in paragraph (2) above,
   (b)     verify that there has been no breach of the ethical wall presently in place, and that the integrity of the ethical wall is maintained
   (c)     notify the Claimant in writing that it has taken the steps referred to in 6) (a) and (b) above.

The 'ethical wall' involved three main steps: software preventing access to any electronic documents relating to restricted matters; allocation of a matter number used in archive management software to prevent given lawyers from being able to retrieve any files; and the files were physically stamped as being restricted. In addition, instructions were disseminated internally to draw attention to the importance of the confidential material not coming to the attention of anybody, particularly those in the team working on the arbitration. The sensitive material related to transactions which had taken place and been concluded some years previously.

It was only upon the basis of these arrangements and the undertakings that the court was persuaded not to restrain the firm from acting by injunction.

It follows that although the issue will remain fact sensitive, arrangements that are less effective and wide ranging would be unlikely to be sufficient, and it would not be lawful for a firm to continue acting, unless it were to be possible – on the basis of informed consent by the affected client – to impose safeguards which were less than is required by the common law.

It is unsurprising in the circumstances that the guidance notes to Chapter 4 emphasise the difficulty of implementing effective safeguards and information barriers if the firm is small; if the physical structure or layout of the firm means that it will be difficult to preserve confidentiality; or if the clients are not sophisticated users of legal services.

While this is not a 'City firm only' rule or '20+ partner only' rule, in reality it is unlikely in the extreme that any small firm would be able achieve the necessary protections and effective barriers.

It is also noted that the protection of confidential information may be at particular risk where two or more firms merge, or one or more lawyers leave one firm and join another, resulting in a team acting against one of its former clients.

## A practical checklist

In O(4.4) both parties are referred to as clients but it may be easier to think of A as the current client who would be interested in receiving information, and B as the former client whose right to confidentiality is in play. Although the outcome refers to A having an adverse interest to B, this is not strictly the position in law (though it is likely to be the case in practice). The important point is not whether they have contrary interests in a litigation sense, but whether A would want to receive the information, because it is 'material'; that is, potentially of value, and whether B would agree to release it or would want the confidential information to remain so.

If this situation arises and B does not consent to disclosure – or plainly cannot be expected to consent if asked – the default position is that the firm must cease to act for A. If the firm wishes to use the exception provided by O(4.4), the following checks need to be made:

- Would it be reasonable, in principle, for the firm to continue to act for A if sufficient safeguards to protect B could be put in place? Would this be in A's interests? One could envisage a situation in which those acting for A within the firm might have been compromised by learning of the confidential information so that, as a minimum, a new team would have to take over immediately, and it might on balance be better if A instructs a new firm. If nevertheless the answer is yes:

- A must give informed consent; that is, A must be informed that the firm has information of potential value that it cannot disclose. The firm would almost certainly not be in a position to identify B as the source of that information or to say anything more about it, although, for example, as a result of a protest by B, A may otherwise learn something of this. A must be content, without knowing more, for the firm to continue acting on the basis that the information will never be disclosed. This would require a sophisticated thought process and an enlightened individual or body who is well able to understand that, amongst other things, there will be 'no cheating'. Although the outcome says that the firm must 'reasonably believe' that A understands and gives informed consent, there is little room here for uncertainty. If A does give informed consent, either:
- B is consulted, agrees that the firm may continue to act and agrees the safeguards to be put in place to protect the confidential information, which could be to a standard sufficient to meet the common law requirements, or something less; or
- In the absence of B's informed consent, which could be, for example, because of an unreasonable refusal or because B cannot be contacted, safeguards are put in place sufficient to meet the firm's obligations at law.

## 5.6 CHAPTER 5 – YOUR CLIENT AND THE COURT

This chapter is the successor to rule 11 of the 2007 Code (Litigation and advocacy) and little has changed.

### 5.6.1 Chapter 5 outcomes

You must achieve these outcomes:

O(5.1)   you do not attempt to deceive or knowingly or recklessly mislead, the court;
O(5.2)   you are not complicit in another person deceiving or misleading the court;
O(5.3)   you comply with court orders which place obligations on you;
O(5.4)   you do not place yourself in contempt of court;
O(5.5)   where relevant, clients are informed of the circumstances in which your duties to the court outweigh your obligations to your client;
O(5.6)   you comply with your duties to the court;
O(5.7)   you ensure that evidence relating to sensitive issues is not misused;
O(5.8)   you do not make or offer to make payments to witnesses dependent upon their evidence or the outcome of the case.

## 5.6.2 Chapter 5 indicative behaviours

Acting in the following way(s) may tend to show that you have achieved these outcomes and therefore complied with the Principles:

IB(5.1)   advising your clients to comply with court orders made against them, and advising them of the consequences of failing to comply;

IB(5.2)   drawing the court's attention to relevant cases and statutory provisions, and any material procedural irregularity;

IB(5.3)   ensuring child witness evidence is kept securely and not released to clients or third parties;

IB(5.4)   immediately informing the court, with your client's consent, if during the course of proceedings you become aware that you have inadvertently misled the court, or ceasing to act if the client does not consent to you informing the court;

IB(5.5)   refusing to continue acting for a client if you become aware they have committed perjury or misled the court, or attempted to mislead the court, in any material matter unless the client agrees to disclose the truth to the court;

IB(5.6)   not appearing as an advocate, or acting in litigation, if it is clear that you, or anyone within your firm, will be called as a witness in the matter unless you are satisfied that this will not prejudice your independence as an advocate, or litigator, or the interests of your clients or the interests of justice.

Acting in the following way(s) may tend to show that you have not achieved these outcomes and therefore not complied with the Principles:

IB(5.7)   constructing facts supporting your client's case or drafting any documents relating to any proceedings containing:

- any contention which you do not consider to be properly arguable; or
- any allegation of fraud, unless you are instructed to do so and you have material which you reasonably believe shows, on the face of it, a case of fraud;

IB(5.8)   suggesting that any person is guilty of a crime, fraud or misconduct unless such allegations:

- go to a matter in issue which is material to your own client's case; and
- appear to you to be supported by reasonable grounds;

IB(5.9)   calling a witness whose evidence you know is untrue;

IB(5.10)  attempting to influence a witness, when taking a statement from that witness, with regard to the contents of their statement;

IB(5.11)  tampering with evidence or seeking to persuade a witness to change their evidence;

IB(5.12)  when acting as an advocate, naming in open court any third party whose character would thereby be called into question, unless it is necessary for the proper conduct of the case;

IB(5.13)  when acting as an advocate, calling into question the character of a witness you have cross-examined unless the witness has had the opportunity to answer the allegations during cross-examination.

## 5.6.3 Chapter 5 notes

1.   If you are a litigator or an advocate there may be occasions when your obligation to act in the best interests of a client may conflict with your duty to the court. In such

situations you may need to consider whether the public interest is best served by the proper administration of justice and should take precedence over the interests of your client.

### 5.6.4 What is new? Chapter 5

There is nothing substantively different from the obligations imposed by the 2007 Code and any practitioner familiar with the proper standards of behaviour for litigators and advocates need have no concern that the new outcomes or indicative behaviours present any traps.

The opportunity has been taken to clarify one situation: both rule 11 of the 2007 Code and the first drafts of the present Chapter 5 included references to the court being misled by others: in rule 11: 'You must never . . . knowingly allow the court to be misled' and in the draft Chapter 5: 'You do not knowingly allow another person to deceive or mislead . . . the court'.

Both could have been interpreted to mean that in the well-known situation in which, in the criminal courts, the prosecution fails to identify that the defendant had previous convictions, a defence advocate would have been under a regulatory obligation to correct the misunderstanding. The former rule was never interpreted in that way because it was well understood that in this respect the 2007 Code served to codify existing principles and guidance and not to change them.

The new Code is to be interpreted as it stands without assistance from the legislative background, as it is part of a complete new regulatory system. An outcome which required defence advocates to prevent the court being innocently misled by the prosecution would, amongst other things, have required different standards to be applied by barristers and solicitors.

The law has always been that:

> A barrister must not wilfully mislead the court as to the law nor may he actively mislead the court as to the facts; although, consistently with the rule that the prosecution must prove its case, he may passively stand by and watch the court being misled by reason of its failure to ascertain facts that are within the barrister's knowledge. (*Saif Ali* v. *Sydney Mitchell & Co* [1980] AC 198, per Lord Diplock at 220)

By changing O(5.2) to its present form, prohibiting a solicitor from being 'complicit' in another person misleading the court, the *status quo* is maintained.

### Practical suggestions

Although the constraint is not new and IB(5.6) is very similarly worded to rule 11.06 of the 2007 Code, it has caused difficulties in the past because it has not seemed to be wholly logical.

The rule was first expressed as guidance in successive Guides to Professional Conduct. There the principle was:

A solicitor must not accept instructions to act as an advocate for a client if it is clear that he or she or a member of the firm will be called as a witness on behalf of the client, unless the evidence is purely formal.

It will be noted that the focus is not only on advocacy, but on the sequence of events. The question was whether a solicitor could 'accept instructions to act' – in other words, the mischief at which the principle is aimed is a situation in which it is *already* clear that the solicitor is or is likely to be a material witness. One can well see that if the solicitor had, for example, been a witness to a road accident and one of the drivers or passengers subsequently instructed that solicitor's firm, professional issues would be likely to arise.

The rule has far less logical application when the solicitor acts for the client perfectly properly, and then something arises as a result of the solicitor/client relationship which makes it appropriate or necessary for the solicitor to give supportive evidence. It is commonplace, as is very well known, for solicitors to give evidence for their clients about matters arising in the course of the retainer, for example, on procedural matters and as to dealings with opposing solicitors in civil proceedings (which probably happens many times every single day if one includes written evidence in support of interlocutory applications), and in criminal proceedings in the circumstances where evidence may be needed that the defendant exercised his or her right of silence on advice. The idea that, in this situation, the solicitor would be obliged to cease to act, for no logical reason but only because the rule appeared to suggest it, would make little sense.

In our view the primary historical concern was the situation where a solicitor who is a material witness to matters unrelated to the solicitor/client relationship is subsequently instructed. In the guidance notes to the former rule 11.06 it was said that it would be 'extremely rare' for it to be proper to act in litigation where you are also a witness. This could not make sense unless the rule is interpreted as we suggest.

The present Code and this specific outcome permit this interpretation more easily than the 2007 Code by shifting the focus from the giving of evidence, *per se*, to whether giving evidence would offend any of the Principles which require independence, the interests of the client and the interests of justice to be considered. No such concerns tend to arise in the everyday situations in which most solicitors find themselves giving evidence on behalf of their clients.

## 5.7  CHAPTER 6 – YOUR CLIENT AND INTRODUCTIONS TO THIRD PARTIES

Chapter 6 derives from rule 9.03 and rule 19.01(1)(a) of the 2007 Code. As will be discussed below, it is doubtful whether the use of apparently more liberal language has actually reduced the solicitor's regulatory obligations, and in one important respect, it has increased them.

### 5.7.1 Chapter 6 introduction

There may be circumstances in which you wish to refer your clients to third parties, perhaps to another lawyer or a financial services provider. This chapter describes the conduct duties which arise in respect of such introductions. It is important that you retain your independence when recommending third parties to your client and that you act in the client's best interests.

### 5.7.2 Chapter 6 outcomes

You must achieve these outcomes:

O(6.1)   whenever you recommend that a client uses a particular person or business, your recommendation is in the best interests of the client and does not compromise your independence;

O(6.2)   clients are fully informed of any financial or other interest which you have in referring the client to another person or business;

O(6.3)   if a client is likely to need advice on investments, such as life insurance with an investment element or pension policies, you refer them only to an independent intermediary.

### 5.7.3 Chapter 6 indicative behaviours

Acting in the following way(s) may tend to show that you have achieved these outcomes and therefore complied with the Principles:

IB(6.1)   any arrangement you enter into in respect of regulated mortgage contracts, general insurance contracts (including after the event insurance) or pure protection contracts, provides that referrals will only be made where this is in the best interests of the particular client and the contract is suitable for the needs of that client;

IB(6.2)   any referral in respect of regulated mortgage contracts, general insurance contracts and pure protection contracts to a third party that can only offer products from one source, is made only after the client has been informed of this limitation.

Acting in the following way(s) may tend to show that you have not achieved these outcomes and therefore not complied with the Principles:

IB(6.3)   entering into any arrangement which restricts your freedom to recommend any particular business, except in respect of regulated mortgage contracts, general insurance contracts or pure protection contracts;

IB(6.4)   being an appointed representative.

### Definitions

It is useful to define the following terms, as per Chapter 14:

• 'arrangement' in relation to financial services, fee sharing and referrals, in Chapters 1, 6 and 9, means any express or tacit agreement between a solicitor and another person, whether contractually binding or not;

- 'regulated mortgage contract' has the meaning given by article 61(3) of the Financial Services and Markets Act 2000 (Regulated Activities) Order 2001, SI 2001/544;
- 'pure protection contract', by rule 8(1) of the SRA Financial Services (Scope) Rules 2001, is defined as:

 (1) a long-term insurance contract
  (a) under which the benefits are payable only in respect of death or of incapacity due to injury, sickness or infirmity;
  (b) which has no surrender value or the consideration consists of a single premium and the surrender value does not exceed that premium; and
  (c) which makes no provision for its conversion or extension in a manner which would result in its ceasing to comply with (a), or (b); or

 (2) a reinsurance contract covering all or part of a risk to which a person is exposed under a long-term insurance contract

- 'appointed representative' has the meaning given in the Financial Services and Markets Act 2000.

### 5.7.4 What is new? Chapter 6

An important change is that the referral provisions in Chapter 6 now apply to referrals between lawyers. Rule 9 of the 2007 Code did not apply to such referrals, by virtue of a specific exception in rule 9.01(3). Solicitors will have to be fully transparent as to any referral fee paid to them by other lawyers to whom they refer work.

Noteworthy features of the old rules included the following:

- By rules 9.03(2) and (3), solicitors could not enter into any agreement which would restrict their freedom to recommend any particular firm, agency or business, save in the case of regulated mortgage contracts, general insurance contracts or pure protection contracts.
- By rule 9.03(5), where solicitors referred clients to a firm, agency or business that could only offer products from one source, they had to notify the client in writing of this limitation.
- By rule 9.03(6), where clients were likely to need an endowment policy, or similar life insurance with an investment element, solicitors could only refer them to an independent intermediary authorised to give investment advice – this rule is substantially re-enacted in O(6.3).

The new rules, at least on the surface, are more liberal. The prohibition against solicitors restricting their freedom to recommend particular firms, etc. has shifted from a rule in the 2007 Code to a non-mandatory indicative behaviour – IB(6.3). However, this is a further example of a supposedly non-mandatory indicative behaviour looking suspiciously like a mandatory rule, particularly as O(6.1) requires that a solicitor's recommendation must be in the best interests of the client and that the solicitor must not compromise their independence. In reality, it is difficult to see how a solicitor can tie themselves to a particular service provider without compromising their independence and in the light of IB(6.3) they would run an unacceptable regulatory risk were they to do so. By O(6.2), full disclosure has to be made to the lay client of any financial interest the solicitor has in making a referral.

Reflections of the pre-existing rules in respect of regulated mortgage contracts, general insurance contracts or pure protection contracts (by which solicitors could tie themselves to particular providers) are found in the non-mandatory indicative behaviours, IB(6.1) and IB(6.2). Solicitors must be satisfied that referrals to the preferred provider are in the best interests of clients, that the contract is suitable for the needs of the client (arguably a matter outside the expertise of the solicitor), and the clients must be made aware of the solicitor's lack of freedom in making the referral before the referral is made. In the light of the terms of O(6.1), it is doubtful if IB(6.1) and (6.2) were actually necessary.

Indicative behaviour 6.4, which states that being an appointed representative may tend to show that a solicitor has not achieved these outcomes and therefore not complied with the Principles, again has all the appearances of a mandatory rule, and was formerly found in rule 19.01(1)(a) of the 2007 Code.

It is no longer formally necessary for solicitors to provide written notification where the client is referred to a business that can only offer products from one source. However, it is difficult to see how a solicitor could be acting in the best interests of their client if they were to opt not to provide such important information to the client.

Although O(6.2), by which solicitors must fully inform clients of any financial or other interest which they have in referring the client to another person or business, is new, it is doubtful whether this ought to make any practical difference. Solicitors have always been prevented by the general law from making a secret profit, although the Law Society created a *de minimis* exception in respect of commissions of £20 or less. Subject to that, solicitors have always been prevented from retaining commissions paid to them unless they have the informed consent of the client. This topic is dealt with in detail at **5.2.6**.

All in all, it is doubtful whether Chapter 6 has significantly altered or liberalised the rules which preceded it. The language is more liberal, but the obligations appear to remain much the same. By extending the rules to referrals between lawyers, the regulatory burden on solicitors has actually been increased.

## 5.8  CHAPTER 7 – YOU AND YOUR BUSINESS

This chapter is the successor to rule 5 of the 2007 Code; it emphasises that everyone has a role to play in the efficient running of a business, although of course that role will depend on the individual's position within the organisation. The responsibility for the management of the business in the broadest sense rests with the managers. The managers should determine what arrangements are appropriate to meet the outcomes, having regard to: the size and complexity of the business; the number, experience and qualifications of the employees; the number of offices; and the nature of the work undertaken.

It will be important to have regard to the roles of compliance officers for legal practice (COLPs) and compliance officers for finance and administration (COFAs) under the SRA Authorisation Rules, and to understand the responsibilities of those individuals on the one hand, and of the managers of the practice on the other (see **7.3**).

There is a new focus on outsourcing, though this is somewhat unformed and indicative of a recognition on the part of the SRA that regulation is needed in this area, but without as yet much in the way of practical detail.

Chapter 7 marks a significant move towards a more aggressive regulation of business management. Many of the words are familiar, but whereas rule 5 was mainly concerned with ensuring that firms had 'systems', including, for example, systems concerned with financial control, there was no regulatory obligation to ensure that the business was financially sound, with the consequence that if it was not, it would become a matter of interest to, and potentially lead to action by, the regulator.

It is in this area of regulation that it is expected we will see the greatest impact of OFR, because of its focus on risk and risk avoidance. For example, a firm in which no partner or employee has ever been guilty of misconduct in the traditional sense, which has complied meticulously with the Accounts Rules and to which any breach of the rules of conduct would be anathema, may nevertheless feel the full force of regulatory interest and supervision if it constantly struggles to stay within its overdraft limit, and to pay VAT, PAYE and rent on time. For these are indications that the firm may not be viable, or that the partners are imprudent in terms of the level of drawings.

Not long ago, if the question were to be asked: 'Is it professional misconduct to fail to pay the office rent?' the answer would have been that the regulator was not a debt collection agency and business debts did not raise issues of conduct (although, depending on the facts, it might trigger a precautionary inspection of the firm's accounts because of the enhanced risk that money might be 'borrowed' from the client account in such circumstances).

The current view would be that the same facts would amount to a breach of O(7.4) – monitoring financial stability and taking steps to address identified issues. A firm might be required to demonstrate the steps that are being taken to deal with the situation, including redundancy programmes, a freeze on drawings or capital injection, or to accept that the business has become unviable and that a plan for the orderly closure of the practice is needed, under the SRA's supervision.

### 5.8.1   Chapter 7 outcomes

You must achieve these outcomes:

O(7.1)   you have a clear and effective governance structure and reporting lines;

O(7.2)   you have effective systems and controls in place to achieve and comply with all the Principles, rules and outcomes and other requirements of the Handbook, where applicable;

O(7.3)   you identify, monitor and manage risks to compliance with all the Principles, rules and outcomes and other requirements of the Handbook, if applicable to you, and take steps to address issues identified;

O(7.4)   you maintain systems and controls for monitoring the financial stability of your firm and risks to money and assets entrusted to you by clients and others, and you take steps to address issues identified;

O(7.5)   you comply with legislation applicable to your business, including anti-money laundering and data protection legislation;

O(7.6)   you train individuals working in the firm to maintain a level of competence appropriate to their work and level of responsibility;

O(7.7)   you comply with the statutory requirements for the direction and supervision of reserved legal activities and immigration work;

O(7.8)   you have a system for supervising clients' matters, to include the regular checking of the quality of work, by suitably competent and experienced people;

O(7.9)   you do not outsource reserved legal activities to a person who is not authorised to conduct such activities;

O(7.10)  subject to Outcome 7.9, where you outsource legal activities, or any operational functions that are critical to the delivery of any legal activities, you ensure such outsourcing:

    (a)   does not adversely affect your ability to comply with, or the SRA's ability to monitor your compliance with, your obligations in the Handbook;

    (b)   is subject to contractual arrangements that enable the SRA or its agent to obtain information from, inspect the records (including electronic records) of, or enter the premises of, the third party, in relation to the outsourced activities or functions;

    (c)   does not alter your obligations towards your clients; and

    (d)   does not cause you to breach the conditions with which you must comply in order to be authorised and to remain so.

### 5.8.2   Chapter 7 indicative behaviours

Acting in the following way(s) may tend to show that you have achieved these outcomes and therefore complied with the Principles:

IB(7.1)   safekeeping of documents and assets entrusted to the firm;

IB(7.2)   controlling budgets, expenditure and cash flow;

IB(7.3)   identifying and monitoring financial, operational and business continuity risks including complaints, credit risks and exposure, claims under legislation relating to matters such as data protection, IT failures and abuses, and damage to offices;

IB(7.4)    making arrangements for the continuation of your firm in the event of absences and emergencies, for example holiday or sick leave, with the minimum interruption to clients' business.

### 5.8.3   What is new? Chapter 7

The references to the regulation of outsourcing in O(7.9) and O(7.10) are completely new and require detailed consideration; see **5.8.4**.

In other respects, the areas of responsibility addressed by Chapter 7 correspond for the most part to words or concepts found in rule 5: an effective governance structure (O(7.1)) in place of 'effective management of the firm'; systems to achieve compliance with the SRA Handbook (O(7.2)) in place of arrangements for compliance with 'key regulatory requirements'; compliance with legislation including anti-money laundering and data protection legislation (O(7.5)), whereas only money laundering regulations were previously mentioned specifically (though one has to question whether there is a need for an outcome in any chapter of the Code which is to the effect that solicitors must comply with the law). The training obligation (O(7.6)) is in virtually identical words to the previous rule.

The requirements for supervision have been split between two concepts: supervision of client matters (O(7.8)), and ensuring that reserved legal activities and immigration work (in other words, work that is reserved to those statutorily entitled to carry it out, either under the Legal Services Act 2007 or the Immigration and Asylum Act 1999), are carried out within a regulated environment (O(7.7)).

The requirements for supervision of client matters have been redrafted to emphasise the need for regular checking of the quality of work by those who are suitably competent and experienced.

Both of these changes are to be expected in a regime in which businesses, through ABSs, may be supplying regulated and unregulated services; O(7.7) is designed to ensure that there is no slippage of regulated services into the unregulated part of the business. An emphasis on checking by suitably competent and experienced people is appropriate when it can no longer be assumed that qualified lawyers will be involved in the day–to-day supply of commoditised legal services, other than in a supervisory role.

As mentioned at **5.8** above, there are significant changes in emphasis. Whereas O(7.2) requires systems designed to ensure compliance, and is not new, O(7.3) requires firms to 'identify, monitor and manage risks to compliance' and to 'take steps to address issues identified'. This is enhanced by O(7.4) requiring firms to monitor risks to financial stability.

A standard question in future might be: 'What are the major risks to compliance and the financial viability of your firm that you have identified, and what steps have you taken to address them?'

These risks and steps could be of the relatively traditional variety – for example, the risk of misappropriation of funds by accounts staff, and the checks and balances established to minimise those risks – but the question will also relate to larger concepts, such as an over-dependence on work of a particular kind, which could dry up or be lost to competition, or an over-dependence on one or a small number of sources of work, the withdrawal of which would threaten the viability of the business.

There is no reference in this chapter of the Code to the concept of the person 'qualified to supervise' – a material part of rule 5 of the 2007 Code. At first blush, this could have appeared to be a deregulatory move entirely consistent with OFR, but Chapter 7 of the Code does not contain a complete list of all the outcomes required for compliant management of the business. Firms must also comply with the SRA Practice Framework Rules, and rule 12 of those rules maintains this aspect of rule 5 of the 2007 Code:

12.1 The following persons must be 'qualified to supervise':

    (a)    a recognised sole practitioner;

    (b)    one of the lawyer managers of an authorised body or of a body corporate which is a legally qualified body and which is a manager of the authorised body;

    (c)    one of the solicitors or RELs employed by a law centre in England and Wales; or

    (d)    one in-house solicitor or in-house REL in any department in England and Wales where solicitors and/or RELs, as part of their employment:

        (i)    do publicly funded work; or

        (ii)    do or supervise advocacy or the conduct of proceedings for members of the public before a court or immigration tribunal.

12.2 To be 'qualified to supervise' under this rule a person must:

    (a)    have completed the training specified from time to time by the SRA for this purpose; and

    (b)    have been entitled to practise as a lawyer for at least 36 months within the last 10 years; and

must be able to demonstrate this if asked by the SRA.

Indicative behaviour 7.1 as to the safekeeping of documents and client assets entrusted to the firm is somewhat otiose, and IB(7.2) as to controlling budgets, expenditure and cashflow is a reflection of rule 5 of the 2007 Code, and thus no change.

Indicative behaviour 7.3 provides a convenient but non-exclusive list of business risks. Indicative behaviour 7.4 dealing with business continuity appears to downgrade this obligation from a rule (rule 5.01(1)(k) of the 2007 Code) to a non-binding recommendation, but a better way of considering the matter is that continuity is a business risk, and a risk to the management of client matters, and thus something to be addressed for compliance with O(7.3) and O(7.4).

### 5.8.4 Outsourcing

There are some indications that this whole subject was a late entrant to the Code. Outsourcing is one of the few material words that is not defined in Chapter 14, possibly the only one (there are a total of 91 words and phrases specifically defined).

On the 'Outcomes-focused regulation at a glance' section of the SRA website under the heading 'Q&A – Outsourcing', the SRA explains that the outsourcing provisions 'are aimed at firms or in-house solicitors who use a third party to undertake work that the firm or in-house solicitor would normally do themselves and for which the firm or in-house solicitor remains responsible'. However, it also says: 'The outsourcing provisions in the Code ... do not apply when you use a specialist service to assist with the provision of legal services to a client, for example instructing counsel, medical experts, tax experts or accountancy services.'

This is not entirely satisfactory nor entirely consistent. Firms may very frequently instruct counsel in circumstances where it would be 'normal' for the firm to have done the work itself, but where such instruction is an efficient use of time and resources, and no more. The firm would nevertheless remain 'responsible' for the service overall, including the choice of counsel and would (perhaps jointly) be liable for any mistakes in the sense that counsel's advice or drafts could not be uncritically passed on. See *Davy-Chiesman* v. *Davy-Chiesman* [1984] 2 WLR 291 (at p. 303) per May LJ:

> ... a solicitor is in general entitled to rely on the advice of counsel properly instructed. However, this does not operate so as to give a solicitor an immunity in every such case. A solicitor is highly trained and rightly expected to be experienced in his particular legal fields. He is under a duty at all times to exercise that degree of care, to both client and the court, that can be expected of a reasonably prudent solicitor. He is not entitled to rely blindly and with no mind of his own on counsel's views.

Outcome 7.9 prohibits the outsourcing of reserved legal activities to a person who is not authorised to conduct such activities (since under the Legal Services Act 2007, s.14, it is unlawful to conduct reserved legal activities when not entitled to do).

Applying the words of the Code, instructing counsel, at least in cases where this is done for reasons of efficiency or expedience and not, for example, to obtain specialist assistance unavailable within the firm, is subject to O(7.10). The SRA website guidance cannot change the interpretation of the Code; that is a matter of statutory construction. It can be a reliable indication as to how the SRA is intending to interpret the rules it has made (always bearing in mind the ephemeral nature of websites and that guidance can change without notice).

What we appear to have here is something of a half-way house where the rules are being supplemented with guidance, where what is needed is a better drafted rule and, in particular, a better definition of what is really meant by outsourcing.

The SRA appears to have two main aims – again, this is apparent from its website rather than the Code: 'It is important that when firms outsource work this does not affect our ability to regulate the firm's activities and that clients remain fully protected.' So in part this element of regulation is intended to ensure that outsourcing does not take matters outside the ability of the SRA to regulate, as well as what might be described as the basic requirement that any practitioner would appreciate.

Outcome 7.10 refers to the outsourcing of 'legal activities or any operational functions that are critical to the delivery of any legal activities'. A legal activity is defined in the Legal Services Act 2007, s.12 and includes reserved legal activities (which include the exercise of a right of audience, the conduct of litigation, reserved instrument activities (key elements of conveyancing), probate activities (limited to the application and grant), notarial activities and the administration of oaths) and also includes the provision of legal advice or assistance, or representation, in connection with the application of the law or with any form of resolution of legal disputes.

The SRA website offers a non-exhaustive list of examples of activities which, if outsourced, would be caught by O(7.10):

- activities which would normally be conducted by a paralegal
- initial drafting of contracts
- legal secretarial services – digital dictation to an outsourced secretarial service for word-processing or typing
- proofreading
- research
- document review
- Companies House filing
- due diligence, for example in connection with the purchase of a company
- IT functions which support the delivery of legal activities
- business process outsourcing

None of these activities could be expected to be within the definition of legal activities in relation to either legal advice or representation (as distinct from 'assistance'). In reality, it seems that the SRA's view of what constitutes outsourcing is in itself uncontroversial, and relates to the delivery of services which support the delivery of legal services, without themselves amounting to legal activities, still less reserved legal activities. The (hopefully transitory) problem is in the form of the Code as currently drafted.

Outcome 7.10(a) is not controversial and may be said to be stating the obvious. Outcome 7.10(b), on the other hand, could become a substantial problem in requiring contractual arrangements with the outsourcing company that 'enable the SRA or its agent to obtain information from, inspect the records (including electronic records) of, or enter the premises of, the third party, in relation to the outsourced activities or functions'. These will have to be in place before 6 October 2011 for all existing firms and from 10 August 2011 for those applying for ABS licences. It is to be hoped that the profession will not have to fund SRA investigation teams jetting off to India or the Philippines.

Further, the existence of a clause in a contract between firm and outsourcing company enabling access by the SRA to the company's premises and records will comply with the solicitors' obligations, but it may not be straightforward to enforce that against an uncooperative company in a foreign jurisdiction. It seems likely that the SRA's remedy will be directed to the regulated firm, requiring the termination of the relationship with a non-cooperative company.

Outcome 7.10(c) and (d) are unexceptionable. Those involved or contemplating involvement in outsourcing arrangements are not doing so to prejudice clients; quite the reverse – this likely to be a client-led initiative in the interests of economy and improved service, particularly where clients are sophisticated users of legal services.

Matters which firms should focus on will include quality control and supervision, security (including data protection issues), confidentiality and informed client consent, in addition to a consideration of the proper limits on what may be outsourced (unlikely to be a significant problem) and the new contractual obligations on SRA accessibility.

The first issue will be the repute of the outsourcing company. This is a growth field and new entrants to the market are to be expected. It will be necessary to investigate the background of the company and to establish reputation by suitable enquiry, including the taking of references if necessary, and to review the company's systems for security of data, the control of conflicts, and the protection of client confidentiality.

Assurances will be required as to the qualifications and competence of those who will be undertaking the work and their supervision, and also as to their ethical standards which can vary by reference to local *mores*.

There will need to be systems for review of the quality of the work undertaken. Other issues are how problems will be rectified and disputes resolved, and what records the outsourcing company will be required to keep.

Although, as mentioned, outsourcing may well be, and is likely to be, driven by clients, particularly sophisticated clients who may themselves be outsourcing business processes and may demand reduced legal costs on the basis of similar efficiencies, inevitably there are enhanced risks because control of things such as access to premises is not in the hands of the firm. It will be important to obtain informed consent, and for there to be openness in charging. There is no reason why a firm cannot take a profit from outsourcing, just as it takes a profit from the product of its own employees (see, for example, *Crane v. Canons Leisure Centre* [2008] 1 WLR 2549). There is no obligation to charge clients for the outsourced services at cost, any more than there is an obligation to charge for the work of employed staff at no more than their overhead cost to the firm, but equally clients will expect savings to be made and charging policies to be clear.

Finally, it is stating the obvious that outsourcing is not abdication of responsibility; the firm remains entirely responsible.

### 5.8.5    Other practical suggestions

Despite public SRA announcements broadly to the effect that firms complying with the 2007 Code will be in compliance with the new Code, this does not hold good for

Chapter 7. There is a real and substantial new emphasis on the need to identify and assess risks to the business, and risks to compliance in the widest sense, including in particular financial viability.

Firms will have to think about their specific business model, its sustainability and threats to its stability, and will have to be able to demonstrate an understanding of those risks and what steps have been taken in the light of them.

## 5.9 CHAPTER 8 – PUBLICITY

This chapter is the successor to rule 7 of the 2007 Code and is not materially different. Publicity is however now comprehensively defined as including:

> ... all promotional material and activity, including the name or description of your firm, stationery, advertisements, brochures, websites, directory entries, media appearances, promotional press releases, and direct approaches to potential clients and other persons, whether conducted in person, in writing, or in electronic form, but does not include press releases prepared on behalf of a client

### 5.9.1 Chapter 8 outcomes

You must achieve these outcomes:

O(8.1)   your publicity in relation to your firm or in-house practice or for any other business is accurate and not misleading, and is not likely to diminish the trust the public places in you and in the provision of legal services;

O(8.2)   your publicity relating to charges is clearly expressed and identifies whether VAT and disbursements are included;

O(8.3)   you do not make unsolicited approaches in person or by telephone to members of the public in order to publicise your firm or in-house practice or another business;

O(8.4)   clients and the public have appropriate information about you, your firm and how you are regulated;

O(8.5)   your letterhead, website and e-mails show the words 'authorised and regulated by the Solicitors Regulation Authority' and either the firm's registered name and number if it is an LLP or company or, if the firm is a partnership or sole practitioner, the name under which it is licensed/authorised by the SRA and the number allocated to it by the SRA.

### 5.9.2 Chapter 8 indicative behaviours

Acting in the following way(s) may tend to show that you have achieved these outcomes and therefore complied with the Principles:

IB(8.1)   where you conduct other regulated activities your publicity discloses the manner in which you are regulated in relation to those activities;

IB(8.2)   where your firm is a multi-disciplinary practice any publicity in relation to that practice makes clear which services are regulated legal services and which are not;

IB(8.3)   any publicity intended for a jurisdiction outside England and Wales complies with the Principles, voluntary codes and the rules in force in that jurisdiction concerning publicity;

IB(8.4)    where you and another business jointly market services, the nature of the services provided by each business is clear.

Acting in the following way(s) may tend to show that you have not achieved these outcomes and therefore not complied with the Principles:

IB(8.5)    approaching people in the street, at ports of entry, in hospital or at the scene of an accident; including approaching people to conduct a survey which involves collecting contact details of potential clients, or otherwise promotes your firm or in-house practice;

IB(8.6)    allowing any other person to conduct publicity for your firm or in-house practice in a way that would breach the Principles;

IB(8.7)    advertising an estimated fee which is pitched at an unrealistically low level;

IB(8.8)    describing overheads of your firm (such as normal postage, telephone calls and charges arising in respect of client due diligence under the Money Laundering Regulations 2007) as disbursements in your advertisements;

IB(8.9)    advertising an estimated or fixed fee without making it clear that additional charges may be payable, if that is the case;

IB(8.10)  using a name or description of your firm or in-house practice that includes the word 'solicitor(s)' if none of the managers are solicitors;

IB(8.11)  advertising your firm or in-house practice in a way that suggests that services provided by another business are provided by your firm or in-house practice;

IB(8.12)  producing misleading information concerning the professional status of any manager or employee of your firm or in-house practice.

### 5.9.3  What is new? Chapter 8

There is very little new material, but one important stipulation, to the advantage of stationers and printers.

The current requirement on all regulated entities and sole practitioners is that letterheads (including fax covers), websites and e-mails should declare that it, he or she is 'regulated by the Solicitors Regulation Authority'.

From 6 October 2011 this must be changed to:

'authorised and regulated by the Solicitors Regulation Authority'

The firm's registered name and number must also be shown as before.

There are new and predictable requirements suitable for the ABS era – O(8.4) and IB(8.1) and IB(8.2) – to ensure that clients are aware of the scope of regulation in a practice supplying regulated and unregulated services.

Indicative behaviour 8.10 reminds us that the title 'solicitors' can only be used for a firm in which there is at least one solicitor manager.

Indicative behaviour 8.8 is somewhat contentious in stipulating (at least by way of non-binding guidance, but we know what they mean) that the client-specific costs of electronic money laundering due diligence checks may not be described as disbursements. There does not, however, appear to be any reason why the cost could not be recharged to the client and designated as costs, with VAT, if this is transparent.

## 5.10  CHAPTER 9 – FEE SHARING AND REFERRALS

### 5.10.1  Chapter 9 introduction

> This chapter is about protecting clients' interests where you have arrangements with third parties who introduce business to you and/or with whom you share your fees. The relationship between clients and firms should be built on trust, and any such arrangement should not jeopardise that trust by, for example, compromising your independence or professional judgement.

By Chapter 14, an 'arrangement' in relation to financial services, fee sharing and referrals, in Chapters 1, 6 and 9, means any express or tacit agreement between the solicitor and another person, whether contractually binding or not.

The introduction masks what are in fact fundamental changes to the rules governing referral arrangements and fee sharing in the new Code. Old prohibitions and conditions have been swept away, and the result will be a far less complex system than existed under the 2007 Code.

### 5.10.2  Chapter 9 outcomes

You must achieve these outcomes:

O(9.1)  your independence and your professional judgement are not prejudiced by virtue of any arrangement with another person;

O(9.2)  your clients' interests are protected regardless of the interests of an introducer or fee sharer or your interest in receiving referrals;

O(9.3)  clients are in a position to make informed decisions about how to pursue their matter;

O(9.4)  clients are informed of any financial or other interest which an introducer has in referring the client to you;

O(9.5)  clients are informed of any fee sharing arrangement that is relevant to their matter;

O(9.6)  you do not make payments to an introducer in respect of clients who are the subject of criminal proceedings or who have the benefit of public funding;

O(9.7)  where you enter into a financial arrangement with an introducer you ensure that the agreement is in writing.

By Chapter 14, an 'introducer' is any person, business or organisation who or that introduces or refers potential clients to the solicitor's business, or recommends that business to clients or otherwise puts solicitors and clients in touch with each other.

### 5.10.3  Chapter 9 indicative behaviours

Acting in the following way(s) may tend to show that you have achieved these outcomes and therefore complied with the Principles:

IB(9.1)    only entering into arrangements with reputable third parties and monitoring the outcome of those arrangements to ensure that clients are treated fairly;

IB(9.2)    in any case where a client has entered into, or is proposing to enter into, an arrangement with an introducer in connection with their matter, which is not in their best interests, advising the client that this is the case;

IB(9.3)    terminating any arrangement with an introducer or fee sharer which is causing you to breach any requirements of the Code;

IB(9.4)    being satisfied that any client referred by an introducer has not been acquired as a result of marketing or other activities which, if done by a person regulated by the SRA, would be contrary to the Principles or any requirements of the Code;

IB(9.5)    drawing the client's attention to any payments you make, or other consideration you provide in connection with any referral;

IB(9.6)    where information needs to be given to clients, ensuring the information is clear and in writing or in a form appropriate to the client's needs.

Acting in the following way(s) may tend to show that you have not achieved these outcomes and therefore not complied with the Principles:

IB(9.7)    entering into any type of business relationship with a third party, such as an unauthorised partnership, which places you in breach of the SRA Authorisation Rules or any other regulatory requirements in the Handbook;

IB(9.8)    allowing an introducer or fee sharer to influence the advice you give to clients;

IB(9.9)    accepting referrals where you have reason to believe that clients have been pressurised or misled into instructing you.

### 5.10.4  What is new? Referral arrangements

The first issue to address under Chapter 9 is that of arrangements between solicitors and introducers of work. No subject has been more controversial for solicitors than the payment of referral fees by solicitors to introducers. The profession itself has been sharply divided over the issue. One side regards the whole idea of buying work, and thereby increasing the basic overhead cost of conducting a client's case, to be distasteful, and damaging in tending to increase costs. The other side maintains that solicitors' practices are businesses, that the payment of commissions for the introduction of work is a common and inevitable feature of business life, and that a return to more restrictive practices would defy the marketplace, which never really works, and in any event it would probably be unlawful as being anti-competitive.

The debate shows no signs of relenting. In his *Review of Civil Litigation Costs: Final Report*, published in December 2009, Lord Justice Jackson recommended the abolition of referral fees, or alternatively capping them at £200. The Government issued a Green Paper late in 2010, and consultation upon it closed at the end of February 2011. The Green Paper did not make any recommendation as to the future of referral fees; the Government was apparently awaiting the report of the Legal

Services Board (LSB) before making its decision. Thus far, the LSB has been supportive of the existence of referral fees. In a recent consultation paper, 'Discussion document on the regulatory treatment of referral fees, referral arrangements and fee sharing' (LSB, September 2010), it was sharply opposed to an outright ban:

> Our preliminary hypothesis is that the simple solutions of an outright ban or a laissez faire free for all are both unacceptable. The first proposition would, in our view, be a wholly disproportionate action when the economic evidence is that consumers do not suffer detriment from the existence of referral fees and, indeed, that there may even be access to justice benefits from their retention. Lawyers are under no obligation to pay such fees: independent marketing is a viable alternative. To outlaw such practices when viable alternatives exist therefore could fail a test of regulatory proportionality.

At the time of writing, the government is under renewed pressure to ban referral fees despite these conclusions and the debate shows no signs of early resolution.

Referral fees do not exist in a vacuum. Solicitors have to consider not only the professional conduct implications of paying those referral fees, but also the overall commercial relationship between the introducer and the client whom it is introducing to the solicitor. Amendments made to the 2007 Code in late 2009, and a small number of decisions of the Solicitors Disciplinary Tribunal, made clear that it could amount to professional misconduct for a solicitor to fail to advise a new client about the wisdom or enforceability of a contract entered into with an introducer before the solicitor was instructed if that contract was manifestly unfair to the lay client. This is discussed in greater detail below.

In order to understand the new rules properly, it is necessary to know the general law and the Law Society's/SRA's approach to this issue hitherto.

## (i) Referral arrangements – the general law

There is no inhibition against the payment by solicitors of referral fees in the general law.

As for agreements between introducers and their clients entered into before the client is introduced to the solicitor, solicitors may need to consider the doctrine of unconscionable bargain. In *Strydom* v. *Vendside Limited* [2009] EWHC 2130 (QB), in which an attempt was made to set aside an agreement with a claims handling company associated with the Union of Democratic Mineworkers, Blair J, on appeal from the County Court judge's decision, summarised the law on unconscionable bargains as follows (at [36]):

> before the court will consider setting a contract aside as an unconscionable bargain, one party has to have been disadvantaged in some relevant way as regards the other party, that other party must have exploited that disadvantage in some morally culpable manner, and the resulting transaction must be overreaching and oppressive. No single one of these factors is sufficient – all three elements must be proved, otherwise the enforceability of contracts is undermined (see the reasoning in Goff & Jones, *The Law of Restitution*, 7th edn, para 12-006). Where all these requirements are met, the burden then passes to the

other party to satisfy the court that the transaction was fair, just and reasonable (*Snell's Equity*, 31st edn, para 8-47).

## (ii) Referral arrangements – the 2007 Code

Payment of referral fees was outlawed by rule 3 of the Solicitors' Practice Rules 1990 and s.2(3) of the Solicitors' Introduction and Referral Code (SIRC) 1990. That outright ban was abolished in March 2004 by amendment to the SIRC and the new relaxed rule was then replicated in rules 9.01 and 9.02 of the 2007 Code without material change, save that: (a) there was a new additional requirement that agreements with introducers had to be in writing (formerly this had been the subject of non-binding guidance); and (b) the information required to be given by way of disclosure to clients by solicitors also had to be in writing.

Rule 9, which was directed at ensuring that a solicitor's duties to their client were not impaired by their relationship with an introducer of work, contained an elaborate framework of information that had to be given by both the solicitor and the introducer at certain defined times. Solicitors had to:

- draw the attention of potential introducers to the relevant rules (rule 9.01(2));
- make the relevant agreement with the introducers in writing (rule 9.02(a));
- ensure that introducers undertook to comply with rule 9.02 (rule 9.02(b));
- be satisfied that the introducers had not referred clients acquired as a result of marketing, etc. activities which would breach SRA rules if done by a solicitor (rule 9.02(c)) – this rule was principally aimed at cold calling;
- ensure that the relevant agreement between solicitor and introducer provided that *the introducer* would reveal all relevant information about the referral before making it, including the fact of the financial arrangement with the solicitor, the amount of any payment made to the introducer by reference to the referral, and the amount paid by the introducer to the solicitor to provide services to the client (rule 9.02(e));
- take all reasonable steps to remedy any breach by the introducer of the terms of the agreement required by rule 9, and, if breaches continued, terminate the agreement (rule 9.02(f));
- *before* accepting instructions, reveal *to the client* all relevant information about the referral in writing, including: the fact of the financial arrangement with the introducer; the amount of any payment made to the introducer by reference to the referral; and the amount paid by the introducer to the solicitor to provide services to the client; that the client could raise questions on all aspects of the transaction; and information concerning confidentiality and conflict of interest (rule 9.02(g)).

In this way, the 2007 Code sought to ensure that solicitors acted throughout in the best interests of their clients, and did not compromise their independence. The requirements were unnecessarily detailed. In particular, it made little sense that solicitors had to provide the relevant information to their clients before accepting instructions. That information made very little difference to the vast majority of clients, who were far less exercised about the payment of referral fees than were the regulatory authorities. The natural manner in which to inform the client was in the client care letter, usually written immediately after the solicitors had accepted instructions but at a time when the client could easily pull out of the retainer if they objected to the payment of a referral fee for their case. A second oft-heard criticism was the unnecessary duplication in solicitors having to ensure that much the same information was given to clients by both the introducer and the solicitor.

### (iii) Referral arrangements – the 2011 Code

The long list of actions that solicitors had to take to comply with rule 9 of the 2007 Code has been removed. The seven outcomes required by Chapter 9 of the new Code centre upon maintaining the solicitor's independence, protecting the best interests of clients and ensuring transparency. The Chapter 1 outcomes are also relevant in this context: the client must be treated fairly. Although O(9.4) requires that clients are informed of any financial interest which an introducer has in referring the client to the solicitor, the rule does not mandate when this has to be done. Indicative behaviour 1.4 in Chapter 1 suggests that solicitors should explain any arrangements such as fee sharing or referral arrangements which are relevant to the client's instructions. Outcome 9.7 requires financial arrangements between solicitors and introducers to be in writing, and O(9.6) outlaws referral fees in respect of clients who are the subject of criminal proceedings or who have the benefit of public funding.

In the light of continuing political controversy on the issue, solicitors should be wary of departing from the transparency requirements of the 2007 Code. The elaborate framework in rule 9 of the 2007 Code was designed to ensure that clients were put fully in the picture about referral fees at the very outset. It is likely to remain best practice for solicitors to inform their clients of the fact and amount of a referral fee at that stage, and the SRA will be able to point to O(9.3), O(9.4) and IB(9.5) in this regard.

The nearest that the SRA has come to giving guidance on the interpretation of the new Code is a series of 'Q&As' on the 'Outcomes-focused regulation at a glance' section of its website. The answer to the question 'When do I have to give this information to clients?' regarding referral arrangements is:

> The outcomes do not specify when the information should be provided. However, in order to achieve outcome 9.3, you will need to consider whether you need to give the information before the client has committed themselves to instructing your firm i.e. at the outset of the matter. The nature of the referral arrangement may affect the client's decision to instruct your firm.

Solicitors must also have in mind IB(9.6), which requires information to be clear and in writing, or in a form appropriate to the client's needs, where, for instance, the client may have difficulty in reading English.

On the other hand, in the absence of any specific rule to that effect, solicitors can now safely abandon any attempt to require the introducer to provide information to clients. Claims management companies and other introducers are regulated by the Ministry of Justice under the Compensation Act 2006, and are subject to their own suite of regulatory rules. In the absence of any specific requirement in the new Code upon solicitors to make introducers behave in a certain way, the old provisions in rules 9.01(2) and 9.02(a), (b) (e) and (f) can no longer apply. They will not be missed.

The provision in rule 9.02(c) of the 2007 Code that solicitors must be satisfied that the introducers had not referred clients acquired as a result of marketing, etc. activities which would breach SRA rules if done by a solicitor (the most obvious example being cold calling) is specifically retained in IB(9.4).

A further important change is that the referral provisions in Chapter 9 now apply to referrals between lawyers. Rule 9 of the 2007 Code did not apply to such referrals, by virtue of a specific exception in rule 9.01(3). Such referrals now have to be disclosed to clients, and if a referral fee is paid, that too must be disclosed in writing (O(9.7)).

## (iv) Pre-retainer arrangements between clients and introducers – IB(9.2)

Indicative behaviour 9.2 requires special mention: it provides that where a client *has entered into* or proposes to enter into an arrangement with an introducer in connection with their matter, which is not in the client's best interests, solicitors should advise the client that this is the case.

Until recent years, it has not been suggested that solicitors are under any duty to advise their clients as to the wisdom or otherwise of contractual arrangements that they (the clients) may have made before instructing the solicitor. Indeed, the imposition of such a duty in the general law is fraught with danger, and the courts have consistently pointed out the limits of a solicitor's retainer. In the words of Lord Jauncey in *Clark Boyce* v. *Mouat* [1994] 1 AC 428, at 437:

> When a client in full command of his faculties and apparently aware of what he is doing seeks the assistance of a solicitor in the carrying out of a particular transaction, that solicitor is under no duty, whether before or after accepting instructions, to go beyond those instructions by proffering unsought advice on the wisdom of the transaction. To hold otherwise could impose intolerable burdens on solicitors.

However, in some of the disciplinary prosecutions arising out of the miners' compensation cases, and later in disciplinary prosecutions arising out of the activities of an organisation known as Justice Direct, the Solicitors Disciplinary Tribunal found that solicitors should have advised clients about agreements with introducers entered into before instruction of the solicitors, by which the client agreed to yield a proportion of their compensation to the introducer.

On 13 November 2009 the SRA amended the guidance to rule 9 of the 2007 Code. Included in that guidance was a new paragraph 3 in the following terms:

> If a client is entering into or has already entered into a scheme or arrangement with an introducer which is not in their best interests then you must advise the client accordingly. Schemes or arrangements which involve the client paying unnecessary or unreasonable fees will not normally be in the client's best interests.

It was most undesirable that such an important new obligation should be introduced by amending the guidance to the rule, rather than the rule itself. The rules had the force of law, whereas the guidance did not. But this was the genesis of IB(9.2), which is couched in similar terms.

There is no doubt that the November 2009 guidance was aimed at cases where introducers were seeking to receive an unjustifiably large proportion of compensation recovered by the lay client in claims for damages (or their equivalent) against third parties. However, the wording of IB(9.2) is very wide. For instance, what is the solicitor to do where the client is introduced by an estate agent who charges significantly more than its competitors, with no apparent added value for the client? Is the solicitor to advise the new client that they are paying far too much to the estate agency which has introduced the client to the solicitor? In the judgment in *Beresford and Smith* v. *The Solicitors Regulation Authority and The Law Society* [2009] EWHC 3155 (Admin), on appeal from the Solicitors Disciplinary Tribunal, the Divisional Court discussed this issue at some length (paras. 61–80 inclusive), but declined to decide it, observing that (at [75]):

> It would for instance be a distraction to set about determining whether the Vendside agreements were indeed unenforceable in law. They were certainly questionable, as Beresfords knew or ought to have known. Vendside were not providing the services for which the fee was stated to be payable.

The court appeared to take the view that there was an obligation to advise that the agreement was 'questionable'. There remains uncertainty. In the *Beresfords* case itself (No. 9666-2007, SDT, 9 April 2009), the Solicitors Disciplinary Tribunal provided some guidance as to what was expected of solicitors acting for claimants in the miners' compensation cases (at [156]):

> The Tribunal had no doubt that it was part of Beresfords' retainer for them to read the agreement and comment on it to ensure the miners fully understood what they had agreed to and to indicate to them that there was some uncertainty about the agreement and therefore about their deductions from their compensation.

After its success in the *Beresfords* case, the SRA prosecuted four separate sole practitioner solicitors who had accepted work from Justice Direct, an organisation that charged a hefty slice of a client's damages for doing little more than finding a solicitor for the client. All four admitted the allegations, and the Solicitors Disciplinary Tribunal followed its approach in *Beresfords* by agreeing that the failure to alert the clients to the disadvantageous nature of the Justice Direct contract amounted to professional misconduct. In the first such case, *Tilbury* (No. 9880-2008, SDT, 8 January 2009), the Tribunal stated (at [86]):

The Tribunal was satisfied that by entering into the agreement with Justice Direct, the Respondent effectively disabled himself from advising his clients as to the desirability of the client becoming liable to pay 25% of any recoverable damages to Justice Direct in return for an introduction to the solicitor. The benefits to the client of entering into the Purchase Order were claimed to be some initial screening of the claim and introduction of a suitably qualified solicitor. Neither in the Tribunal's view could justify the payment to Justice Direct of so disproportionate a share of the damages awarded to the client and the Tribunal considered that no competent solicitor rendering advice in the best interests of the client could recommend the client to enter into such an agreement.

The Justice Direct cases and *Beresfords* are therefore consistent with a duty to advise in relation to a pre-existing contract, if on the facts there is something obviously inaccurate or uncertain, or a fee that is apparently wholly unreasonable and disproportionate. The question remains open as to what, in the case of a lawful contract, which is unreasonable and unfair, but not unconscionable and liable to be set aside, the solicitor is expected to advise. The solicitor may find themselves in an unenviable position, in breach of regulatory duty if they stay silent, and at risk of committing the tort of inducing a breach of contract if they advise in accordance with IB(9.2).

### (v) Involvement of the introducer after the case has been referred to the solicitor

One of the legitimate concerns of the SRA in policing referral fee arrangements is that solicitors may develop an unhealthy dependence upon a flow of work from a particular introducer, and then permit the introducer an inappropriate degree of control over how the solicitor carries out the work. An introducer has a legitimate interest in ensuring that the chosen solicitor carries out the work to a reasonable standard, as the introducer has entrusted his or her client to the solicitor. It is commonplace to see agreements between solicitors and introducers by which the introducer has the right to audit the work of the solicitor. However, unless dealt with in the agreement between introducer and client and/or the retainer letter between solicitor and client, such a right of audit may cut across the confidentiality that is owed by the solicitor to his or her client. Appropriate contractual provisions can reduce or eliminate any regulatory concern on that front, but solicitors should be aware that the SRA remains very concerned at the ability of introducers to weaken the independence of the solicitor's advice to his or her client. Indicative behaviour 9.8 warns specifically against allowing an introducer or fee sharer to influence the advice given by a solicitor to their client. Likewise, IB(9.9) warns against accepting referrals where the solicitor has reason to believe that clients have been pressurised or misled into instructing them.

## (vi) Introducers operating on a contingency fee basis

As already noted in the commentary on Chapter 1, the prohibition in rule 9.01(4) of the 2007 Code against solicitors having arrangements in personal injury work with introducers who operate on a contingency fee basis has gone entirely (see **5.2.5**).

### 5.10.5 What is new? Fee sharing

The rule against solicitors fee sharing with non-solicitors was traditionally based upon the risk of a non-solicitor having an inappropriate amount of influence over a solicitor in the handling of a claim for a client. The strength of the rule was steadily eroded over the years. Historically there was an absolute prohibition, but that was relaxed in March 2004 to permit fee sharing with those who introduce capital or services into a firm. Under rule 8.02 of the 2007 Code of Conduct, this exception took the following form:

>   (1)   You may share your professional fees with another person or business ('the fee sharer') if:
>
>       (a)   the purpose of the fee sharing arrangement is solely to facilitate the introduction of capital and/or the provision of services to your firm;
>       (b)   neither the fee sharing agreement nor the extent of the fees shared permits any fee sharer to influence or constrain your professional judgement in relation to the advice which you give to any client;

The advent of ABSs in October 2011 means that the old objection to fee sharing between solicitors and non-solicitors has fallen away. The whole purpose of the reforms is to permit non-lawyers to share profits with solicitors. Fee sharing will be inevitable where, for instance, a company merges with a firm of solicitors to create an ABS, or sets up an SRA-regulated subsidiary to provide legal services to existing clients. If fee sharing will be permissible *within* one overall corporate structure from October 2011, there is no logical reason why fee sharing *between* two independent corporate structures should be outlawed. In order to make such an important distinction, clear rules would have to be made so that solicitors could know where they stood.

The only specific references to fee sharing in the new Code are in Chapter 1 at IB(1.4) – 'explaining any arrangements, such as fee sharing or referral arrangements, which are relevant to the client's instructions' – and Chapter 9, particularly O(9.2), IB(9.3) and IB(9.8). These make clear that fee sharing is no longer outlawed. In a nutshell, solicitors will simply have to: (a) be transparent to clients about arrangements with fee sharers; (b) ensure that there is no sacrifice of their independence (i.e. permitting the fee sharer inappropriate influence); and (c) ensure that the best interests of clients remain paramount.

## 5.11    CHAPTER 10 – YOU AND YOUR REGULATOR

### 5.11.1    Chapter 10 introduction

This chapter is about co-operation with your regulators and ombudsmen, primarily the SRA and the Legal Ombudsman.

The information which we request from you will help us understand any risks to clients, and the public interest more generally.

### 5.11.2    Chapter 10 outcomes

You must achieve these outcomes:

O(10.1)    you ensure that you comply with all the reporting and notification requirements in the Handbook that apply to you;

O(10.2)    you provide the SRA with information to enable the SRA to decide upon any application you make, such as for a practising certificate, registration, recognition or a licence and whether any conditions should apply;

O(10.3)    you notify the SRA promptly of any material changes to relevant information about you including serious financial difficulty, action taken against you by another regulator and serious failure to comply with or achieve the Principles, rules, outcomes and other requirements of the Handbook;

O(10.4)    you report to the SRA promptly, serious misconduct by any person or firm authorised by the SRA, or any employee, manager or owner of any such firm (taking into account, where necessary, your duty of confidentiality to your client);

O(10.5)    you ensure that the SRA is in a position to assess whether any persons requiring prior approval are fit and proper at the point of approval and remain so;

O(10.6)    you co-operate fully with the SRA and the Legal Ombudsman at all times including in relation to any investigation about a claim for redress against you;

O(10.7)    you do not attempt to prevent anyone from providing information to the SRA or the Legal Ombudsman;

O(10.8)    you comply promptly with any written notice from the SRA;

O(10.9)    pursuant to a notice under Outcome 10.8, you:

(a)    produce for inspection by the SRA documents held by you, or held under your control;

(b)    provide all information and explanations requested; and

(c)    comply with all requests from the SRA as to the form in which you produce any documents you hold electronically, and for photocopies of any documents to take away;

in connection with your practice or in connection with any trust of which you are, or formerly were, a trustee;

O(10.10)    you provide any necessary permissions for information to be given, so as to enable the SRA to:

(a)    prepare a report on any documents produced; and

(b)    seek verification from clients, staff and the banks, building societies or other financial institutions used by you;

O(10.11)    when required by the SRA in relation to a matter specified by the SRA, you:

(a) act promptly to investigate whether any person may have a claim for redress against you;

(b) provide the SRA with a report on the outcome of such an investigation, identifying persons who may have such a claim;

(c) notify persons that they may have a right of redress against you, providing them with information as to the nature of the possible claim, about the firm's complaints procedure and about the Legal Ombudsman; and

(d) ensure, where you have identified a person who may have a claim for redress, that the matter is dealt with under the firm's complaints procedure as if that person had made a complaint;

O(10.12) you do not attempt to abrogate to any third party your regulatory responsibilities in the Handbook, including the role of Compliance Officer for Legal Practice (COLP) or Compliance Officer for Finance and Administration (COFA);

O(10.13) once you are aware that your firm will cease to practise, you effect the orderly and transparent wind-down of activities, including informing the SRA before the firm closes.

Chapter 14 clarifies the following definitions:

- 'documents' includes documents, whether written or electronic, relating to the firm's client accounts and office accounts;
- 'claim for redress' has the same meaning as in s.158 of the Legal Services Act 2007, which does not contain any definition, but provides:

> Section 157 does not prohibit the regulatory arrangements of an approved regulator from making provision requiring, or authorising the approved regulator to require, a relevant authorised person –
>
> (a) to investigate whether there are any persons who may have a claim against the relevant authorised person in relation to a matter specified by the approved regulator;

### 5.11.3 Chapter 10 indicative behaviours

Acting in the following way(s) may tend to show that you have achieved these outcomes and therefore complied with the Principles:

IB(10.1) actively monitoring your achievement of the outcomes in order to improve standards and identify non-achievement of the outcomes;

IB(10.2) actively monitoring your financial stability and viability in order to identify and mitigate any risks to the public;

IB(10.3) notifying the SRA promptly of any indicators of serious financial difficulty, such as inability to pay your professional indemnity insurance premium, or rent or salaries, or breach of bank covenants;

IB(10.4) notifying the SRA promptly when you become aware that your business may not be financially viable to continue trading as a going concern, for example because of difficult trading conditions, poor cash flow, increasing overheads, loss of managers or employees and/or loss of sources of revenue;

IB(10.5) notifying the SRA of any serious issues identified as a result of monitoring referred to in IB10.1 and IB10.2 above, and producing a plan for remedying issues that have been identified;

IB(10.6) responding appropriately to any serious issues identified concerning competence and fitness and propriety of your employees, managers and owners;

IB(10.7) reporting disciplinary action taken against you by another regulator;

IB(10.8) informing the SRA promptly when you become aware of a significant change to your firm, for example:

- key personnel, such as a manager, COLP or COFA, joining or leaving the firm;
- a merger with, or an acquisition by or of, another firm;

IB(10.9) having appropriate arrangements for the orderly transfer of clients' property to another authorised body if your firm closes;

IB(10.10) having a 'whistle-blowing' policy.

Acting in the following way(s) may tend to show that you have not achieved these outcomes and therefore not complied with the Principles:

IB(10.11) entering into an agreement which would attempt to preclude the SRA or the Legal Ombudsman from investigating any actual or potential complaint or allegation of professional misconduct;

IB(10.12) unless you can properly allege malice, issuing defamation proceedings in respect of a complaint to the SRA.

By Chapter 14, 'manager' means a partner in a partnership, a member of an LLP, a director of a company, or a member of the governing body of any other body.

## 5.11.4 What is new? Chapter 10

Chapter 10 appears to represent a return to the type of prescriptive rule making which has been abandoned in the remainder of the Code. Consisting of 13 outcomes and 12 indicative behaviours, it is second only to Chapter 1 in the amount of regulation that it contains. Much of the content has been drawn from rules 20.05 to 20.10 of the 2007 Code. The clear message for solicitors is that all of those regulated by the SRA must co-operate in all respects with their regulator.

The following alterations to what has gone before are particularly worthy of note:

- *Reporting obligations.* Outcome 10.4 requires the reporting of serious misconduct by any regulated entity or individual. Prior to 2007, solicitors had a duty to report serious misconduct by *another* solicitor, and this included the situation where the other solicitor's integrity was in question. Similarly, solicitors had a duty to report serious misconduct within their own firm (see generally *The Guide to the Professional Conduct of Solicitors 1999* (8th edn), pp.361–2). In the 2007 Code, the obligation under rule 20.06 was to report to the SRA where: (a) the solicitor became aware of serious misconduct by solicitors, managers and employees of regulated entities; (b) there was reason to doubt the integrity of those individuals; and (c) the solicitor had reason to believe that entities or senior individuals within them were in serious financial difficulty. There is no longer such an obligation where there is reason to doubt integrity (although the wide terms of O(10.5) should be noted). Importantly, the solicitor must report serious misconduct by *any* person or authorised firm: there is now clearly an obligation to self-report.

- *Continuing obligations.* The terms of O(10.5) are very wide – the SRA must be put in the picture about those who require prior approval, not only at the point of the application for such approval, but at all times thereafter.
- *Non-delegation of regulatory duties.* O(10.12) is new, and is designed to prevent solicitors from delegating performance of their regulatory duties to third parties, particularly the role of COLP or COFA.
- *Financial difficulty.* There is a new emphasis upon informing the SRA when financial difficulties arise in a regulated entity (see O(10.3), O(10.13), IB(10.2), IB(10.3), IB(10.4) and IB(10.9)). This is a direct result of the recession and the difficult trading conditions faced by solicitors since 2008. It can also be seen as a corollary of the obligations in Chapter 7 concerning the management of the business, and the identification and management of the risks to financial stability. The SRA was successful in ensuring the orderly wind-down of one large firm of solicitors in a high-profile case, and so avoided the costs and distress of an intervention. The sooner that the SRA is informed about an entity's financial problems, the greater will be the opportunity to avoid an intervention. Costs of interventions tend to be very high, and fall for the most part upon the profession rather than the intervened-upon solicitor, who rarely has the funds to discharge the obligation to pay those costs. (The costs of an intervention are recoverable from the intervened-upon solicitor as a debt by virtue of the Solicitors Act 1974, Sched. 1, para. 13.)

## 5.12 CHAPTER 11 – RELATIONS WITH THIRD PARTIES

### 5.12.1 Chapter 11 introduction

The Introduction to Chapter 11 states that:

> This chapter is about ensuring you do not take unfair advantage of those you deal with and that you act in a manner which promotes the proper operation of the legal system . . .
>
> The conduct requirements in this area extend beyond professional and business matters. They apply in any circumstances in which you may use your professional title to advance your personal interests.

The last two sentences contain an important reminder and warning to solicitors. If they choose to use their status as solicitors, or their firm's notepaper, to conduct essentially private business, they are as much at risk of regulatory action as when they are acting in their ordinary professional capacity.

## 5.12.2 Chapter 11 outcomes

You must achieve these outcomes:

O(11.1)  you do not take unfair advantage of third parties in either your professional or personal capacity;

O(11.2)  you perform all undertakings given by you within an agreed timescale or within a reasonable amount of time;

O(11.3)  where you act for a seller of land, you inform all buyers immediately of the seller's intention to deal with more than one buyer;

O(11.4)  you properly administer oaths, affirmations or declarations where you are authorised to do so.

## 5.12.3 Chapter 11 indicative behaviours

Acting in the following way(s) may tend to show that you have achieved these outcomes and therefore complied with the Principles:

IB(11.1)  providing sufficient time and information to enable the costs in any matter to be agreed;

IB(11.2)  returning documents or money sent subject to an express condition if you are unable to comply with that condition;

IB(11.3)  returning documents or money on demand if they are sent on condition that they are held to the sender's order;

IB(11.4)  ensuring that you do not communicate with another party when you are aware that the other party has retained a lawyer in a matter, except:

- to request the name and address of the other party's lawyer; or
- the other party's lawyer consents to you communicating with the client; or
- where there are exceptional circumstances;

IB(11.5)  maintaining an effective system which records when undertakings have been given and when they have been discharged;

IB(11.6)  where an undertaking is given which is dependent upon the happening of a future event and it becomes apparent the future event will not occur, notifying the recipient of this.

Acting in the following way(s) may tend to show that you have not achieved these outcomes and therefore not complied with the Principles:

IB(11.7)  taking unfair advantage of an opposing party's lack of legal knowledge where they have not instructed a lawyer;

IB(11.8)  demanding anything for yourself or on behalf of your client, that is not legally recoverable , such as when you are instructed to collect a simple debt, demanding from the debtor the cost of the letter of claim since it cannot be said at that stage that such a cost is legally recoverable;

IB(11.9)  using your professional status or qualification to take unfair advantage of another person in order to advance your personal interests;

IB(11.10) taking unfair advantage of a public office held by you, or a member of your family, or a member of your firm or their family.

### 5.12.4  What is new? Chapter 11

*Unfair advantage*

Outcome 11.1 reflects a long-standing rule of professional conduct, previously contained in rule 10.01 of the 2007 Code, that solicitors must not take unfair advantage of anyone. However, the wording of O(11.1) is significantly wider than rule 10.01, which provided 'You must not use your position to take unfair advantage of anyone either for your own benefit or for another person's benefit.' The important addition in the new Code is that the outcome specifically includes actions taken in the solicitor's personal capacity. A solicitor will be taking unfair advantage when acting in a personal capacity if using their status as a solicitor, or the trappings of the profession, such as their firm's headed notepaper, to gain advantage over a third party. The golden rule is that when transacting in a private capacity, solicitors should not state that they are solicitors, and should not use their firm's notepaper or e-mail address.

Practitioners will need to consider virtually all of the indicative behaviours set out above when considering the issue of taking unfair advantage of third parties.

*Undertakings*

Outcome 11.2 is concerned with undertakings. An undertaking is defined in Chapter 14 to mean:

> a statement, given orally or in writing, whether or not it includes the word 'undertake' or 'undertaking', made by or on behalf of you or your firm, in the course of practice, or by you outside the course of practice but as a solicitor or REL, to someone who reasonably places reliance on it, that you or your firm will do something or cause something to be done, or refrain from doing something

This definition is similar in meaning, though different in sentence construction, to the definition in the 2007 Code, which for the first time placed a solicitor's duty to perform undertakings on a statutory footing. The new Code also includes for the first time within the definition of undertaking a statement made outside the course of practice but as a solicitor or REL. This significantly widens the ambit of a professional undertaking, and exposes solicitors to liability and regulatory action for breach of an undertaking given outside the course of practice.

Outcome 11.2 is a great deal simpler than the equivalent provision in rule 10.05 of the 2007 Code. Two specific provisions that have been dropped are:

(3)  If you give an undertaking which is dependent upon the happening of a future event, you must notify the recipient immediately if it becomes clear that the event will not occur.

(4)  When you give an undertaking to pay another's costs, the undertaking will be discharged if the matter does not proceed unless there is an express agreement that the costs are payable in any event.

It should be noted, however, that these provisions do reappear as a non-mandatory guidance in IB(11.6) and IB(11.4).

## Multiple buyers

Similarly, O(11.3) greatly simplifies rule 10.06 of the 2007 Code and is reduced to a single obligation, i.e. to inform all buyers of the seller's intention to deal with more than one buyer. Rule 10.06 had required the solicitor to stop acting where the seller refused to agree to such disclosure, and had provided that the solicitor should not act for both the seller and any of the prospective buyers, or for more than one of the prospective buyers. These prohibitions are not carried forward into the new Code. For the position in relation to acting for seller and buyer, see **5.4**.

## Administration of oaths, etc.

The equivalent provision in the 2007 Code (rule 10.03) prevented solicitors from administering oaths or affirmations or taking declarations if their firm was acting for any party in the matter or was otherwise 'interested' in the subject matter. This prohibition has apparently been removed, in the sense that there is simply no reference to it at all, but that is not actually so. The outcome requires solicitors to administer oaths properly when 'authorised to do so', leaving the practitioner to apply the law. The former rule simply reflected the prohibition to the same effect in the Solicitors Act 1974, s.81(1). Section 81 has been repealed by the Legal Services Act 2007. However, the Legal Services Act 2007 specifies who may properly carry out the reserved legal activity of administering oaths, and defines this activity by reference (primarily) to the Commissioners for Oaths Act 1889. Section 1(3) of the Commissioners for Oaths Act 1889 contains exactly the same provision:

> Provided that a commissioner for oaths shall not exercise any of the powers given by this section in any proceeding in which he is interested.

## Omissions

Matters contained in rule 10 of the 2007 Code which have not found their way into the outcomes of the new Code are:

- an obligation to give sufficient information about costs when they are payable by a third party (rule 10.02);
- restrictions on contacting directly the client of another lawyer (rule 10.04);
- the obligation to pay the fees of foreign lawyers if such lawyers have been instructed in the course of a solicitor's practice (rule 10.07).

## 5.13   CHAPTER 12 – SEPARATE BUSINESSES

Chapter 12 not only replaces rule 21 of the 2007 Code, but also sweeps up some of rule 19, which was devoted to financial services.

The philosophy behind rule 21 of the 2007 Code was that clients should not be confused into believing that they are dealing with a firm regulated by the SRA (which is highly controlled and provides them with the benefit of minimum levels of insurance and the Compensation Fund) when they are not. The rule was also designed to ensure that core legal services are only provided through a properly regulated firm and by properly regulated individuals, and to prevent part of a case or matter being severed so as to remove statutory protections available to the client. In a regulatory world which permits ABSs, the rule needed to be relaxed, although much has been retained.

### 5.13.1   Chapter 12 introduction

The purpose of this chapter is to ensure clients are protected when they obtain mainstream legal services from a firm regulated by the SRA. This is accomplished by restricting the services that can be provided through a separate business that is not authorised by the SRA or another approved regulator.

When read with the Chapter 14 interpretations, there are prescriptive lists of *permitted* separate businesses (the kind of services a member of the public would not necessarily expect to be provided only by a regulated lawyer but which are 'solicitor-like' services), and *prohibited* separate business activities (mainstream legal services which members of the public would expect to be offered by a regulated lawyer).

A *permitted* separate business means, for the purpose of Chapter 12:

a separate business offering any of the following services:

(a)     alternative dispute resolution;
(b)     financial services;
(c)     estate agency;
(d)     management consultancy;
(e)     company secretarial services;
(f)     acting as a parliamentary agent;
(g)     practising as a lawyer of another jurisdiction;
(h)     acting as a bailiff;
(i)     acting as nominee, trustee or executor outside England and Wales;
(j)     acting as a nominee, trustee or executor in England and Wales where such activity is provided as a subsidiary but necessary part of a separate business providing financial services;
(k)     providing legal advice or drafting legal documents not included in (a) to (j) above, where such activity is provided as a subsidiary but necessary part of some other service which is one of the main services of the separate business; and

(l)   providing any other business, advisory or agency service which could be provided through a firm or in-house practice but is not a prohibited separate business activity;

*Prohibited* separate business activities are:

(a)   the conduct of any matter which could come before a court [defined as 'any court, tribunal or enquiry of England and Wales, or a British court martial, or any court of another jurisdiction'], whether or not proceedings are started;
(b)   advocacy before a court, tribunal or enquiry;
(c)   instructing counsel in any part of the UK;
(d)   immigration work [defined as 'the provision of immigration advice and immigration services as defined in section 82 of the Immigration and Asylum Act 1999'];
(e)   any activity in relation to conveyancing, applications for probate or letters of administration, or drawing trust deeds or court documents, which is reserved to solicitors and others under the LSA;
(f)   drafting wills;
(g)   acting as nominee, trustee or executor in England and Wales, where such activity is not provided as a subsidiary but necessary part of a separate business providing financial services; and
(h)   providing legal advice or drafting legal documents not included in (a) to (g) above where such activity is not provided as a subsidiary but necessary part of some other service which is one of the main services of the separate business;

The list of permitted businesses, previously found in rule 21.04 of the 2007 Code, has been increased by those at (j) and (k). The list of prohibited activities is to all intents and purposes identical to that in rule 21.02 of the 2007 Code, save for the addition of the phrases in (g) 'where such activity is not provided as a subsidiary but necessary part of a separate business providing financial services' and (h) 'where such activity is not provided as a subsidiary but necessary part of some other service which is one of the main services of the separate business'.

### 5.13.2   Chapter 12 outcomes

You must achieve these outcomes:

O(12.1)   you do not:

    (a)   own;
    (b)   have a significant interest in; or
    (c)   actively participate in,

    a separate business which conducts prohibited separate business activities;

O(12.2)   if you are a firm:

    (a)   you are not owned by; or
    (b)   connected with,

    a separate business which conducts prohibited separate business activities;

O(12.3)   where you:

    (a)   have a significant interest in;
    (b)   actively participate in;

(c)      own; or

(d)      are a firm and owned by or connected with,

a permitted separate business, you have safeguards in place to ensure that clients are not misled about the extent to which the services that you and the separate business offer are regulated;

O(12.4)   you do not represent any permitted separate business as being regulated by the SRA or any of its activities as being provided by an individual who is regulated by the SRA;

O(12.5)   you are only connected with reputable separate businesses;

O(12.6)   you are only connected with a permitted separate business which is an appointed representative if it is an appointed representative of an independent financial adviser.

Definitions in Chapter 14 state that:

- 'owner' means a person having a substantial ownership interest in and 'own' and 'owned by' shall be construed accordingly;
- 'actively participate in' means, in relation to a separate business, having any active involvement in the separate business, and includes:

    (a)      any direct control over the business, and any indirect control through another person such as a spouse; and

    (b)      any active participation in the business or the provision of its services to customers;

- 'connected with' means in relation to a separate business for the purpose of Chapter 12:

    (a)      having one or more partner(s), owner(s), director(s) or member(s) in common with the separate business;

    (b)      being a subsidiary company of the same holding company as the separate business; or

    (c)      being a subsidiary company of the separate business

- 'appointed representative' has the meaning given in the Financial Services and Markets Act 2000.

### 5.13.3   Chapter 12 indicative behaviours

Acting in the following way(s) may tend to show that you have achieved these outcomes and therefore complied with the Principles:

IB(12.1)   ensuring that client information and records are not disclosed to the permitted separate business, without the express consent of the client;

IB(12.2)   complying with the SRA Accounts Rules and not allowing the client account to be used to hold money for the permitted separate business;

IB(12.3)   where you are referring a client to a permitted separate business, informing clients of your interest in the separate business;

IB(12.4) terminating any connection with a permitted separate business where you have reason to doubt the integrity or competence of that separate business.

### 5.13.4 What is new? Chapter 12

The first two outcomes are self-evident, as is the fifth. Outcomes 12.3 and 12.4 amount to ensuring that clients are not misled about the extent to which the separate business is regulated, or as to the identity of the regulator.

The Chapter 12 outcomes are a good example of OFR in action. Under rule 21.05 of the 2007 Code, there was a long list of safeguards that had to be in place for solicitors undertaking a separate business:

(2) You must ensure that the following safeguards are in place in relation to a separate business which offers or provides any of the services listed in 21.04(1):

    (a) the separate business must not be held out or described in such a way as to suggest that the separate business is carrying on a practice regulated by the Solicitors Regulation Authority or another approved regulator, or that any lawyer connected with your firm is providing services through the separate business as a practising lawyer regulated by the Solicitors Regulation Authority or another approved regulator;

    (b) all paperwork, documents, records or files relating to the separate business and its customers must be kept separate from those of any firm or in-house practice, even where a customer of the separate business is also a client of the firm or in-house practice;

    (c) the client account or other account used to hold money for the clients of any firm or in-house practice must not be used to hold money for the separate business, or for customers of the separate business in their capacity as such;

    (d) if the separate business shares premises, office accommodation or reception staff with any firm or in-house practice:

        (i) the areas used by the firm or in-house practice must be clearly differentiated from the areas used by the separate business; and

        (ii) all customers of the separate business must be informed that it is not regulated by the Solicitors Regulation Authority and that the statutory protections attaching to clients of a lawyer regulated by the Authority are not available to them as customers of that business;

    (e) if you or your firm refer a client to the separate business, the client must first be informed of your interest in the separate business, that the separate business is not regulated by the Solicitors Regulation Authority, and that the statutory protections attaching to clients of a lawyer regulated by the Authority are not available to them as customers of the separate business; and

    (f) if the separate business is an estate agency, then without prejudice to the provisions of these rules regarding conflicts of interests, neither you nor any firm through which you practise may act in the conveyance for the buyer of any property sold through the estate agency unless:

        (i) the firm shares ownership of the estate agency with at least one other business in which neither you nor the firm have any financial interest;

        (ii) neither you nor anyone else in the firm is dealing with or has dealt with the sale of the seller's property for the separate business; and

(iii)    the buyer has given written consent to you or the firm acting, after your financial interest in the sale going through has been explained to the buyer.

The six safeguards in rule 21.05 have not been reproduced in the new Code, save that in the notes, solicitors are warned that particular care needs to be taken over the name and branding of the separate business, misleading publicity, and geographical proximity of the two businesses, particularly where premises are shared. The prescriptive safeguards have been abandoned and hence solicitors are freer in the manner in which they can run the separate business. However, the safeguards remain of value in indicating to solicitors where problems may occur, and solicitors must constantly have in mind the Principles to act in the best interests of each client and not to allow their independence to be compromised. In particular, it will remain best practice for the solicitor to give the client the information set out in safeguard rule 21.05(2)(e) above, and this is reflected in IB(12.3).

## Financial services

Solicitors who provide 'mainstream' financial services must be regulated by the Financial Services Authority (FSA), but if the financial services offered are incidental to other legal work and are within the limits set by what will be the SRA Financial Services (Scope) Rules 2011 (as the successors to the Solicitors' Financial Services (Scope) Rules 2001), solicitors will be engaged in 'exempt regulated activities' and can be regulated by the SRA. Solicitors regulated by the SRA (as opposed to the FSA) must comply with what will be the SRA Financial Services (Conduct of Business) Rules 2011 (likewise, as successors to the Solicitors' Financial Services (Conduct of Business) Rules 2001).

Under the 2007 Code, services which could be provided through a separate business included financial services, except for those that could not form part of a solicitors' practice such as banking, stockbroking and insurance underwriting – see rule 21.04 and guidance note 17 thereto. This exception has not been retained in the 2011 Code.

Rule 19 of the 2007 Code was devoted to financial services. Rule 19(1) provided:

(1)    You must not, in connection with any regulated activity:

(a)    be an appointed representative; or

(b)    have any arrangement with other persons under which you could be constrained to recommend to clients or effect for them (or refrain from doing so) transactions:

(i)      in some investments but not others;
(ii)     with some persons but not others; or
(iii)    through the agency of some persons but not others; or

(c)    have any arrangement with other persons under which you could be constrained to introduce or refer clients or other persons with whom you deal to some persons but not others.

The rule against solicitors becoming appointed representatives is now found in the theoretically non-mandatory IB(6.4) (see **5.7.4**), but solicitors can now (at least in theory) have arrangements which constrain them to recommend a limited number of investments, investment management companies, etc. The practical difficulty in the way of that is that the recommendation must be in the best interests of the client, and the solicitor cannot compromise his or her independence.

The only other provision of rule 19 which finds its way directly into the new Code is rule 19.01(2), which has become O(12.6), i.e. that solicitors can only be concerned in a separate business that is an appointed representative if it is an appointed representative of an independent financial adviser. This is retained in order to safeguard the independence of the solicitor and the best interests of the lay client.

The four indicative behaviours should all be self-evident to the conscientious practitioner.

# CHAPTER 6

# Application of the Code to in-house practice and overseas practice

Most of the Code applies to both in-house and overseas practice. The modifications are set out here, but first we have to fight our way through the definitions as to what constitutes in-house and overseas practice.

## 6.1 APPLICATION OF THE CODE TO IN-HOUSE PRACTICE

### 6.1.1 In-house practice defined

Rather obscurely, 'in-house practice' is defined in Chapter 14 of the Code in a manner which involves a great deal of page-turning. The definition is:

> ... practice as a solicitor, REL or RFL (as appropriate) in accordance with Rules 1.1(c)(B), 1.1(d)(B), 1.1(e), 1.2(f), 2.1(c)(B), 2.1(d)(B), 2.1(e), 2.2(f), 3.1(b)(B) or 3.1(c)(B) of the SRA Practice Framework Rules.

In translation, this means practice:

- covered by rule 1.1(c)(B) of the SRA Practice Framework Rules, which is practise as a solicitor from an office in England and Wales:

> (c) as a manager, employee, member or interest holder of:
> (i) an authorised body; or
> (ii) a body corporate which is a manager, member or interest holder of an authorised body,
> provided that all work you do is:
> . . .
> (B) done for the body itself, or falls within Rule 4.1 to 4.11 (In-house practice: Work colleagues, Related bodies and Pro bono work), and where this sub-paragraph applies, references in Rule 4 to 'employer' shall be construed as referring to that body, accordingly;

(Rule 1.1(c)(A) authorises the individual to work through his or her employer for clients to the extent that the firm is authorised to do so by the SRA.)

- covered by rule 1.1(d)(B) of the SRA Practice Framework Rules, which is practice as a solicitor from an office in England and Wales:

> (d)  as a manager, employee, member or interest holder of:
> (i)  an authorised non-SRA firm; or
> (ii)  a body corporate which is a manager, member or interest holder of an authorised non-SRA firm,
>
> provided that all work you do is:
>
> ...
>
> (B)  done for the firm itself, or falls within Rule 4.1 to 4.11 (In-house practice: Work colleagues, Related bodies and Pro bono work), and where this sub-paragraph applies, references in Rule 4 to 'employer' shall be construed as referring to that firm, accordingly;

(Rule 2.1(d)(A) makes the same provision for employees of firms authorised by another regulator.)

- covered by rule 1.1(e) of the SRA Practice Framework Rules, which is practice as a solicitor from an office in England and Wales:

> (e)  as the employee of another person, business or organisation, provided that you undertake work only for your employer, or as permitted by Rule 4 (In-house practice).

- covered by rule 1.2(f) of the SRA Practice Framework Rules, which is practice as a solicitor from an office outside England and Wales:

> (f)  as the employee of another person, business or organisation, provided that you undertake work only for your employer, or as permitted by Rule 4.22 to 4.25 (In-house practice overseas).

Rules 2.1(c)(B), 2.1(d)(B), 2.1(e) and 2.2(f) are identical provisions applicable to RELs as distinct from solicitors. Rules 3.1(b)(B) and 3.1(c)(B) are the equivalent provisions for RFLs.

Obviously, those further definitions are not sufficient in themselves, because there are cross-references to rule 4 of the SRA Practice Framework Rules.

So far as relevant, rule 4 is in two parts: in-house practice within England and Wales, and in-house practice overseas.

The normal rule (rule 4.1) is that if you are an in-house lawyer you must not act for clients other than your employer. Rules 4.4 to 4.11 of the SRA Practice Framework Rules provide exceptions which relate to (expressed informally):

- work done for work colleagues: past or present fellow employees and similar persons, and when employed by a media organisation includes work on behalf of a contributor to a broadcast or publication in defamation claims;
- work for companies and the like associated with the employer;
- pro bono work subject to specified limitations and exceptions.

Further exceptions, rules 4.12 to 4.18, cover practitioners who are employed not by law firms (entities regulated either by the SRA or other approved regulators) but by other organisations, and therefore to whom rule 1.1(e) applies, and therefore to whom the whole of rule 4 applies, not just 4.4 to 4.11. These are in short:

- acting for members of an association which employs the practitioner, subject to express restrictions (4.12);
- acting on behalf of an insured when employed by an insurer, in certain circumstances (4.13);
- working for commercial legal advice services, principally telephone legal advice helplines (4.14);
- when employed in local government, working for other persons or bodies in specified limited circumstances (4.15);
- acting for members of the public through law centres, charities and other non-commercial providers of advice and other legal services, subject to express conditions (4.16);
- when employed in central government or by other public bodies, including the Legal Services Commission, acting for other persons if doing so in pursuance of the lawful functions of the employer (4.18);
- the provision of legal services to clients of a foreign law firm (lawyers qualified in foreign jurisdictions practising as such, but within England and Wales), subject to specified controls and restrictions (4.19 to 4.21);
- when employed by a regulatory body, giving advice to other persons and acting for them if carrying out the employer's statutory functions (4.26).

Rules 4.22 to 4.25 of the SRA Practice Framework Rules cover in-house practice overseas:

- Rule 4.22 enables the exception permitting pro bono work to be done for clients other than the employer (rules 4.10 and 4.11) to apply to in-house practice overseas.
- Rule 4.23 disapplies the remainder of rule 4 and substitutes an obligation to comply only with the overseas-specific rules 4.24 and 4.25.
- By rule 4.25, a solicitor registered with the professional body for a local legal profession in another EU state under the Establishment Directive may practise in-house to the extent that a member of that legal profession is permitted to do so.
- Otherwise, by rule 4.24, an in-house solicitor in overseas practice may only act for his or her employer, a company substantially controlled by the employer, or another group company or parent company, or for fellow employees subject to specified limitations.

## 6.1.2 Application of the Code to in-house practice by chapter

*Chapter 1*

All the Chapter 1 outcomes (client care) apply directly or indirectly, apart from O(1.8) (compulsory professional indemnity insurance), which is replaced by an outcome specific to in-house practice.

Outcomes 1.1 to 1.5, O(1.7), O(1.15) and O(1.16) apply to in-house practice without any variation.

Outcome 1.6 and O(1.9) to O(1.14) apply to in-house practice where the practitioner acts for someone other than his or her employer unless it is clear that the outcome is not relevant to the particular circumstances.

An in-house-specific outcome is substituted for O(1.8): IHP(1.1), which requires compliance with the SRA Practice Framework Rules in relation to professional indemnity insurance.

This means that if acting for a client other than the employer by taking advantage of the exceptions for pro bono work (rule 4.10), commercial advice services (rule 4.14), law centres, charities, etc. (rule 4.16) or foreign law firms (rule 4.19), professional indemnity cover must be in place. In all other cases, the practitioner must consider whether the employer has appropriate indemnity insurance, and if it does not, the client must be informed in writing.

*Chapter 2*

All the Chapter 2 outcomes apply depending on the status of the employed lawyer.

Outcome 2.1 and O(2.2) (avoiding discrimination and respecting diversity) apply to all in-house practice.

Outcomes 2.3 to 2.5 envisage a management responsibility (practical arrangements to accommodate disability, recruitment policies and complaints handling). In place of those provisions an in-house solicitor who has management·responsibilities must take all reasonable steps to encourage equality of opportunity and respect for diversity in the workplace (IHP(2.1)).

*Chapter 3*

All the Chapter 3 outcomes apply depending on the status of the employed lawyer.

Outcomes 3.1 to 3.3 (systems and controls relating to conflicts of interest) apply if the employed solicitor has management responsibilities.

All other outcomes, O(3.4) to O(3.7), apply without variation.

## Chapters 4, 5 and 6

All the outcomes in Chapter 4 (confidentiality and disclosure); Chapter 5 (duties to the court); and Chapter 6 (clients introduced to third parties) apply to in-house practice without variation.

## Chapter 7

Chapter 7 is concerned with business management. All save two outcomes only apply to in-house solicitors if they have management responsibilities. The exceptions are O(7.5) and O(7.7), which apply to all in-house solicitors – compliance with legislation, including anti-money laundering and data protection provisions, and compliance with the statutory requirements for the carrying on of reserved legal activities and immigration work.

## Chapter 8

The first four outcomes of Chapter 8 (publicity) apply to in-house practice unless it is clear from the context that the outcome is not relevant in the particular circumstances. These are the requirements as to publicity being accurate and not misleading, clarity of charges, the prohibition on cold calling, and clarity as to the extent of regulation.

Outcome 8.5 is concerned with the proper content of a law firm's letterhead, etc. and has no application.

## Chapter 9

Chapter 9 (fee sharing and referrals) applies to in-house practice with practical modifications.

Outcomes 9.1 to 9.3 apply without variation, and are concerned with independence, the protection of clients' interests and the ability of clients to make informed decisions.

Outcomes 9.4 to 9.7 apply unless it is clear from the context that the outcome is not relevant in the particular circumstances. These outcomes are concerned with disclosure of financial arrangements with introducers, disclosure of any fee sharing arrangement relevant to the client, exclusion of criminal matters and publicly funded matters from any referral fee arrangement, and the requirement that an agreement with an introducer must be in writing.

*Chapters 10 and 11*

The outcomes of Chapter 10 (duties to the regulator) and Chapter 11 (relations with third parties – the duty not to take advantage, undertakings, contract races, the proper administration of oaths and affirmations) apply to in-house practice without variation.

*Chapter 12*

Chapter 12 (separate businesses) applies to in-house practice with one exception: O(12.2) only applies to a regulated firm and prohibits ownership of the firm by a separate business which provides core legal services, or a connection with such an entity (connection meaning something like common ownership or closely associated companies).

## 6.2   APPLICATION OF THE CODE TO OVERSEAS PRACTICE

### 6.2.1   Overseas practice defined

'Overseas practice' means:

> practice from an office outside England and Wales, except in the case of an REL, where it means practice from an office in Scotland or Northern Ireland.

### 6.2.2   Application of the Code of Conduct in relation to practice from an office outside England and Wales

Chapter 13 of the Code (application and waivers provisions) contains the following:

3.   Subject to 5 and 6 below, the Code applies to you, in relation to practice from an office in Scotland or Northern Ireland, if you are:

   (a)   a solicitor or an REL practising as such, whether or not your firm or employer is subject to this Code;
   (b)   a lawyer-controlled body;
   (c)   an REL-controlled body;
   (d)   any other person who is a manager of an authorised body; or
   (e)   a solicitor who was formerly an REL, when practising as a lawyer of an Establishment Directive profession.

4.   Subject to 5 and 6 below, the Code applies to you, in relation to practice from an office outside the UK, if you are:

   (a)   a solicitor practising as such, whether or not your firm or employer is subject to this Code;
   (b)   a lawyer-controlled body; or
   (c)   any other person who is a manager of an authorised body.

5.   If any outcome in the Code does not apply to your overseas practice, you may

disregard that Outcome in relation to your overseas practice, but you must comply with any alternative provision substituted for overseas practice.

6.     If compliance with any outcome in the Code would result in your breaching local law, you may disregard that outcome to the extent necessary to comply with that local law.

### 6.2.3   Application of the Code to overseas practice by chapter

*Chapter 1*

The normal outcomes required by Chapter 1 (client care) do not apply to overseas practice. A different overseas-specific set of outcomes is substituted:

OP(1.1)   you properly account to your clients for any financial benefit you receive as a result of your instructions unless it is the prevailing custom of your local jurisdiction to deal with financial benefits in a different way;

OP(1.2)   clients have the benefit of insurance or other indemnity in relation to professional liabilities which takes account of:

(a)     the nature and extent of the risks you incur in your overseas practice;
(b)     the local conditions in the jurisdiction in which you are practising; and
(c)     the terms upon which insurance is available;

and you have not attempted to exclude liability below the minimum level required for practice in the local jurisdiction;

OP(1.3)   you do not enter into unlawful contingency fee arrangements.

*Chapter 2*

The normal outcomes required by Chapter 2 (equality and diversity) do not apply to overseas practice. A different overseas-specific outcome is substituted:

OP(2.1)   you do not discriminate unlawfully according to the jurisdiction in which you are practising.

*Chapters 3 and 4*

The outcomes in Chapter 3 (conflicts of interest) and Chapter 4 (confidentiality and disclosure) apply to overseas practice without variation.

*Chapter 5*

The outcomes in Chapter 5 (duties to the court) apply to overseas practice only in relation to proceedings conducted by the overseas practice in England and Wales: that is in relation to litigation or advocacy conducted before a court, tribunal or enquiry in England and Wales or a British court martial.

*Chapters 6 and 7*

The outcomes in Chapter 6 (introductions to third parties) and Chapter 7 (business management) apply to overseas practice without variation.

*Chapter 8*

Both O(8.1) (accurate and not misleading publicity) and O(8.4) (information about the extent of regulation) apply to overseas practice.

Outcome 8.2 (clarity of information about charges), O(8.3) (cold calling) and O(8.5) (the requirements for the content of letterheads, etc.) do not apply. Instead, there is an overseas-specific outcome:

OP(8.1)  publicity intended for a jurisdiction outside England and Wales must comply with any applicable law or rules regarding lawyers' publicity in the jurisdiction in which your office is based; and the jurisdiction for which the publicity is intended.

*Chapter 9*

The outcomes in Chapter 9 (fee sharing and referrals) apply to overseas practice, except where they conflict with the SRA European Cross-Border Practice Rules, which will prevail in the event of any conflict.

The provisions in the SRA European Cross-Border Practice Rules relating to fee sharing and referrals are:

**4.  Fee sharing with non-lawyers**

4.1   You must not share your professional fees with a non-lawyer situated in a CCBE [Council of the Bars and Law Societies of Europe] state other than the UK except:

(a)   within a firm and only as permitted under the SRA Practice Framework Rules 2011; or

(b)   with a retired manager, member, owner or predecessor of the firm, or the dependants or personal representatives of a deceased manager, member, owner or predecessor.

4.2   If you are practising from an office in a CCBE state other than the UK, whether or not you are actually present at that office, you must not share your professional fees from that practice with a non-lawyer, except:

(a)   within a firm, and only as permitted under the SRA Practice Framework Rules 2011; or

(b)   with a retired manager, member, owner or predecessor of the firm, or the dependants or personal representatives of a deceased manager, member, owner or predecessor.

. . .

**7. Paying referral fees to non-lawyers**

7.1   You must not pay a fee, commission or any other compensation to a non-lawyer as a consideration for referring a client to you:

(a)   if the non-lawyer is situated in a CCBE state other than the UK; or

(b)   if you are practising from an office in a CCBE state other than the UK, whether or not you are physically present at that office.

## Chapter 10

The Chapter 10 outcomes (duties to the regulator) apply to overseas practice without variation.

## Chapter 11

The Chapter 11 (relations with third parties) outcomes (no unfair advantage, undertakings, contract races, administration of oaths, etc.) apply to overseas practice, except that O(11.3) – the duty when acting for a seller of land to inform buyers immediately of the seller's intention to deal with more than one buyer, usually referred to as the rule on contract races – only applies if the land in question is situated in England and Wales.

## Chapter 12

In relation to overseas practice, if the practitioner also has a separate business, O(12.3) to O(12.6) apply. These are: safeguards to ensure clients are not misled as to the extent of regulation; prohibition on holding out the separate business or any individual providing services through it as being regulated by the SRA; requirement to be connected only with reputable separate businesses; and, in relation to financial services, the requirement that any separate business should be independent, and not a tied financial adviser.

Outcome 12.1 and O(12.2), which prohibit participation through or ownership by a separate business which conducts 'prohibited separate business activities' – essentially core legal practice matters which cannot properly be hived off to a separate entity – do not apply to overseas practice.

# CHAPTER 7

# Other important changes

## 7.1 INTRODUCTION

This book is primarily concerned with the new Principles and Code, which are intended to replace the Solicitors' Code of Conduct 2007. These comprise no more than 55 pages. However, the whole of the SRA's new 'SRA Handbook' comprises 574 pages. The complete list of new regulations (excluding the Code and Principles and all carrying the provisional date of '2011') is:

- SRA Accounts Rules;
- SRA Practice Framework Rules;
- SRA Authorisation Rules for Legal Services Bodies and Licensable Bodies;
- SRA Practising Regulations;
- SRA Recognised Bodies Regulations;
- SRA Training Regulations;
- SRA Admission Regulations;
- SRA Qualified Lawyers Transfer Scheme Regulations;
- SRA Higher Rights of Audience Regulations;
- SRA Suitability Test;
- Solicitors Keeping of the Roll Regulations;
- SRA Indemnity Insurance Rules;
- SRA Indemnity (Enactment) Rules;
- SRA Compensation Fund Rules;
- SRA Intervention Powers (Statutory Trust) Rules;
- SRA Disciplinary Procedure Rules;
- SRA (Cost of Investigations) Regulations;
- SRA Property Selling Rules;
- SRA Financial Services (Scope) Rules;
- SRA Financial Services (Conduct of Business) Rules;
- SRA European Cross-border Practice Rules;
- SRA Handbook glossary.

A commentary on all this material is beyond the scope of this book. More detailed consideration will be available in the next edition of the *Solicitor's Handbook*, scheduled to be published a short time after all the rules are expected to come into force.

There are a modest number of specific changes to which firms should be giving particular attention, however, as they require attention as soon as the rules are in force.

## 7.2 SRA ACCOUNTS RULES

The (new) introduction to the SRA Accounts Rules includes a reference to desired outcomes:

- client money is safe;
- clients and the public have confidence that client money held by firms will be safe;
- firms are managed in such a way, and with appropriate systems and procedures in place, so as to safeguard client money;
- client accounts are used for appropriate purposes only; and
- the SRA is aware of issues in a firm relevant to the protection of client money.

Because, following the introduction of ABSs, businesses may be supplying both regulated and unregulated services (through multi-disciplinary practices (MDPs)), in relation to MDPs the rules apply only in respect of those activities for which the practice is regulated by the SRA, and are concerned only with money handled by the practice which relates to those regulated activities.

This results in there being a third category of money handled by the firm. As well as client money and office money there will be 'out-of-scope money' – funds held by an MDP which relate to activities which are not regulated by the SRA.

For traditional firms unaffected by such changes, there are two matters to note: (1) in relation to client interest; and (2) as to who may be an authorised signatory on client account.

There is no longer any list or specific guidance as to when interest, or a sum in lieu of interest, must be paid. Instead, there is a general requirement to account for interest 'when it is fair and reasonable to do so in all the circumstances' (rule 22(1)), but, importantly, rule 22(3) provides:

> You must have a written policy on the payment of interest, which seeks to provide a fair outcome. The terms of the policy must be drawn to the attention of the client at the outset of a retainer, unless it is inappropriate to do so in the circumstances.

So there is another item to be included in client care information, and the firm must first design the policy.

There is no reason why firms should not adopt a policy which bears a close resemblance to the current rules (rules 24 and 25 of the Solicitors' Accounts Rules

1998), including the £20 *de minimis* provision, if that is suitable having regard to the nature of the practice.

Secondly, there is no longer a specific list of persons who may be authorised to withdraw money from client account (rule 23 of the 1998 Rules).

Instead, by rule 21 of the 2011 rules:

(1)   A withdrawal from a client account may be made only after a specific authority in respect of that withdrawal has been signed by an appropriate person or persons in accordance with the firm's procedures for signing on client account. An authority for withdrawals from client account may be signed electronically, subject to appropriate safeguards and controls.

(2)   Firms must put in place appropriate systems and procedures governing withdrawals from client account, including who should be permitted by the firm to sign on client account. A non-manager owner or a non-employee owner of a licensed body is not an appropriate person to be a signatory on client account and must not be permitted by the firm to act in this way ...

**Guidance notes**

(i)   A firm should select suitable people to authorise withdrawals from the client account. Firms will wish to consider whether any employee should be able to sign on client account, and whether signing rights should be given to all managers of the practice or limited to those managers directly involved in providing legal services. Someone who has no day-to-day involvement in the business of the practice is unlikely to be regarded as a suitable signatory because of the lack of proximity to client matters. An appropriate understanding of the requirements of the rules is essential ...

So, again, the onus is on the firm to determine a policy and put in place suitable systems. All responsible firms will already have addressed these issues in detail, so this is , in reality, a deregulatory development, allowing firms to decide who is best suited and qualified to authorise withdrawals from client account, rather than being restricted to persons of particular professional qualifications.

## 7.3   SRA AUTHORISATION RULES

These rules are the core of the SRA's control mechanism for all forms of practice. They will apply to ABSs from the planned commencement date (which at the time of writing is probably going to be before the end of 2011) and to all other more traditional forms of practice ('recognised bodies' as they are at present) including legal disciplinary partnerships from 31 March 2012. On a date yet to be determined but which will not be before 31 March 2012. Also on 31 March 2012, as planned, the SRA Recognised Bodies Regulations will be repealed. They are only being maintained for a transitional period because the SRA Authorisation Rules will not apply to non-ABS businesses – recognised bodies – until 31 March 2012.

There are three key elements:

•   the process of authorisation;

- information requirements; and
- the roles of compliance officers – the COLP and the COFA.

'Authorisation' is the word being used to describe the recognition process for recognised bodies, and the licensing process for ABSs. Once authorised, a firm will not need to renew its authorisation (recognition or licence); it will continue until withdrawn or revoked, although there will be requirements to make annual returns with specified information and pay annual fees.

By rule 6.2 of the Authorisation Rules, the SRA may only grant an application for authorisation if the applicant satisfies, in terms of the business structure, the requirements for a legal services body (non-ABS) or a licensable body (ABS); if it is a partnership, the body has adopted a name under which it is to be registered, and which complies with Chapter 8 (publicity) of the SRA Code of Conduct; and that upon authorisation, the body will be in compliance with the SRA Indemnity Insurance Rules and SRA Compensation Fund Rules. The applicant will also have to satisfy the requirements as to the appointment of compliance officers, and obtain the SRA's approval; demonstrate that all managers and owners of the business are approved as necessary, and not disqualified (for example, as a result of having been struck off); demonstrate compliance with rule 12 of the SRA Practice Framework Rules in relation to persons who must be 'qualified to supervise'; and demonstrate compliance with rules 15 and 16 of those Rules as to formation, registered office, practising address and composition of the body.

By rule 6.3, the SRA may refuse an application even if these conditions are satisfied if:

(a)   it is not satisfied that the applicant body's managers and interest holders are suitable, as a group, to operate or control a business providing regulated legal services;

(b)   it is not satisfied that the applicant body's management or governance arrangements are adequate to safeguard the regulatory objectives;

(c)   it is not satisfied that if the authorisation is granted, the applicant body will comply with the SRA's regulatory arrangements including [the Authorisation Rules] and any conditions imposed on the authorisation;

(d)   the applicant body has provided inaccurate or misleading information in its application or in response to any requests by the SRA for information;

(e)   the applicant body has failed to notify the SRA of any changes in the information provided in the application in accordance with Rule 3; or

(f)   for any other reason, the SRA considers that it would be against the public interest or otherwise inconsistent with the regulatory objectives to grant authorisation.

All authorisations will be subject to general conditions (under rule 8 of the Authorisation Rules) as well as any specific conditions the SRA decides to impose (under rule 9; these are broadly comparable with the purposes for which conditions may be imposed currently on recognitions and practising certificates).

The general conditions impose duties as to: regulatory compliance (rule 8.1); making suitable arrangements to ensure compliance (rule 8.2); the payment of periodical fees (rule 8.3); any limits on the activities that may be carried out (rule

8.4); the appointment of compliance officers (rule 8.5); those permitted to have management responsibilities and control (rule 8.6); and the provision of information, including information requirements specific to partnerships, recognised bodies and licensed bodies (rules 8.7 to 8.10).

As information requirements occur in various places throughout the Authorisation Rules, a summary of all of them can be found at **8.2.2**.

### 7.3.1 COLPs and COFAs

Rule 8.5 of the SRA Authorisation Rules provides:

(a)  An authorised body must have suitable arrangements in place to ensure that its compliance officers are able to discharge their duties in accordance with these rules.

(b)  An authorised body must at all times have an individual:

    (i)  who is a manager or an employee of the authorised body;

    (ii)  who is designated as its COLP;

    (iii)  who is of sufficient seniority and in a position of sufficient responsibility to fulfil the role; and

    (iv)  whose designation is approved by the SRA.

(c)  The COLP of an authorised body must:

    (i)  take all reasonable steps to:

        (A)  ensure compliance with the terms and conditions of the authorised body's authorisation except any obligations imposed under the SRA Accounts Rules;

        (B)  ensure compliance with any statutory obligations of the body, its managers, employees or interest holders in relation to the body's carrying on of authorised activities; and

        (C)  record any failure so to comply and make such records available to the SRA on request; and

    (ii)  as soon as reasonably practicable, report to the SRA any failure so to comply, provided that:

        (A)  in the case of non-material failures, these shall be taken to havebeen reported as soon as reasonably practicable if they are reported to the SRA together with such information as the SRA may require in accordance with Rule 8.7(a); and

        (B)  a failure may be material either taken on its own or as part of a pettern of failures so to comply.

(d)  An authorised body must at all times have an individual:

    (i)  who is a manager or an employee of the authorised body;

    (ii)  who is designated as its COFA;

    (iii)  who is of sufficient seniority and in a position of sufficient responsibility to fulfil the role; and

    (iv)  whose designation is approved by the SRA.

(e)  The COFA of an authorised body must:

      (i)    take all reasonable steps to ensure that the body and its employees and managers comply with any obligations imposed upon them under the SRA Accounts Rules;

      (ii)   record any failure so to comply and make such records available to the SRA on request; and

      (iii)  as soon as reasonably practicable, report to the SRA any failure so to comply which is material either taken on its own or as part of a pattern of failures so to comply, provided that:

            (A)   in the case of non-material failures, these shall be taken to have been reported as soon as reasonably practicable if they are reported to the SRA together with such other information as the SRA may require in accordance with Rule 8.7(a); and

            (B)   a failure may be material either taken on its own or as part of a pattern of failures so to comply.

(f)    The SRA may approve an individual's designation as a COLP or COFA if it is satisfied, in accordance with Part 4, that the individual is a suitable person to carry out his or her duties.

(g)    A designation of an individual as a COLP or COFA has effect only while the individual:

      (i)    consents to the designation;

      (ii)   in the case of a COLP:

            (A)   is not disqualified from acting as a HOLP [Head of Legal Practice] [under the Legal Services Act 2007 [LSA], s.99]; and

            (B)   is:

                (Aa)   a lawyer of England and Wales;

                (Bb)   an REL; or

                (Cc)   registered with the BSB [Bar Standards Board] under regulation 17 of the European Communities (Lawyer's Practice) Regulations 2000 (SI 2000/1119);

              and is an authorised person in relation to one or more of the reserved legal activities which the body is authorised to carry on; and

      (iii)  in the case of a COFA, is not disqualified from acting as a HOFA [Head of Finance and Administration] [under the LSA, s.99].

The reference in rules 8.5(c)(ii)(A) and 8.5(e)(iii)(A) to information required by the SRA 'in accordance with Rule 8.7(a)' is a reference to the annual report to the SRA which all authorised bodies must provide. Accordingly, while all breaches have to be reported by the COLP or COFA 'as soon as reasonably practicable', non-material breaches have only to be reported in the annual information report.

There are helpful guidance notes, reproduced here:

(v)    Rule 8.5 requires all authorised bodies to have a COLP and a COFA. For COLPs and COFAs of licensed bodies, compliance with their obligations under Rule 8.5 will assist in complying with their duties as Head of Legal Practice and Head of Finance and Administration under sections 91 and 92 respectively of the LSA.

(vi)   The roles of COLP and COFA are a fundamental part of a firm's compliance and governance arrangements. COLPs' and COFAs' ability to take the steps they need to ensure compliance is dependent on the firm having suitable arrangements in place under Rule 8.2. The firm must therefore ensure that any person designated as its COLP or COFA is of sufficient seniority, in a position of sufficient power and responsibility and has clear reporting lines to enable them to have access to all management systems and arrangements and all other relevant information including client files and business information. The existence of compliance officers in a firm and the requirements on them to ensure that the firm, as well as its managers and employees, are complying with the regulatory arrangements (COLP) and the SRA Accounts Rules (COFA) is not a substitute for the firm's and managers' responsibilities and their obligations to comply with Rule 8.1 (Regulatory compliance). Firms and managers need to take care not to obstruct, whether intentionally or unwittingly, a COLP or COFA in fulfilling their role.

(vii)   COLPs and COFAs are responsible for ensuring that the firm has systems and controls in place to enable the firm, as well as its managers and employees, to comply with the requirements on them. The firm and its managers are not absolved from any of their own obligations and remain fully responsible for compliance (see Rule 8.1).

(viii)  Those designated as COLP will need to be in a position to be able to discharge the role. They will need to consider whether they are in a position to, for example:

- take all reasonable steps to ensure compliance with the terms of the firm's authorisation; compliance with the SRA's regulatory arrangements by the firm, its employees and managers; and with relevant statutory obligations, e.g.

    - that non-authorised persons comply with the duty imposed by section 90 of the LSA (duty not to do anything which causes or substantially contributes to a breach of the SRA's regulatory arrangements by an authorised body or its employee or manager)
    - that authorised persons and other managers and employees comply with the duty imposed by section 176 of the LSA (duty to comply with the SRA's regulatory arrangements)
    - under the LSA, [Administration of Justice Act 1985] and the [Solicitors Act 1974] in respect of practice matters.

- as soon as reasonably practicable, report to the SRA any failure to comply where such failure is material either on its own or as part of a pattern.

(ix)    Those designated as COFA will need to be in a position to be able to discharge the role. They will need to consider whether they are in a position to, for example:

- ensure that they have access to all accounting records
- carry out regular checks on the accounting systems
- carry out file and ledger reviews
- ensure that the reporting accountant has prompt access to all the information needed to complete the accountant's report
- take steps to ensure that breaches of the SRA Accounts Rules are remedied promptly, and report any breach, which is material either on its own or as part of a pattern, to the SRA
- monitor, review and manage risks to compliance with the SRA Accounts Rules.

(x)     In considering whether a failure is 'material' and therefore reportable, the COLP or COFA, as appropriate, will need to take account of various factors, such as:

- the detriment, or risk of detriment, to clients
- the extent of any risk of loss of confidence in the firm or in the provision of legal services

- the scale of the issue
- the overall impact on the firm, its clients and third parties.

In addition, the COLP/COFA will need to keep appropriate records of failures in compliance to:

- monitor overall compliance with obligations
- assess the effectiveness of the firm's systems
- be able to comply with the duty to report breaches which are material because they form a pattern.

(xi) In developing their governance and administrative arrangements firms will need to consider how they approach unexpected risks such as the absence of key staff, including COLP and COFA, and whether the nature of the absence will trigger the need to notify the SRA (see Rule 8.7) and to obtain approval for a replacement.

(xii) The statutory obligations of a recognised body are contained in the AJA and the SA, and for licensed bodies are contained in sections 90 and 176 of the LSA. An important aspect of the roles of COLP and COFA is the need to report breaches to the SRA. Although it will commonly be appropriate for the firm to take steps to remedy breaches immediately, this does not obviate the need for compliance officers to make a report in compliance with Rule 8.5 where appropriate.

(xiii) Approval (see Rules 8.5 and 8.6) relates only to the role for which it is granted. Any change from one role that requires approval to another, will require a further approval . . .

It is important to appreciate the distinction between the responsibilities of compliance officers and managers. The COLPs and COFAs are responsible for systems, and for recording and reporting compliance failings. The obligation to 'ensure compliance' does not mean, in our view, that the compliance officer is personally liable if there is non-compliance. Both COLPs and COFAs can expect to face disciplinary consequences if there are no adequate systems in place to minimise risks or to monitor the effectiveness of controls, or if there is a failure to keep adequate records, or to report when it was appropriate to do so.

However, the managers remain responsible for the firm, and individuals for their own conduct. If the compliance officer is not provided with adequate facilities and resources, that will be the responsibility of the managers, but that in itself will be a failure of compliance which is likely to mean that the compliance officer cannot carry out his or her duties, which would trigger an obligation to report.

There can be expected to be some tensions between COLPs and COFAs and managers.

In small firms, and sole practices in particular, one person may fulfil all roles, and there is no requirement that it should be otherwise. Small firms, however, must bear in mind that compliance officers must be expressly approved by the SRA, and if there is no COLP or COFA the firm cannot maintain its authorisation, and would have to close.

Withdrawal of approval of a COLP or COFA could be terminal for a practice. If for any reason a firm ceases to have an approved COLP and COFA, it must notify the SRA within seven days and designate a replacement or replacements within the same time; temporary approval may be granted for 28 days.

Larger firms may find it desirable to have more than one compliance officer of each class in a position to take over the role in the event of unforeseen circumstances.

# CHAPTER 8

# Summary of reporting and similar obligations

There are now so many obligations of this kind that it seems sensible and helpful to list them.

## 8.1 STATUTORY REQUIREMENTS

- Solicitors Act 1974, s.84: notification of a change in a solicitor's place of business;
- Legal Services Act 2007, Sched. 13, para. 21: notification by non-authorised persons (investors) who propose to acquire an interest in a licensed body (ABS) which would amount to a restricted interest (currently 10 per cent) or who have acquired such an interest must notify the proposal or the acquisition. Failure to do so is a criminal offence.

## 8.2 SRA REQUIREMENTS

### 8.2.1 Under the Code of Conduct

- O(10.2): providing information required by the SRA to deal with any application (such as for a practising certificate);
- O(10.3): prompt notification of any material changes to relevant information including serious financial difficulty, action taken by another regulator and serious failure to comply with or achieve the Principles, rules, outcomes and other requirements of the SRA Handbook;
- O(10.4): prompt reporting of serious misconduct by any person or firm authorised by the SRA, or any employee, manager or owner of any such firm (taking into account, where necessary, the duty of confidentiality to clients);
- O(10.5): ensuring that the SRA is in a position to assess whether any persons requiring prior approval are fit and proper at the point of approval and remain so;

- O(10.6): full co-operation with the SRA and the Legal Ombudsman at all times, including in relation to any investigation about a claim for redress;
- O(10.7): prohibition of any attempt to prevent anyone from providing information to the SRA or the Legal Ombudsman;
- O(10.8): prompt compliance with any written notice from the SRA;
- O(10.9): pursuant to any notice by the SRA the production of any documents; the provision of all information and explanations requested; compliance with all requests from the SRA as to the form in which any documents held electronically are produced, and for photocopies of any documents to be taken, provided that they are in connection with the individual's practice or in connection with any trust of which he or she is, or formerly was, a trustee;
- O(10.11): when required by the SRA to investigate whether any person may have a claim for redress, acting promptly to do so, reporting to the SRA the outcome of the investigation and identifying the persons who may have a claim, notifying those persons about the possible claim, about the firm's complaints procedures and about the Legal Ombudsman (as well as dealing with the matter as if a complaint had been made);
- O(10.13): informing the SRA before a firm closes as part of the orderly wind-down of a firm ceasing to practise.

### 8.2.2 Under the SRA Authorisation Rules for Legal Services Bodies and Licensable Bodies

- Rule 3: notification of any change in information provided in an application for authorisation;
- Rule 8.5(c)(ii): report by a COLP of any material non-compliance as soon as reasonably practicable;
- Rule 8.5(e)(iii): report by a COFA of any material non-compliance as soon as reasonably practicable;
- Rule 8.7(a): provision of an annual information report containing such information as may be specified in the prescribed form by the prescribed date;
- Rule 8.7(c): notification of any changes to relevant information about the firm, its employees, managers or interest holders, including non-compliance with the Authorisation Rules and the conditions on its authorisation;
- Rule 8.7(d): immediate notification of any information which reasonably suggests that the firm has or may have provided the SRA with information which was or may have been false, misleading, incomplete or inaccurate, or has or may have changed in a materially significant way;
- Rule 8.8: notification by the sole surviving partner of a partnership in the event that they are the sole active partner by reason of the imprisonment or incapacity of, the imposition of relevant conditions on or abandonment of the practice by the other partner or partners;

- Rule 8.9: notification in similar circumstances by a legal services body of the loss of the sole remaining solicitor or REL whose role ensured the status of the body as a legal services body;
- Rule 8.10: notification in similar circumstances by a licensed body (ABS) of the loss of the sole remaining authorised individual whose role enabled the body to be a licensable body;
- Rule 18: notification that the firm ceases to have an approved COLP or COFA;
- Rule 23: notification of unforeseen temporary breach of conditions or eligibility criteria to be a legal services body or licensed body;
- Rule 24: notification of relevant changes in the composition of a partnership where temporary emergency recognition of a sole practitioner or new firm is required;
- Rule 25: applications for temporary emergency authorisations.

### 8.2.3 Under the SRA Practice Framework Rules

- Rule 18.1: any information and documentation relating to the composition and structure of the firm, or about its managers, employees or shareowners, as and when requested by the SRA;
- Rule 18.2: notification of any change to the firm's name, registered office or practising addresses, managers, members if it is a company, interest holders if it is a recognised body, owners if it is a licensed body, COLP or COFA;
- Rule 18.3: notification by an unlimited company of re-registration under the Companies Acts (the Companies Act 1985 and the Companies Act 2006) as a limited company;
- Rule 18.4: notification of a relevant insolvency event.

### 8.2.4 Under the SRA Accounts Rules

- Rule 35: strictly not a duty to inform, but to have a standard letter of engagement with reporting accountants enabling and requiring them to make a report to the SRA on discovery of relevant matters.

### 8.2.5 Under the SRA Practising Regulations

- Regulation 4.3: notification of a change in a firm's composition resulting in a solicitor or REL becoming a sole principal;
- Regulation 4.5: notification of the death of a recognised sole practitioner;
- Regulation 14.1: notification by a solicitor, REL or RFL if he or she:

    (a) is committed to prison in civil or criminal proceedings;

    (b) is charged with or convicted of an indictable offence;

    (c) is made the subject of bankruptcy proceedings;

(d)    makes a proposal for an individual voluntary arrangement or is a manager of a firm which makes a proposal for a company voluntary arrangement or a partnership voluntary arrangement under the Insolvency Act 1986;

(e)    is admitted as:
    (i)    a member of a legal profession of a jurisdiction other than England and Wales;
    (ii)    a lawyer of England and Wales other than a solicitor;

(f)    is made subject to disciplinary proceedings as:
    (i)    a member of a legal profession of a jurisdiction other than England and Wales; or
    (ii)    a lawyer of England and Wales other than a solicitor;

(g)    becomes a manager of or acquires any interest in a firm which is a recognised body, or becomes a manager or owner of a firm which is a licensed body or an authorised non-SRA firm;

(h)    sets up a sole practice as:
    (i)    a member of a legal profession of a jurisdiction other than England and Wales; or
    (ii)    a lawyer of England and Wales other than a solicitor;

(i)    changes his or her name as shown on the register of holders of practising certificates, the register of European lawyers or the register of foreign lawyers, and must at the same time provide details of his or her new name.

A number of events or occurrences are reportable under more than one regulation, which does not indicate a completely integrated approach.

Where requirements are not referred to as 'immediate' or 'prompt' or 'as soon as reasonably practicable' and refer to the happening of a particular event, the obligation is generally to notify within seven days.

# CHAPTER 9

# OFR in practice: what will it be like?

*We acknowledge with grateful thanks the major contribution to this chapter by Vanessa Shenton of The Compliance Partner*

Historically, most 'close encounters' with the SRA by the majority of the profession have been through visits by the Practice Standards Unit. Here we try to guess what might be different in future, as visits in one form or another will undoubtedly continue, having regard to the SRA's stated policies (see **9.2**).

## 9.1 A FOCUS ON SYSTEMS

The focus in future will be likely to be on firms' internal governance and the ability of managers to develop workable monitoring systems. These systems will need to be capable of identifying serious breaches of the Principles and outcomes, and other business risks, and firms will need to demonstrate how they will respond appropriately. The SRA supervision process, which will include visits to firms, will need to be able to review and assess these systems.

The SRA intends to risk-rate firms in order to apply its finite resource to firms who pose serious risks or to those who are unable or unwilling to identify and manage risk.

To achieve what it wants to, the SRA will need far more information from firms than previously required. New firms will go through a rigorous authorisation process, with the possibility of conditions being applied (perhaps restricting the nature of the work that can be undertaken if adequate expertise cannot be demonstrated). Existing firms will be passported, but all firms will have to provide an annual report from October 2012 and, in the meantime, through the compliance officers which each firm will have to appoint, and for whom approval will be required (see **7.3.1**), will have to notify the SRA of serious misconduct, serious financial difficulty, and material breaches of the SRA Handbook.

## 9.2    SRA 'RISK RATING' AND VISIT PROCESS

The SRA's Risk Centre will risk-rate firms and information received. However, the Risk Centre is not a new concept. Since April 2008, the SRA has employed the resources of its Risk Assessment and Designation Centre (RADC). Since then, following Practice Standards Unit (PSU) visits, the percentage of firms judged to exhibit serious breaches of the SRA rules and regulations or require a referral to another part of the SRA for further investigation has risen dramatically. This is despite the PSU continuing throughout the period to be the front line unit responsible for visiting *lower risk* firms.

Those within this (broadly equivalent) PSU classification in September 2007 amounted to 25 per cent. By September 2009, using RADC classifications, this had risen to 81 per cent. It has subsequently dropped back, but towards the end of 2010 the figure remained broadly above 65 per cent. It is noteworthy, however, that only around 10–15 per cent of firms visited were actually referred to other parts of the SRA, so it may be that the statistical classification erred towards caution.

The SRA's risk assessment focus will change from a consideration of compliance or non-compliance with detailed rules, to an assessment of the risks to the Principles and outcomes, and the risks associated with firms failing to have adequate processes and systems in place.

It is not, however, entirely clear how the SRA will go about risk-rating firms and what, in the future, it will consider to be serious (which may not be what firms consider to be serious). What will the SRA's risk appetite be? Will it take an overzealous approach, even if with a different focus?

Another potential hurdle is that the new guidance-free Code could lead to inconsistencies in decision making by both regulator and regulated alike. There has, for instance, already been much debate about the outcomes and indicative behaviours around conveyancing conflicts of interest and how these might be applied (see **5.4**). Another issue relates to the regulation of outsourcing, a new area of interest (see **5.8.4**).

### 9.2.1    Old tried and tested visit processes

Another factor in considering how a new visit process might take shape is that, although the theory behind the new Code might have changed, much of the content remains very similar to the 2007 Code, albeit without guidance. The old process, particularly that employed by the PSU, has become a tried and tested formula. One might imagine that SRA officers will still need to assess how outcomes are being complied with at fee earner level. They will presumably also need to consider what level of judgement is apparent at casework level to demonstrate why an indicative behaviour has not been followed. It is likely officers will still want to select and review a range of case files to be able to monitor these requirements.

The tried and tested formula for selecting cases for review is likely, therefore, to remain. This is not random. It is influenced by the officer having conducted a pre-visit review of the background of the firm and its regulatory and complaints history. One of the techniques employed in the past (and therefore likely in the future) is to select files from a case list which includes information on the type of matter, the file open date, the work in progress figure against the date and amount of the last bill, and client and office balances. SRA officers are adept at finding case files that the firm would rather they did not see. They are likely to continue to be so.

One might also imagine that the SRA will still review how referral arrangements operate. This remains a sensitive area, transparency with clients being crucial. It is unlikely that the SRA will discontinue its detailed assessment of how third party relationships are managed at central and case level.

Some elements of the new arrangements are not open to an outcomes focused approach. Most of the SRA Accounts Rules remain rules-based. Some regulation is imposed by third parties. Examples are the Money Laundering Regulations and the financial services rules. A new visit process will still have to assess compliance in these areas to satisfy the expectations of other regulators. Co-operation with the Legal Ombudsman is a regulatory requirement, and complaints handling can be expected to continue to be an area of interest

Chapter 15 of the new Code (transitional provisions) stresses that:

> ... where a breach of any provision of the Solicitors' Code of Conduct 2007 comes to the attention of the SRA after 6 October 2011, this shall be subject to action by the SRA notwithstanding any repeal of the relevant provision.

It would be sensible to assume that at least some successful past visit processes will re-emerge in one guise or another in the future. Although the visit processes of the future will inevitably require the SRA to assess the strength of a firm's management, including risks to its financial stability, and reporting systems, it would be a mistake to conclude that they will not be interested in reviewing case level detail as well.

### 9.2.2 The SRA's new supervision function

The visit process of the future will fall within the SRA's new function of supervision. Within this function a range of supervisory tools is envisaged. These include desk-based supervision, written or telephone contact, risk-based visits and a new concept of relationship management.

The intention is that the SRA will be able to respond to potential risk before its impact is felt upon clients or the wider public. Put into diagrammatic form, supervision might operate as Figure 9.1.

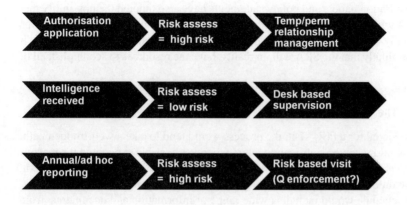

**Figure 9.1** Possible SRA supervision processes

### 9.2.3 Selection for a visit

Historically, some visits were random or theme-based, for instance to assess a range of firms known to have referral arrangements. In addition, firms were selected by reference to what was known about them.

The sources of information that the SRA had (and still has) range from regulatory and complaints histories and information on practising certificate or recognition application forms, intelligence reports from a range of potential contributors to the SRA's Fraud and Confidential Intelligence Bureau, annual accountants' reports and additional information received from reporting accountants in compliance with their mandatory whistle-blowing duties (introduced from 31 March 2009). Individuals within firms also had a duty to comply with rule 20 requirements to report serious misconduct and serious financial difficulty.

Information would be sifted by the RADC and a decision made as to whether a visit should take place and if so which of a number of visiting units should conduct that visit. The two main candidates were the Forensic Investigation Unit for more serious risk and financial concerns and, more commonly, the PSU for lower level compliance issues.

So what is likely to change in terms of selection for visits under the new regime?

The SRA will have additional information to decide whether a risk-based visit, relationship management or desk-based supervision might be appropriate. The information requirements, which have not as yet been fully devised, will no doubt focus on finding out what systems firms have in place and the risks which they consider themselves exposed to.

Firms can expect to receive a visit, not necessarily because of rule breaches, but because the SRA does not consider that a firm's systems are effective in the light of the identified risks, or because of failures to comply with the obligations of disclosure and notification.

Consultation papers and policy statements have also mooted the possibility that the SRA will consider visits to new firms, firms in the assigned risk pool, to all firms potentially every five years, random visits and a continuation of thematic visits. It seems unlikely that the SRA will, in reality, have the resources to accomplish all of that.

### 9.2.4 The past PSU visit process

Once selected for a PSU visit, the process would tend to take a well-trodden path. Firms would receive a notification letter, wherever possible explaining the reasons for the visit. This would enclose a schedule of information required for the visit, which would help firms prepare, and questionnaires for completion in advance.

The schedule would include a wide range of information and documents, from management structure and risk management procedures, standard client care letters, complaints and claims information, client account reconciliations, information about referral arrangements, records of periodic reviews and so on. This information would enable the PSU to review the activities of the firm against most, if not all, elements of the rules.

The schedule would ask for access to complaint and case files and a case list which would enable the PSU officer to conduct a targeted selection of cases for review.

Visits would tend to be for one or two days. They would generally include an initial meeting with the managing partner, case selection and review, an assessment of complaints, complaints handling procedures and any apparent trends, an accounts review and a meeting with the chief cashier or accounts manager.

Other than perhaps in relation to referral arrangements, there would be a fairly cursory consideration given to the firm's procedures and systems. Time would be spent for the most part on file reviews to uncover specific rule breaches, rather than in testing whether documented procedures were actually followed and worked satisfactorily.

### 9.2.5 A future visit process

For new firms, the SRA will have more information about the structure and systems of those that it regulates as part of the more detailed authorisation process. For existing firms passported into the new regime, the SRA will eventually have more information as a result of annual reporting commencing in October 2012. Of course, firms must comply, in the meantime, with their events-driven notification requirements as soon as the Code comes into force in October 2011.

It is possible that, if more information is needed to determine an individual firm's risk in accordance with the SRA's risk appetite and its priorities of the day, this might be dealt with initially as a desk-based exercise through contact with the firm by telephone or correspondence, and by other enquiries. It may be, therefore, that a supervision visit will involve less generic fact-finding than previously, as the basic information will already have been acquired.

Visits are more likely to focus attention on perceived gaps in internal governance, risk management procedures and reporting structures. A visit may also take place in response to discrete areas of identified risk arising from a firm's business activities and third party relationships.

One might imagine that a future visit would assess, in far greater detail, how documented procedures actually operate in practice, for instance, file reviews. This may replace the document review element of the former PSU visit, which was largely a quick 'flick through' exercise.

Meetings and detailed discussions with compliance officers (COLPs and COFAs), who must take all reasonable steps to record *any* failure to comply with the SRA Handbook, and make records available to the SRA on request, are likely to be a key focus. Meetings with heads of higher risk or financially fragile departments might also feature.

There is insight into how the SRA might go about its visit process within various consultation papers and other documents it has issued. In its 'Delivering Outcomes-focused Regulation – Policy Statement' (November 2010), the SRA indicated that a visit to a firm under 'close or continuous supervision' might entail an assessment of (para.78):

- The environmental risks affecting the firm, for example, the economic environment for conveyancing firms.
- The firm's business model, for example the spread of the firm's business, how is it financed, and what services it offers.
- The firm's business processes, for example:

  - the firm's structure and ownership
  - the extent of any risks posed by staff, including owners or managers
  - controls over its financial position
  - IT systems
  - exposure to legal/litigation risk
  - conflict and client care procedures
  - quality control and management of client matters;

- The firm's control functions, for example the work done by the COLP and COFA, together with internal audit (if the firm has an internal audit function – many smaller firms will not need one). We will consider the firm's governance arrangements, the strength of the relationship with the SRA (and its other regulators, if any), together with the strength of its management and its internal culture.

However, as mentioned, some rules are not outcomes-focused; the SRA can be expected to assess compliance in these areas too. For example, a review of the accounts and accounting procedures will clearly still occur. Moreover, in the future this will include an assessment of the two outcomes-focused elements in the SRA Accounts Rules, where firms must develop their own policies. These relate to payments in lieu of interest and those with authority to withdraw money from client account (see **7.2**).

In the Code, the SRA states that a failure to follow indicative behaviours 'may help us to decide whether an outcome has been achieved'. It is likely, therefore, that a future visit regime would be designed to test whether appropriate judgement has been applied to ethical dilemmas, particularly if a firm centrally, or a fee earner individually, chooses *not* to follow a particular indicative behaviour. It is unlikely, therefore, that targeted file reviews will be abandoned.

### 9.2.6 Conclusion and follow up – the past

The previous PSU visit process included a closing meeting to discuss breaches of the rules the PSU had uncovered, and to provide information on how the firm might manage compliance with the rules in the future. Usually, a report itemising each area of breach would follow to which the firm would have to respond. Sometimes firms would instead receive a detailed 'summary of breaches' report handed to them at the end of the visit.

Internally, the PSU officer would categorise the firm in accordance with centralised criteria and, in some cases, refer the firm on to other departments for further investigation.

'Hot topics' for further investigation included:

- suspicions of money laundering or fraud;
- accounts breaches, including dormant client balances;
- referrals, fee sharing, separate business rule and other breaches to independence including 'anticipatory' ABSs in breach of the rules at the time;
- secret profits, including misdescribing telegraphic transfer fees;
- retaining commission without strict rule 2.06 compliance;
- misleading clients;
- rule 5 breaches, if breaches were found to be systematic;
- failure to comply with actions from a previous visit.

### 9.2.7 Conclusion and follow up – the future

It is not clear whether an equivalent to the visit report or summary of breaches will survive. The outcome of an SRA supervision visit might be different.

It is also not clear, at this stage, how the SRA may respond to a departure from listed indicative behaviours. It does seem unlikely that the 'hot topics' will be significantly different from what they were previously, although 'jump the gun' ABSs will soon cease to be relevant.

What might well change is the stance taken if the SRA, in its opinion, maintains that internal systems to monitor compliance and financial viability and notification responsibilities are lacking. Due to the intensified focus on these issues, it is not hard to imagine a far sterner view being taken than has been the case hitherto.

The November 2010 policy statement says that 'where firms knowingly or recklessly fail in their responsibilities or show no commitment to achieving compliance, we will take swift and appropriate action'.

Consultation papers, policy statements and the guidance notes to rule 8 of the SRA Authorisation Rules on what might comprise 'suitable arrangements for compliance' refer to the concept of a 'compliance plan'. Agreeing a compliance plan with the SRA supervisor is mentioned as a possibility in the enforcement strategy.

A little troubling is reference to a regulatory settlement agreement also being a potential outcome of the supervision process itself. These publishable agreements have previously been part of the SRA's enforcement armoury. They have been used if a case would otherwise be fit to be referred to the SDT, but where a firm is willing to accept its wrongdoing, pay costs and remedy any defects, as an alternative to being referred to the SDT.

Another possible outcome of the supervisory visit process is that a firm's systems may be seen as so inadequate, and the risks that the SRA perceives to exist so harmful to clients and the public interest, that a firm's authorisation could be withdrawn, bringing a risk of intervention. It is perhaps more likely that this type of firm would enter a form of relationship management and be required to produce a plan for recovery or orderly closure.

The SRA wishes to 'constructively engage'. However, it also wishes to 'credibly deter'. It is possible that the SRA, depending on its risk appetite and what it considers to be serious, may be inclined to select firms for enforcement in order to draw attention to the importance of complying with the Code's new requirements.

The SRA Authorisation Rules enable the SRA to impose further conditions 'at any time', for example, to 'limit, halt or prevent a risk . . . arising from a business agreement or association' or to 'take specified steps conducive to the proper, effective or efficient carrying on of a legal activity'. Broadly equivalent provisions in the former Recognised Bodies Regulations have been used to impose (and publish) conditions, such as a requirement to undertake a training course.

The SRA will be increasing the resources of its authorisation function. This is key to the new risk-based approach. It is possible, therefore, that an outcome of a supervisory visit might be a reference to the authorisation function for conditions to be applied and published, possibly for failure to comply with new responsibilities.

## 9.3  LAW FIRM PRIORITIES

Existing firms will be passported into the new arrangements. Annual reporting will not commence until October 2012. However, the requirements within the new Code and the SRA's new approach will be in existence from October 2011. Firms will need to apply for approval of role holders, including compliance officers, by 31 March 2012.

Firms would, therefore, be ill advised to wait before considering how they will respond to OFR. They need to consider where there are gaps or insecurity in their governance, monitoring systems and lines of communication. They should, as far as possible, position themselves so as to be able to demonstrate that they are low risk for the purpose of risk-rating by the SRA.

# Introduction to the SRA Handbook

1.  Consumer interests and the general public interest are the key justifications for any regulatory scheme. Users of legal services are, therefore, the focus of the Solicitors Regulation Authority's (SRA's) regulatory framework.

2.  This Handbook sets out the standards and requirements which we expect our regulated community to achieve and observe, for the benefit of the clients they serve and in the general public interest. Our approach to regulation (i.e. authorisation, supervision and enforcement) is outcomes-focused and risk-based so that clients receive services in a manner which best suits their own particular needs, and depending on how services are provided (e.g. whether in-house or through private practice).

3.  Our Handbook brings together the key regulatory elements in the following sections:

    - **SRA Principles** – these are the ten Principles which are mandatory and apply to all those we regulate and to all aspects of practice. They define the fundamental ethical and professional standards that we expect of all firms (including owners who may not be lawyers) and individuals when providing legal services. In some circumstances they apply outside practice.

    - **SRA Code of Conduct ('the Code')** – this section contains the 'Outcomes' we require which, when achieved, benefit users of legal services and the public at large. These Outcomes are mandatory and, when achieved, will help ensure compliance with the Principles in the particular contexts covered by the various chapters in the Code. We recognise that these mandatory Outcomes may be achieved in a variety of ways depending on the particular circumstances, and we have supplemented the mandatory Outcomes with non-mandatory 'Indicative Behaviours' to aid compliance. The Indicative Behaviours which we set out are not exhaustive: the Outcomes can be achieved in other ways. We encourage firms to consider how they can best achieve the Outcomes taking into account the nature of the firm, the particular circumstances and, crucially, the needs of their particular clients.
        - Introduction
        - SRA Code of Conduct

    - **Accounts** – this section contains the SRA Accounts Rules – requirements aimed at protecting client money.
        - Introduction
        - SRA Accounts Rules

    - **Authorisation and Practising Requirements** – this section includes key requirements for the training and admission for individuals intending to become solicitors; exercising higher rights of audience; for individuals and firms setting up in practice and for the holding certain roles in a practice.
        - Introduction
        - SRA Practice Framework Rules
        - SRA Authorisation Rules for Legal Services Bodies and Licensable Bodies
        - SRA Practising Regulations

- – SRA Recognised Bodies Regulations
- – SRA Training Regulations:

  - – Training Regulations – Part 1 – Qualification Regulations
  - – Training Regulations – Part 2 – Training Provider Regulations
  - – Training Regulations – Part 3 – CPD Regulations

- – SRA Admission Regulations
- – SRA Qualified Lawyers Transfer Scheme Regulations[1]
- – SRA Higher Rights of Audience Regulations[2]
- – SRA Suitability Test
- – Solicitors Keeping of the Roll Regulations
- **Client Protection** – this section contains key elements for the financial protection of clients.
  - – Introduction
  - – SRA Indemnity Insurance Rules
  - – SRA Indemnity (Enactment) Rules 2011
  - – SRA Compensation Fund Rules
  - – SRA Intervention Powers (Statutory Trust) Rules
- **Discipline and Costs Recovery** – this section contains provisions upon which our disciplinary and costs recovery powers are based.
  - – Introduction
  - – SRA Disciplinary Procedure Rules
  - – SRA Cost of Investigations Regulations
- **Specialist Services** – this section contains provisions which are only applicable when certain services are being provided to clients.
  - – Introduction
  - – SRA European Cross-border Practice Rules
  - – SRA Property Selling Rules
  - – SRA Financial Services (Scope) Rules
  - – SRA Financial Services (Conduct of Business) Rules
- **Glossary** – this is a draft. The final version of the Glossary, which we will publish in the summer, will comprise all the terms used throughout the Handbook, and set out their definitions. [Terms which are defined, and which are being used in their defined sense, will appear in the text in italics.]

  The Glossary will be central to all the rules and regulations within the Handbook.

  When we publish the final version of the Glossary, we will have removed all the individual interpretation clauses which currently appear within these rules and regulations.
  - – Introduction
  - – Glossary

4. Non-mandatory guidance and notes appear, as appropriate, throughout the Handbook as an aid to compliance.
5. Our approach to regulation has two elements: firm-based requirements and individual requirements. It focuses on the practices of regulated entities as well as the conduct and competence of regulated individuals. This approach allows us to take regulatory action

---

[1] A previous version of these Rules (the Qualified Lawyers Transfer Regulations 2009) remain in force and will form part of the Handbook.

[2] A previous version of these Rules (the Higher Courts Qualification Regulations 2000) remain in force and will form part of the Handbook.

against firms or individuals, or both, in appropriate cases. This could include action against anyone in the firm including non-lawyer owners, managers and employees. We exercise our regulatory powers in a proportionate manner, focusing on risk and outcomes for clients.

6.  Firms will need to ensure that all employees (even if non-qualified and non-fee earners) receive appropriate training on the requirements in the Handbook, but only to the extent necessary for the role they undertake in the firm. For example, all staff will need to understand that they should keep clients' affairs confidential and behave with integrity; however it is likely that only those in fee-earning roles need be aware of the procedures required for checking for conflicts of interests and giving undertakings.

7.  Although firms now have greater freedom in the way they offer services (e.g. outsourcing certain functions), they may not abrogate responsibility for compliance with regulatory requirements.

8.  We are confident that the contents of this Handbook, coupled with our modern, outcomes-focused, risk-based approach to authorisation, supervision and effective enforcement will:

    – benefit the public interest;
    – support the rule of law;
    – improve access to justice;
    – benefit consumers' interests;
    – promote competition;
    – encourage an independent, strong, diverse and effective legal profession;
    – increase understanding of legal rights and duties; and
    – promote adherence to the professional principles set out in the Legal Services Act 2007.

    The Handbook will, therefore, support not only consumers of legal services, but will also support the independence of the legal profession and its unique role in safeguarding the legal rights of those it serves.

9.  These regulatory objectives can only be achieved if we and our regulated community work together in a spirit of mutual trust for the benefit of clients and the ultimate public interest.

# APPENDIX 2

# SRA Principles 2011[1]

**Preamble**

The SRA Principles dated [xx] commencing [10 August 2011] made by the Solicitors Regulation Authority Board under sections 31, 79 and 80 of the Solicitors Act 1974, sections 9 and 9A of the Administration of Justice Act 1985 and section 83 of the Legal Services Act 2007, with the approval of the Legal Services Board under paragraph 19 of Schedule 4 to the Legal Services Act 2007, regulating the conduct of solicitors and their employees, registered European lawyers, recognised bodies and their managers and employees, and licensed bodies and their managers and employees.

## 1. SRA PRINCIPLES

These are mandatory *Principles* which apply to all.
   You must:

1.   uphold the rule of law and the proper administration of justice;
2.   act with integrity;
3.   not allow your independence to be compromised;
4.   act in the best interests of each *client*;
5.   provide a proper standard of service to *your clients*;
6.   behave in a way that maintains the trust the public places in you and in the provision of legal services;
7.   comply with your legal and regulatory obligations and deal with your regulators and ombudsmen in an open, timely and co-operative manner;
8.   run your business or carry out your role in the business effectively and in accordance with proper governance and sound financial and risk management principles;
9.   run your business or carry out your role in the business in a way that encourages equality of opportunity and respect for diversity;
10.  protect *client money* and *assets*.

## SRA PRINCIPLES – NOTES

1.   The Principles embody the key ethical requirements on firms and individuals who are involved in the provision of legal services. You should always have regard to the Principles and use them as your starting point when faced with an ethical dilemma.
2.   Where two or more Principles come into conflict, the Principle which takes precedence

---

[1]   Published on SRA website as a draft – correct at 19 August 2011.

134

is the one which best serves the public interest in the particular circumstances, especially the public interest in the proper administration of justice.

3. These Principles:

- apply to individuals and firms we regulate, whether traditional firms of solicitors or ABSs, in-house and overseas;
- will be breached by you if you permit another person to do anything on your behalf which if done by you would breach the Principles; and
- apply to you to the fullest extent if a sole practitioner or manager in a firm, but still apply to you if you work within a firm or in-house and have no management responsibility (for example, even if you are not a manager you may have an opportunity to influence, adopt and implement measures to comply with Principles 8 and 9).

4. Compliance with the Principles is also subject to any overriding legal obligations.

5. **Principle 1: You must uphold the rule of law and the proper administration of justice**
You have obligations not only to clients but also to the court and to third parties with whom you have dealings on your clients' behalf – see, e.g., Chapter 5 (Your client and the court) and Chapter 11 (Relations with third parties) of the Code.

6. **Principle 2: You must act with integrity**
Personal integrity is central to your role as the client's trusted adviser and should characterise all your professional dealings with clients, the court, other lawyers and the public.

7. **Principle 3: You must not allow your independence to be compromised**
'Independence' means your own and your firm's independence, and not merely your ability to give independent advice to a client. You should avoid situations which might put your independence at risk – e.g. giving control of your practice to a third party which is beyond the regulatory reach of the SRA or other approved regulator.

8. **Principle 4: You must act in the best interests of each client**
You should always act in good faith and do your best for each of your clients. Most importantly, you should observe:

(a) your duty of confidentiality to the client – see Chapter 4 (Confidentiality and disclosure) of the Code; and

(b) your obligations with regard to conflicts of interests – see Chapter 3 (Conflicts of interests) of the Code.

9. **Principle 5: You must provide a proper standard of service to your clients**
You should, e.g., provide a proper standard of client care and of work. This would include exercising competence, skill and diligence, and taking into account the individual needs and circumstances of each client.

10. **Principle 6: You must behave in a way that maintains the trust the public places in you and in the provision of legal services**
Members of the public should be able to place their trust in you. Any behaviour either within or outside your professional practice which undermines this trust damages not only you, but also the ability of the legal profession as a whole to serve society.

11. **Principle 7: You must comply with your legal and regulatory obligations and deal with your regulators and ombudsmen in an open, timely and co-operative manner**
You should, e.g., ensure that you comply with all the reporting and notification requirements – see Chapter 10 (You and your regulator) of the Code – and respond promptly and substantively to communications.

12. **Principle 8: You must run your business or carry out your role in the business effectively and in accordance with proper governance and sound financial and risk management principles**

Whether you are a manager or an employee, you have a part to play in helping to ensure that your business is well run for the benefit of your clients and, e.g. in meeting the outcomes in Chapter 7 (Management of your business) of the Code.

13. **Principle 9: You must run your business or carry out your role in the business in a way that encourages equality of opportunity and respect for diversity**

Whether you are a manager or an employee, you have a role to play in achieving the outcomes in Chapter 2 (Your clients and equality and diversity) of the Code. Note that a finding of unlawful discrimination outside practice could also amount to a breach of Principles 1 and 6.

14. **Principle 10: You must protect client money and assets**

This Principle goes to the heart of the duty to act in the best interests of your clients. You should play your part in e.g. protecting money, documents or other property belonging to your clients which has been entrusted to you or your firm.

15. *Breach of the Principles*

Our approach to enforcement is proportionate, outcomes-focused and risk-based. Therefore, how we deal with failure to comply with the Principles will depend on all the particular circumstances of each case. Our primary aim is to achieve the right outcomes for clients.

## 2. SRA PRINCIPLES – APPLICATION PROVISIONS

The *Principles* apply to you in the following circumstances (and 'you' must be construed accordingly).

### Application of the SRA Principles in England and Wales

2.1 Subject to paragraphs 2.2 to 2.6 below and any other provisions in the *SRA Code of Conduct*, the *Principles* apply to you, in relation to your activities carried out from an office in England and Wales, if you are:

(a) a *solicitor, REL* or *RFL* who is *practising* as such, whether or not the entity through which you *practise* is subject to these *Principles*;

(b) a *solicitor, REL* or *RFL* who is:

    (i) a *manager, employee* or *owner* of a body which should be a *recognised body*, but has not been recognised by the *SRA*;

    (ii) a *manager, employee* or *owner* of a body that is a *manager* or *owner* of a body that should be a *recognised body*, but has not been recognised by the *SRA*;

    (iii) an *employee* of a *sole practitioner* which should be a *recognised sole practitioner*, but has not been recognised by the *SRA*;

    (iv) an *owner* of an *authorised body* or of a body which should be a *recognised body* but has not been recognised by the *SRA*, even if you undertake no work for the body's *clients*;

    (v) a *manager* or *employee* of an *authorised non-SRA firm*, or a *manager* of a body which is a *manager* of an *authorised non-SRA firm*, when doing work of a sort authorised by the *SRA*, for that firm;

(c) an *authorised body*, or a body which should be a *recognised body* but has not been recognised by the *SRA*;

(d) any other person who is a *manager* or *employee* of an *authorised body*, or of a body which should be a *recognised body* but has not been recognised by the *SRA*;

(e) any other person who is an *employee* of a *recognised sole practitioner*, or of a *sole practitioner* who should be a *recognised sole practitioner* but has not been recognised by the *SRA*;

and 'you' includes 'your' as appropriate.

2.2 The *Principles* apply to you if you are a *solicitor*, *REL* or *RFL*, and you are:

(a) *practising* as a *manager* or *employee* of an *authorised non-SRA firm* when doing work of a sort authorised by the *authorised non-SRA firm's approved regulator*, or

(b) an *owner* of an *authorised non-SRA firm* even if you undertake no work for the body's *clients*.

### Application of the SRA Principles in relation to practice from an office outside England and Wales

2.3 The *Principles* apply to you, in relation to *practice* from an office in Scotland or Northern Ireland if you are:

(a) a *solicitor* or an *REL practising* as such, whether or not your firm or *employer* is subject to these *Principles*;

(b) a *lawyer-controlled body*;

(c) an *REL-controlled body*;

(d) any other person who is a *manager* of an *authorised body*; or

(e) a solicitor who was formerly an *REL*, when *practising* as a *lawyer* of an *Establishment Directive profession*.

2.4 The *Principles* apply to you in relation to *practice* from an office outside the *UK* if you are:

(a) a s*olicitor practising* as such, whether or not your *firm* or *employer* is subject to these *Principles*;

(b) a *lawyer-controlled body*; or

(c) any other person who is a *manager* of an *authorised body*.

### Application of the SRA Principles outside practice

2.5 In relation to activities which fall outside *practice*, as defined in Chapter 14 (Interpretation) of the *SRA Code of Conduct*, whether undertaken as a *lawyer* or in some other business or private capacity, *Principles* 1, 2 and 6 apply to you if you are a *solicitor*, *REL* or *RFL*.

### General provisions

2.6 You must comply with the *Principles* at all times, but the extent to which you are expected to implement the requirements of the *Principles* will depend on your role in the *firm*, or your way of *practising*. For example, those who are managing a business will be expected to have more influence on how the *firm* or business is run than those *practising* in-house but not managing a legal department, or those *practising* as *employees* of a *firm*.

## 3. TRANSITIONAL PROVISIONS

3.1 For the avoidance of doubt, where a breach of any provision of the Solicitors' Code of Conduct 2007 comes to the attention of the *SRA* after 6 October 2011, this shall be subject to action by the *SRA* notwithstanding any repeal of the relevant provision.

3.2 From 31 March 2012, paragraph 2 shall have effect subject to the following amendments:

(a) paragraph 2.1(b) (iii) and 2.1(e) shall be omitted.

## 4. INTERPRETATION

All italicised terms in these rules are to be interpreted in accordance with Chapter 14 (Interpretation) of the *SRA Code of Conduct*.

# APPENDIX 3

# SRA Code of Conduct

The text has been updated to incorporate the Legal Services Board approved changes made on 17 June 2011.

**Introduction to the SRA Code of Conduct**

## OVERVIEW

Outcomes-focused regulation concentrates on providing positive outcomes which when achieved will benefit and protect *clients* and the public. The SRA Code of Conduct (the Code) sets out our outcomes-focused conduct requirements so that you can consider how best to achieve the right outcomes for your *clients* taking into account the way that your *firm* works and its *client* base. The Code is underpinned by effective, risk-based supervision and enforcement.

Those involved in providing legal advice and representation have long held the role of trusted adviser. There are fiduciary duties arising from this role and obligations owed to others, especially the *court*. No code can foresee or address every issue or ethical dilemma which may arise. You must strive to uphold the intention of the Code as well as its letter.

## THE PRINCIPLES

The Code forms part of the Handbook, in which the 10 mandatory *Principles* are all-pervasive. They apply to all those we regulate and to all aspects of *practice*. They define the fundamental ethical and professional standards that we expect of all *firms* and individuals (including *owners* who may not be *lawyers*) when providing legal services. You should always have regard to the *Principles* and use them as your starting point when faced with an ethical dilemma.

Where two or more *Principles* come into conflict the one which takes precedence is the one which best serves the public interest in the particular circumstances, especially the public interest in the proper administration of justice. Compliance with the *Principles* is also subject to any overriding legal obligations.

You must:

1 uphold the rule of law and the proper administration of justice;
2 act with integrity;
3 not allow your independence to be compromised;
4 act in the best interests of each *client*;
5 provide a proper standard of service to your *clients*;
6 behave in a way that maintains the trust the public places in you and in the provision of legal services;

7    comply with your legal and regulatory obligations and deal with your regulators and ombudsmen in an open, timely and co-operative manner;

8    run your business or carry out your role in the business effectively and in accordance with proper governance and sound financial and risk management principles;

9    run your business or carry out your role in the business in a way that encourages equality of opportunity and respect for diversity;

10   protect *client* money and *assets*.

## STRUCTURE OF THE CODE

The Code is divided into 5 sections:

- You and your client
- You and your business
- You and your regulator
- You and others
- Application, waivers and interpretation

Each section is divided into chapters dealing with particular regulatory issues, for example, client care, *conflicts of interests*, and *publicity*.

These chapters show how the *Principles* apply in certain contexts through mandatory and non-mandatory provisions.

## MANDATORY PROVISIONS

The following provisions are mandatory:

- the outcomes;
- the application and waivers provisions in Chapter 13;
- the interpretations; and
- the transitional provisions in Chapter 15.

The outcomes describe what *firms* and individuals are expected to achieve in order to comply with the relevant *Principles* in the context of the relevant chapter. In the case of *in-house* and *overseas practice*, we have set out at the end of each chapter which outcomes apply and in some cases have specified different outcomes.

In respect of *in-house practice*, different outcomes may apply depending on whether you are acting for your employer or for a *client* other than your employer as permitted by rules 4.1 to 4.10 of the SRA Practice Framework Rules.

The outcomes contained in each chapter are not an exhaustive list of the application of all the *Principles*. We have tried to make them as helpful as possible.

## NON-MANDATORY PROVISIONS

The following provisions are non-mandatory:

- indicative behaviours;
- notes.

The outcomes are supplemented by indicative behaviours. The indicative behaviours specify, but do not constitute an exhaustive list of, the kind of behaviour which may establish compliance with, or contravention of the *Principles*. These are not mandatory but they may help us to decide whether an outcome has been achieved in compliance with the *Principles*.

We recognise that there may be other ways of achieving the outcomes. Where you have chosen a different method from those we have described as indicative behaviours, we might require you to demonstrate how you have nevertheless achieved the outcome. We encourage *firms* to consider how they can best achieve the outcomes, taking into account the nature of the *firm*, the particular circumstances of the matter and, crucially, the needs of their particular *clients*.

## Waivers

Due to the flexibility of approach this structure allows, we do not anticipate receiving many applications for waivers from the mandatory outcomes. The *SRA*, nonetheless, reserves power to waive a provision in exceptional circumstances.

## Sources of help

You can access the Code and other elements of the Handbook and find information on particular issues on the *SRA* website. You can also seek guidance on professional conduct from our Professional Ethics Guidance Team.

## List of contents of the Code

*1st section – You and your client*

Chapter 1 Client care

Chapter 2 Equality and diversity

Chapter 3 Conflicts of interests

Chapter 4 Confidentiality and disclosure

Chapter 5 Your client and the court

Chapter 6 Your client and introductions to third parties

*2nd section – You and your business*

Chapter 7 Management of your business

Chapter 8 Publicity

Chapter 9 Fee sharing and referrals

*3rd section – You and your regulator*

Chapter 10 You and your regulator

*4th section – You and others*

Chapter 11 Relations with third parties

Chapter 12 Separate businesses

*5th section – Application, waivers and interpretation*

Chapter 13 Application and waivers provisions

Chapter 14 Interpretation

Chapter 15 Transitional provisions

**Preamble**

The SRA Code of Conduct dated [ ] commencing [ ] made by the Solicitors Regulation Authority Board under sections 31, 79 and 80 of the Solicitors Act 1974, sections 9 and 9A of the Administration of Justice Act 1985 and section 83 of the Legal Services Act 2007, with the approval of the Legal Services Board under paragraph 19 of Schedule 4 to the Legal Services Act 2007, regulating the conduct of solicitors and their employees, registered European lawyers and their employees, registered foreign lawyers, recognised bodies and their managers and employees and licensed bodies and their managers and employees.

**1st Section – You and your client**

**CHAPTER 1 – CLIENT CARE**

This chapter is about providing a proper standard of service, which takes into account the individual needs and circumstances of each *client*. This includes providing *clients* with the information they need to make informed decisions about the services they need, how these will be delivered and how much they will cost. This will enable you and your *client* to understand each other's expectations and responsibilities. This chapter is also about ensuring that if *clients* are not happy with the service they have received they know how to make a *complaint* and that all *complaints* are dealt with promptly and fairly.

Your relationship with your *client* is a contractual one which carries with it legal, as well as conduct, obligations. This chapter focuses on your obligations in conduct.

You are generally free to decide whether or not to accept instructions in any matter, provided you do not discriminate unlawfully (see Chapter 2).

The outcomes in this chapter show how the *Principles* apply in the context of client care.

**Outcomes**

You must achieve these outcomes:

**O(1.1)** you treat your *clients* fairly;

**O(1.2)** you provide services to your *clients* in a manner which protects their interests in their matter, subject to the proper administration of justice;

**O(1.3)** when deciding whether to act, or terminate your instructions, you comply with the law and the Code;

**O(1.4)** you have the resources, skills and procedures to carry out your *clients'* instructions;

**O(1.5)** the service you provide to *clients* is competent, delivered in a timely manner and takes account of your *clients'* needs and circumstances;

**O(1.6)** you only enter into fee agreements with your *clients* that are legal, and which you consider are suitable for the *client's* needs and take account of the *client's* best interests;

**O(1.7)** you inform *clients* whether and how the services you provide are regulated and how this affects the protections available to the *client*;

**O(1.8)** *clients* have the benefit of your *compulsory professional indemnity insurance* and you do not exclude or attempt to exclude liability below the minimum level of cover required by the SRA Indemnity Insurance Rules;

**O(1.9)** *clients* are informed in writing at the outset of their matter of their right to complain and how *complaints* can be made;

**O(1.10)** *clients* are informed in writing, both at the time of engagement and at the conclusion of your *complaints* procedure, of their right to complain to the *Legal Ombudsman*, the time frame for doing so and full details of how to contact the *Legal Ombudsman*;

**O(1.11)** *clients' complaints* are dealt with promptly, fairly, openly and effectively;

**O(1.12)** *clients* are in a position to make informed decisions about the services they need, how their matter will be handled and the options available to them;

**O(1.13)** *clients* receive the best possible information, both at the time of engagement and when appropriate as their matter progresses, about the likely overall cost of their matter;

**O(1.14)** *clients* are informed of their right to challenge or complain about your bill and the circumstances in which they may be liable to pay interest on an unpaid bill;

**O(1.15)** you properly account to *clients* for any *financial benefit* you receive as a result of your instructions;

**O(1.16)** you inform *clients* if you discover any act or omission which could give rise to a claim by them against you.

### Indicative behaviours

Acting in the following way(s) may tend to show that you have achieved these outcomes and therefore complied with the *Principles*:

*Dealing with the client's matter*

**IB(1.1)** agreeing an appropriate level of service with your *client*, for example the type and frequency of communications;

**IB(1.2)** explaining your responsibilities and those of the *client*;

**IB(1.3)** ensuring that the *client* is told, in writing, the name and status of the person(s) dealing with the matter and the name and status of the person responsible for its overall supervision;

**IB(1.4)** explaining any *arrangements*, such as fee sharing or *referral arrangements*, which are relevant to the *client's* instructions;

**IB(1.5)** explaining any limitations or conditions on what you can do for the *client*, for example, because of the way the *client's* matter is funded;

**IB(1.6)** in taking instructions and during the course of the retainer, having proper regard to your *client's* mental capacity or other vulnerability, such as incapacity or duress;

**IB(1.7)** considering whether you should decline to act or cease to act because you cannot act in the *client's* best interests;

**IB(1.8)**   if you seek to limit your liability to your *client* to a level above the minimum required by the SRA Indemnity Insurance Rules, ensuring that this limitation is in writing and is brought to the *client's* attention;

**IB(1.9)**   refusing to act where your *client* proposes to make a gift of significant value to you or a member of your family, or a member of your *firm* or their family, unless the *client* takes independent legal advice;

**IB(1.10)**   if you have to cease acting for a *client*, explaining to the *client* their possible options for pursuing their matter;

**IB(1.11)**   you inform *clients* if they are not entitled to the protections of the SRA Compensation Fund;

**IB(1.12)**   considering whether a *conflict of interests* has arisen or whether the *client* should be advised to obtain independent advice where the *client* notifies you of their intention to make a claim or if you discover an act or omission which might give rise to a claim;

*Fee arrangements with your client*

**IB(1.13)**   discussing whether the potential outcomes of the *client's* matter are likely to justify the expense or risk involved, including any risk of having to pay someone else's legal fees;

**IB(1.14)**   clearly explaining your fees and if and when they are likely to change;

**IB(1.15)**   warning about any other payments for which the *client* may be responsible;

**IB(1.16)**   discussing how the *client* will pay, including whether public funding may be available, whether the *client* has insurance that might cover the fees, and whether the fees may be paid by someone else such as a trade union;

**IB(1.17)**   where you are acting for a *client* under a fee arrangement governed by statute, such as a conditional fee agreement, giving the *client* all relevant information relating to that arrangement;

**IB(1.18)**   where you are acting for a publicly funded *client*, explaining how their publicly funded status affects the costs;

**IB(1.19)**   providing the information in a clear and accessible form which is appropriate to the needs and circumstances of the *client*;

**IB(1.20)**   where you receive a *financial benefit* as a result of acting for a *client*, either:

- paying it to the *client*;
- offsetting it against your fees; or
- keeping it only where you can justify keeping it, you have told the *client* the amount of the benefit (or an approximation if you do not know the exact amount) and the *client* has agreed that you can keep it;

**IB(1.21)**   ensuring that *disbursements* included in your bill reflect the actual amount spent or to be spent on behalf of the *client*;

*Complaints handling*

**IB(1.22)**   having a written *complaints* procedure which:

- is brought to *clients'* attention at the outset of the matter;
- is easy for *clients* to use and understand, allowing for *complaints* to be made by any reasonable means;
- is responsive to the needs of individual *clients*, especially those who are vulnerable;

- enables *complaints* to be dealt with promptly and fairly, with decisions based on a sufficient investigation of the circumstances;
- provides for appropriate remedies; and
- does not involve any charges to *clients* for handling their *complaints*;

**IB(1.23)** providing the *client* with a copy of the *firm's complaints* procedure on request;

**IB(1.24)** in the event that a *client* makes a *complaint*, providing them with all necessary information concerning the handling of the *complaint*.

Acting in the following way(s) may tend to show that you have not achieved these outcomes and therefore not complied with the *Principles*:

*Accepting and refusing instructions*

**IB(1.25)** acting for a *client* when instructions are given by someone else, or by only one *client* when you act jointly for others unless you are satisfied that the *person* providing the instructions has the authority to do so on behalf of all of the *clients*;

**IB(1.26)** ceasing to act for a *client* without good reason and without providing reasonable notice;

**IB(1.27)** entering into unlawful fee arrangements such as an unlawful contingency fee;

**IB(1.28)** acting for a *client* when there are reasonable grounds for believing that the instructions are affected by duress or undue influence without satisfying yourself that they represent the *client's* wishes.

## In-house practice

Outcomes 1.1 to 1.5, 1.7, 1.15 and 1.16 apply to your *in-house practice*.

Outcomes 1.6 and 1.9 to 1.14 apply to your *in-house practice* where you act for someone other than your employer unless it is clear that the outcome is not relevant to your particular circumstances.

**IHP(1.1)** Instead of Outcome 1.8 you comply with the SRA Practice Framework Rules in relation to professional indemnity insurance.

## Overseas practice

The outcomes in this chapter do not apply to your *overseas practice*. Instead you must achieve the following outcomes:

**OP(1.1)** you properly account to your *clients* for any *financial benefit* you receive as a result of your instructions unless it is the prevailing custom of your local jurisdiction to deal with *financial benefits* in a different way;

**OP(1.2)** *clients* have the benefit of insurance or other indemnity in relation to professional liabilities which takes account of:

(a) the nature and extent of the risks you incur in your *overseas practice*;
(b) the local conditions in the jurisdiction in which you are *practising*; and
(c) the terms upon which insurance is available;

and you have not attempted to exclude liability below the minimum level required for practice in the local jurisdiction;

**OP(1.3)** you do not enter into unlawful contingency fee arrangements.

**NOTES**

1.  The information you give to *clients* will vary according to the needs and circumstances of the individual *client* and the type of work you are doing for them, for example an individual instructing you on a conveyancing matter is unlikely to need the same information as a sophisticated commercial *client* who instructs you on a regular basis.
2.  Information about the *Legal Ombudsman*, including the scheme rules, contact details and time limits, can be found at **www.legalombudsman.org.uk**.

**CHAPTER 2 – EQUALITY AND DIVERSITY**

This chapter is about encouraging equality of opportunity and respect for diversity, and preventing unlawful discrimination, in your relationship with your *clients* and others. The requirements apply in relation to age, disability, gender reassignment, marriage and civil partnership, pregnancy and maternity, race, religion or belief, sex and sexual orientation.

Everyone needs to contribute to compliance with these requirements, for example by treating each other, and *clients*, fairly and with respect, by embedding such values in the workplace and by challenging inappropriate behaviour and processes. Your role in embedding these values will vary depending on your role.

As a matter of general law you must comply with requirements set out in legislation – including the Equality Act 2010 – as well as the conduct duties contained in this chapter.

The outcomes in this chapter show how the *Principles* apply in the context of equality and diversity.

**Outcomes**

You must achieve these outcomes:

**O(2.1)**   you do not discriminate unlawfully, or victimise or harass anyone, in the course of your professional dealings;

**O(2.2)**   you provide services to *clients* in a way that respects diversity;

**O(2.3)**   you make reasonable adjustments to ensure that disabled *clients*, *employees* or *managers* are not placed at a substantial disadvantage compared to those who are not disabled, and you do not pass on the costs of these adjustments to these disabled *clients*, *employees* or *managers*;

**O(2.4)**   your approach to recruitment and employment encourages equality of opportunity and respect for diversity;

**O(2.5)**   *complaints* of discrimination are dealt with promptly, fairly, openly, and effectively.

**Indicative behaviours**

Acting in the following way(s) may tend to show that you have achieved these outcomes and therefore complied with the *Principles*:

**IB(2.1)**   having a written equality and diversity policy which is appropriate to the size and nature of the *firm* and includes the following features:

- a commitment to the principles of equality and diversity and legislative requirements;
- a requirement that all *employees* and *managers* comply with the outcomes;
- provisions to encompass your recruitment and interview processes;
- details of how the *firm* will implement, monitor, evaluate and update the policy;

- details of how the *firm* will ensure equality in relation to the treatment of *employees*, *managers*, *clients* and third parties instructed in connection with *client* matters;
- details of how *complaints* and disciplinary issues are to be dealt with;
- details of the *firm*'s arrangements for workforce diversity monitoring; and
- details of how the *firm* will communicate the policy to *employees*, *managers* and *clients*.

**IB(2.2)** providing *employees* and *managers* with training and information about complying with equality and diversity requirements;

**IB(2.3)** monitoring and responding to issues identified by your policy and reviewing and updating your policy.

Acting in the following way(s) may tend to show that you have not achieved these outcomes and therefore not complied with the *Principles*:

**IB(2.4)** being subject to any decision of a court or tribunal of the *UK*, that you have committed, or are to be treated as having committed, an unlawful act of discrimination;

**IB(2.5)** discriminating unlawfully when accepting or refusing instructions to act for a *client*.

### In-house practice

Outcomes 2.1 and 2.2 apply to all *in-house practice*.
   Instead of outcomes 2.3 to 2.5 you must achieve the following outcome:

**IHP(2.1)** if you have management responsibilities you take all reasonable steps to encourage equality of opportunity and respect for diversity in your workplace.

### Overseas practice

The outcomes in this chapter do not apply to your *overseas practice*. Instead you must achieve the following outcome:

**OP(2.1)** you do not discriminate unlawfully according to the jurisdiction in which you are *practising*.

### NOTES

1. The obligations in this chapter closely mirror your legal obligations. You can obtain further information from the Equality and Human Rights Commission, **www. equalityhumanrights.com**.
2. See also Chapter 1 (Client care) for the handling of *client complaints*.
3. See also Chapter 7 (Management of your business) for your obligation to have in place appropriate systems and controls for complying with the outcomes in this chapter.

### CHAPTER 3 – CONFLICTS OF INTERESTS

This chapter deals with the proper handling of *conflicts of interests*, which is a critical public protection. It is important to have in place systems that enable you to identify and deal with potential conflicts.
   *Conflicts of interests* can arise between:

(a) you and current *clients* ('*own interest conflict*'); and

(b)    two or more current *clients* (*'client conflict'*).

You can never act where there is a conflict, or a significant risk of conflict, between you and your *client*.

If there is a conflict, or a significant risk of a conflict, between two or more current *clients*, you must not act for all or both of them unless the matter falls within the scope of the limited exceptions set out at Outcomes 3.6 and 3.7. In deciding whether to act in these limited circumstances, the overriding consideration will be the best interests of each of the *clients* concerned and, in particular, whether the benefits to the *clients* of you acting for all or both of the *clients* outweigh the risks.

You should also bear in mind that *conflicts of interests* may affect your duties of confidentiality and disclosure which are dealt with in Chapter 4.

The outcomes in this chapter show how the *Principles* apply in the context of *conflicts of interests*.

**Outcomes**

You must achieve these outcomes:

*Systems*

**O(3.1)**    you have effective systems and controls in place to enable you to identify and assess potential *conflicts of interests*;

**O(3.2)**    your systems and controls for identifying *own interest conflicts* are appropriate to the size and complexity of the *firm* and the nature of the work undertaken, and enable you to assess all the relevant circumstances, including whether your ability as an individual, or that of anyone within your *firm*, to act in the best interests of the *client(s)*, is impaired by:

- any financial interest;
- a personal relationship;
- the appointment of you, or a member of your *firm* or family, to public office;
- commercial relationships; or
- your employment;

**O(3.3)**  your systems and controls for identifying *client conflicts* are appropriate to the size and complexity of the *firm* and the nature of the work undertaken, and enable you to assess all relevant circumstances, including whether:

- the *clients'* interests are different;
- your ability to give independent advice to the *clients* may be fettered;
- there is a need to negotiate between the *clients*;
- there is an imbalance in bargaining power between the *clients*; or
- any *client* is vulnerable;

*Prohibition on acting in conflict situations*

**O(3.4)**    you do not act if there is an *own interest conflict* or a significant risk of an *own interest conflict*;

**O(3.5)**    you do not act if there is a *client conflict*, or a significant risk of a *client conflict*, unless the circumstances set out in Outcomes 3.6 and 3.7 apply;

*Exceptions where you may act, with appropriate safeguards, where there is a client conflict*

**O(3.6)**   where there is a *client conflict* and the *clients* have a *substantially common interest* in relation to a matter or a particular aspect of it, you only act if:

(a)   you have explained the relevant issues and risks to the *clients* and you have a reasonable belief that they understand those issues and risks;

(b)   all the *clients* have given informed consent in writing to you acting;

(c)   you are satisfied that it is reasonable for you to act for all the *clients* and that it is in their best interests; and

(d)   you are satisfied that the benefits to the *clients* of you doing so outweigh the risks;

**O(3.7)**   where there is a *client conflict* and the *clients* are *competing for the same objective*, you only act if:

(a)   you have explained the relevant issues and risks to the *clients* and you have a reasonable belief that they understand those issues and risks;

(b)   the *clients* have confirmed in writing that they want you to act, in the knowledge that you act, or may act, for one or more other *clients* who are *competing for the same objective;*

(c)   there is no other *client conflict* in relation to that matter;

(d)   unless the *clients* specifically agree, no individual acts for, or is responsible for the supervision of work done for, more than one of the *clients* in that matter; and

(e)   you are satisfied that it is reasonable for you to act for all the *clients* and that the benefits to the *clients* of you doing so outweigh the risks.

**Indicative behaviours**

Acting in the following way(s) may tend to show that you have achieved these outcomes and therefore complied with the *Principles*:

**IB(3.1)**   training *employees* and *managers* to identify and assess potential *conflicts of interests*;

**IB(3.2)**   declining to act for *clients* whose interests are in direct conflict, for example claimant and defendant in litigation;

**IB(3.3)**   declining to act for *clients* where you may need to negotiate on matters of substance on their behalf, for example negotiating on price between a buyer and seller of a property;

**IB(3.4)**   declining to act where there is unequal bargaining power between the *clients*, for example acting for a seller and buyer where a builder is selling to a non-commercial *client*;

**IB(3.5)**   declining to act for *clients* under Outcome 3.6 (*substantially common interest*) or Outcome 3.7 (*competing for the same objective*) where the *clients* cannot be represented even-handedly, or will be prejudiced by lack of separate representation;

**IB(3.6)**   acting for *clients* under Outcome 3.7 (*competing for the same objective*) only where the *clients* are sophisticated users of legal services;

**IB(3.7)**   acting for *clients* who are the lender and borrower on the grant of a mortgage of land only where:

(a)   the mortgage is a standard mortgage (i.e. one provided in the normal course of the lender's activities, where a significant part of the lender's activities consists of lending and the mortgage is on standard terms) of property to be used as the borrower's private residence;

(b)   you are satisfied that it is reasonable and in the *clients'* best interests for you to act; and

(c)   the certificate of title required by the lender is in the form approved by the *Society* and the Council of Mortgage Lenders.

Acting in the following way(s) may tend to show that you have not achieved these outcomes and therefore not complied with the *Principles*:

**IB(3.8)**   in a personal capacity, selling to or buying from, lending to or borrowing from a *client*, unless the *client* has obtained independent legal advice;

**IB(3.9)**   advising a *client* to invest in a business, in which you have an interest which affects your ability to provide impartial advice;

**IB(3.10)**   where you hold a power of attorney for a *client*, using that power to gain a benefit for yourself which in your professional capacity you would not have been prepared to allow to a third party;

**IB(3.11)**   acting for two or more *clients* in a *conflict of interests* under Outcome 3.6 (*substantially common interest*) where the *clients'* interests in the end result are not the same, for example one partner buying out the interest of the other partner in their joint business or a seller transferring a property to a buyer;

**IB(3.12)**   acting for two or more *clients* in a *conflict of interests* under Outcome 3.6 (*substantially common interest*) where it is unreasonable to act because there is unequal bargaining power;

**IB(3.13)**   acting for two buyers where there is a *conflict of interests* under Outcome 3.7 (*competing for the same objective*), for example where two buyers are competing for a residential property;

**IB(3.14)**   acting for a buyer (including a lessee) and seller (including a lessor) in a transaction relating to the transfer of land for value, the grant or assignment of a lease or some other interest in land for value.

### In-house practice

Outcomes 3.4 to 3.7 apply to your *in-house practice*.
   Outcomes 3.1 to 3.3 apply if you have management responsibilities.

### Overseas practice

The outcomes in this chapter apply to your *overseas practice*.

## CHAPTER 4 – CONFIDENTIALITY AND DISCLOSURE

This chapter is about the protection of *clients'* confidential information and the disclosure of material information to *clients*.
   Protection of confidential information is a fundamental feature of your relationship with *clients*. It exists as a concept both as a matter of law and as a matter of conduct. This duty continues despite the end of the retainer and even after the death of the *client*.
   It is important to distinguish the conduct duties from the concept of law known as legal professional privilege.
   Bear in mind that all members of the *firm* or *in-house practice*, including support staff, consultants and locums, owe a duty of confidentiality to your *clients*.
   The duty of confidentiality to all *clients* must be reconciled with the duty of disclosure to *clients*. This duty of disclosure is limited to information of which you are aware which is material to your *client's* matter. Where you cannot reconcile these two duties, then the

protection of confidential information is paramount. You should not continue to act for a *client* for whom you cannot disclose material information, except in very limited circumstances, where safeguards are in place. Such situations often also give rise to a *conflict of interests* which is discussed in Chapter 3.

The outcomes in this chapter show how the *Principles* apply in the context of confidentiality and disclosure.

## Outcomes

You must achieve these outcomes:

**O(4.1)**   you keep the affairs of *clients* confidential unless disclosure is required or permitted by law or the *client* consents;

**O(4.2)**   any individual who is advising a *client* makes that *client* aware of all information material to that retainer of which the individual has personal knowledge;

**O(4.3)**   you ensure that where your duty of confidentiality to one *client* comes into conflict with your duty of disclosure to another *client*, your duty of confidentiality takes precedence;

**O(4.4)**   you do not act for A in a matter where A has an interest adverse to B, and B is a *client* for whom you hold confidential information which is material to A in that matter, unless the confidential information can be protected by the use of safeguards, and:

    (a)   you reasonably believe that A is aware of, and understands, the relevant issues and gives informed consent;

    (b)   either:

        (i)   B gives informed consent and you agree with B the safeguards to protect B's information; or

        (ii)   where this is not possible, you put in place effective safeguards including information barriers which comply with the common law; and

    (c)   it is reasonable in all the circumstances to act for A with such safeguards in place;

**O(4.5)**   you have effective systems and controls in place to enable you to identify risks to *client* confidentiality and to mitigate those risks.

## Indicative behaviours

Acting in the following way(s) may tend to show that you have achieved these outcomes and therefore complied with the *Principles*:

**IB(4.1)**   your systems and controls for identifying risks to *client* confidentiality are appropriate to the size and complexity of the *firm* or *in-house practice* and the nature of the work undertaken, and enable you to assess all the relevant circumstances;

**IB(4.2)**   you comply with the law in respect of your fiduciary duties in relation to confidentiality and disclosure;

**IB(4.3)**   you only outsource services when you are satisfied that the provider has taken all appropriate steps to ensure that your *clients'* confidential information will be protected;

**IB(4.4)**   where you are an individual who has responsibility for acting for a *client* or supervising a *client's* matter, you disclose to the *client* all information material to the *client's* matter of which you are personally aware, except when:

- the *client* gives specific informed consent to non-disclosure or a different standard of disclosure arises;
- there is evidence that serious physical or mental injury will be caused to a person(s) if the information is disclosed to the *client*;
- legal restrictions effectively prohibit you from passing the information to the *client*, such as the provisions in the money-laundering and anti-terrorism legislation;
- it is obvious that privileged documents have been mistakenly disclosed to you;
- you come into possession of information relating to state security or intelligence matters to which the Official Secrets Act 1989 applies;

**IB(4.5)**   not acting for A where B is a *client* for whom you hold confidential information which is material to A unless the confidential information can be protected.

Acting in the following way(s) may tend to show that you have not achieved these outcomes and therefore not complied with the *Principles*:

**IB(4.6)**   disclosing the content of a will on the death of a *client* unless consent has been provided by the personal representatives for the content to be released;

**IB(4.7)**   disclosing details of bills sent to *clients* to third parties, such as debt factoring companies in relation to the collection of book debts, unless the *client* has consented.

### In-house practice

The outcomes listed above apply to your *in-house practice*.

### Overseas practice

The outcomes listed above apply to your *overseas practice*.

### NOTES

1.   The protection of confidential information may be at particular risk where:

- two or more *firms* merge;
- when you leave one *firm* and join another, such as if you join a *firm* acting against one of your former *clients*.

2.   The following circumstances may make it difficult to implement effective safeguards and information barriers:

- you are a small *firm*;
- the physical structure or layout of the *firm* means that it will be difficult to preserve confidentiality; or
- the *clients* are not sophisticated users of legal services.

### CHAPTER 5 – YOUR CLIENT AND THE COURT

This chapter is about your duties to your *client* and to the *court* if you are exercising a right to conduct litigation or acting as an advocate. The outcomes apply to both litigation and advocacy but there are some indicative behaviours which may be relevant only when you are acting as an advocate.

The outcomes in this chapter show how the *Principles* apply in the context of your *client* and the *court*.

## Outcomes

You must achieve these outcomes:

**O(5.1)**  you do not attempt to deceive or knowingly or recklessly mislead the *court*;

**O(5.2)**  you are not complicit in another person deceiving or misleading the *court*;

**O(5.3)**  you comply with *court* orders which place obligations on you;

**O(5.4)**  you do not place yourself in contempt of *court*;

**O(5.5)**  where relevant, *clients* are informed of the circumstances in which your duties to the *court* outweigh your obligations to your *client*;

**O(5.6)**  you comply with your duties to the *court*;

**O(5.7)**  you ensure that evidence relating to sensitive issues is not misused;

**O(5.8)**  you do not make or offer to make payments to witnesses dependent upon their evidence or the outcome of the case.

## Indicative behaviours

Acting in the following way(s) may tend to show that you have achieved these outcomes and therefore complied with the *Principles*:

**IB(5.1)**  advising your *clients* to comply with *court* orders made against them, and advising them of the consequences of failing to comply;

**IB(5.2)**  drawing the *court's* attention to relevant cases and statutory provisions, and any material procedural irregularity;

**IB(5.3)**  ensuring child witness evidence is kept securely and not released to *clients* or third parties;

**IB(5.4)**  immediately informing the *court*, with your *client's* consent, if during the course of proceedings you become aware that you have inadvertently misled the *court*, or ceasing to act if the *client* does not consent to you informing the *court*;

**IB(5.5)**  refusing to continue acting for a *client* if you become aware they have committed perjury or misled the *court*, or attempted to mislead the *court*, in any material matter unless the *client* agrees to disclose the truth to the *court*;

**IB(5.6)**  not appearing as an advocate, or acting in litigation, if it is clear that you, or anyone within your *firm*, will be called as a witness in the matter unless you are satisfied that this will not prejudice your independence as an advocate, or litigator, or the interests of your *clients* or the interests of justice.

Acting in the following way(s) may tend to show that you have not achieved these outcomes and therefore not complied with the *Principles*:

**IB(5.7)**  constructing facts supporting your *client's* case or drafting any documents relating to any proceedings containing:

- any contention which you do not consider to be properly arguable; or
- any allegation of fraud, unless you are instructed to do so and you have material which you reasonably believe shows, on the face of it, a case of fraud;

**IB(5.8)**  suggesting that any *person* is guilty of a crime, fraud or misconduct unless such allegations:

- go to a matter in issue which is material to your own *client's* case; and
- appear to you to be supported by reasonable grounds;

**IB(5.9)**  calling a witness whose evidence you know is untrue;

**IB(5.10)** attempting to influence a witness, when taking a statement from that witness, with regard to the contents of their statement;

**IB(5.11)** tampering with evidence or seeking to persuade a witness to change their evidence;

**IB(5.12)** when acting as an advocate, naming in open *court* any third party whose character would thereby be called into question, unless it is necessary for the proper conduct of the case;

**IB(5.13)** when acting as an advocate, calling into question the character of a witness you have cross-examined unless the witness has had the opportunity to answer the allegations during cross-examination.

### In-house practice

The outcomes in this chapter apply to your *in-house practice*.

### Overseas practice

The outcomes in this chapter apply to your *overseas practice* in relation to litigation or advocacy conducted before a court, tribunal or enquiry in England and Wales or a British court martial.

### NOTES

1.  If you are a litigator or an advocate there may be occasions when your obligation to act in the best interests of a *client* may conflict with your duty to the *court*. In such situations you may need to consider whether the public interest is best served by the proper administration of justice and should take precedence over the interests of your *client*.

### CHAPTER 6 – YOUR CLIENT AND INTRODUCTIONS TO THIRD PARTIES

There may be circumstances in which you wish to refer your *clients* to third parties, perhaps to another *lawyer* or a financial services provider. This chapter describes the conduct duties which arise in respect of such introductions. It is important that you retain your independence when recommending third parties to your *client* and that you act in the *client*'s best interests.

The outcomes in this chapter show how the *Principles* apply in the context of your *client* and introductions to third parties.

### Outcomes

You must achieve these outcomes:

**O(6.1)** whenever you recommend that a *client* uses a particular *person* or business, your recommendation is in the best interests of the *client* and does not compromise your independence;

**O(6.2)** *clients* are fully informed of any financial or other interest which you have in referring the *client* to another *person* or business;

**O(6.3)** if a *client* is likely to need advice on investments, such as life insurance with an investment element or pension policies, you refer them only to an independent intermediary.

## Indicative behaviours

Acting in the following way(s) may tend to show that you have achieved these outcomes and therefore complied with the *Principles*:

**IB(6.1)** any *arrangement* you enter into in respect of *regulated mortgage contracts, general insurance contracts* (including after the event insurance) or *pure protection contracts*, provides that referrals will only be made where this is in the best interests of the particular *client* and the contract is suitable for the needs of that *client*;

**IB(6.2)** any referral in respect of *regulated mortgage contracts, general insurance contracts* and *pure protection contracts* to a third party that can only offer products from one source, is made only after the *client* has been informed of this limitation.

Acting in the following way(s) may tend to show that you have not achieved these outcomes and therefore not complied with the *Principles*:

**IB(6.3)** entering into any *arrangement* which restricts your freedom to recommend any particular business, except in respect of *regulated mortgage contracts, general insurance contracts* or *pure protection contracts*;

**IB(6.4)** being an *appointed representative*.

## In-house practice

The outcomes in this chapter apply to your *in-house practice*.

## Overseas practice

The outcomes in this chapter apply to your *overseas practice*.

## NOTES

1. See Outcome 1.15, in relation to *financial benefits* that you may receive in respect of introductions to third parties.
2. If the introduction is in connection with the provision of financial services, and your *firm* is not authorised by the Financial Services Authority, you will need to comply with the SRA Financial Services (Scope) Rules 2001 and the SRA Financial Services (Conduct of Business) Rules 2001. Where an introduction is not a *regulated activity* because you can rely on an exclusion in the *Regulated Activities Order*, you will need nevertheless to consider Outcome 1.15.
3. This chapter should be read in conjunction with Chapter 12 (Separate businesses).

## 2nd Section – You and your business

## CHAPTER 7 – MANAGEMENT OF YOUR BUSINESS

This chapter is about the management and supervision of your *firm* or *in-house practice*.

Everyone has a role to play in the efficient running of a business, although of course that role will depend on the individual's position within the organisation. However, overarching responsibility for the management of the business in the broadest sense rests with the *manager(s)*. The *manager(s)* should determine what arrangements are appropriate to meet the outcomes. Factors to be taken into account will include the size and complexity of the

155

business; the number, experience and qualifications of the *employees*; the number of offices; and the nature of the work undertaken.

Where you are using a third party to provide services that you could provide, (often described as 'outsourcing'), this chapter sets out the outcomes you need to achieve.

The outcomes in this chapter show how the *Principles* apply in the context of the management of your business.

**Outcomes**

You must achieve these outcomes:

**O(7.1)**     you have a clear and effective governance structure and reporting lines;

**O(7.2)**     you have effective systems and controls in place to achieve and comply with all the *Principles*, rules and outcomes and other requirements of the Handbook, where applicable;

**O(7.3)**     you identify, monitor and manage risks to compliance with all the *Principles*, rules and outcomes and other requirements of the Handbook, if applicable to you, and take steps to address issues identified;

**O(7.4)**     you maintain systems and controls for monitoring the financial stability of your *firm* and risks to money and *assets* entrusted to you by *clients* and others, and you take steps to address issues identified;

**O(7.5)**     you comply with legislation applicable to your business, including anti-money laundering and data protection legislation;

**O(7.6)**     you train individuals working in the *firm* to maintain a level of competence appropriate to their work and level of responsibility;

**O(7.7)**     you comply with the statutory requirements for the direction and supervision of *reserved legal activities* and *immigration work*;

**O(7.8)**     you have a system for supervising *clients'* matters, to include the regular checking of the quality of work by suitably competent and experienced people;

**O(7.9)**     you do not outsource *reserved legal activities* to a *person* who is not authorised to conduct such activities;

**O(7.10)** subject to Outcome 7.9, where you outsource *legal activities* or any operational functions that are critical to the delivery of any legal activities, you ensure such outsourcing:

     (a)   does not adversely affect your ability to comply with, or the *SRA's* ability to monitor your compliance with, your obligations in the Handbook;

     (b)   is subject to contractual arrangements that enable the *SRA* or its agent to obtain information from, inspect the records (including electronic records) of, or enter the premises of, the third party, in relation to the outsourced activities or functions;

     (c)   does not alter your obligations towards your *clients*; and

     (d)   does not cause you to breach the conditions with which you must comply in order to be authorised and to remain so.

**Indicative behaviours**

Acting in the following way(s) may tend to show that you have achieved these outcomes and therefore complied with the *Principles*:

**IB(7.1)**     safekeeping of documents and *assets* entrusted to the *firm*;

**IB(7.2)**     controlling budgets, expenditure and cash flow;

**IB(7.3)**     identifying and monitoring financial, operational and business continuity risks including *complaints*, credit risks and exposure, claims under legislation relating to matters such as data protection, IT failures and abuses, and damage to offices;

**IB(7.4)** making arrangements for the continuation of your *firm* in the event of absences and emergencies, for example holiday or sick leave, with the minimum interruption to *clients'* business.

**In-house practice**

Outcomes 7.5 and 7.7 apply to your *in-house practice*.

Outcomes 7.1 to 7.3, and 7.6 and 7.8 to 7.10 apply to you if you have management responsibilities.

**Overseas practice**

The outcomes in this chapter apply to your *overseas practice*.

**NOTES**

1. All of the chapters in the Code will be relevant to the management of your business, in particular those which require you to have systems and controls in place.
2. This chapter should also be read with the *SRA Authorisation Rules*, the SRA Financial Services (Conduct of Business) Rules 2001 and the SRA Indemnity Insurance Rules.

**CHAPTER 8 – PUBLICITY**

This chapter is about the manner in which you publicise your *firm* or *in-house practice* or any other businesses. The overriding concern is that *publicity* is not misleading and is sufficiently informative to ensure that *clients* and others can make informed choices.

In your *publicity*, you must comply with statutory requirements and have regard to voluntary codes.

The outcomes in this chapter show how the *Principles* apply in the context of *publicity*.

**Outcomes**

You must achieve these outcomes:

**O(8.1)** your *publicity* in relation to your *firm* or *in-house practice* or for any other business is accurate and not misleading, and is not likely to diminish the trust the public places in you and in the provision of legal services;

**O(8.2)** your *publicity* relating to charges is clearly expressed and identifies whether VAT and *disbursements* are included;

**O(8.3)** you do not make unsolicited approaches in person or by telephone to *members of the public* in order to publicise your *firm* or *in-house practice* or another business;

**O(8.4)** *clients* and the public have appropriate information about you, your *firm* and how you are regulated;

**O(8.5)** your letterhead, website and e-mails show the words 'authorised and regulated by the Solicitors Regulation Authority' and either the *firm*'s registered name and number if it is an *LLP* or *company* or, if the *firm* is a *partnership* or *sole practitioner*, the name under which it is licensed/authorised by the *SRA* and the number allocated to it by the *SRA*.

### Indicative behaviours

Acting in the following way(s) may tend to show that you have achieved these outcomes and therefore complied with the *Principles*:

**IB(8.1)** where you conduct other regulated activities your *publicity* discloses the manner in which you are regulated in relation to those activities;

**IB(8.2)** where your *firm* is a multi-disciplinary *practice*, any *publicity* in relation to that *practice* makes clear which services are regulated legal services and which are not;

**IB(8.3)** any *publicity* intended for a jurisdiction outside England and Wales complies with the *Principles*, voluntary codes and the rules in force in that jurisdiction concerning *publicity*;

**IB(8.4)** where you and another business jointly market services, the nature of the services provided by each business is clear.

Acting in the following way(s) may tend to show that you have not achieved these outcomes and therefore not complied with the *Principles*:

**IB(8.5)** approaching people in the street, at ports of entry, in hospital or at the scene of an accident; including approaching people to conduct a survey which involves collecting contact details of potential *clients*, or otherwise promotes your *firm* or *in-house practice*;

**IB(8.6)** allowing any other *person* to conduct *publicity* for your *firm* or *in-house practice* in a way that would breach the *Principles*;

**IB(8.7)** advertising an estimated fee which is pitched at an unrealistically low level;

**IB(8.8)** describing overheads of your *firm* (such a normal postage, telephone calls and charges arising in respect of client due diligence under the Money Laundering Regulations 2007) as *disbursements* in your advertisements;

**IB(8.9)** advertising an estimated or fixed fee without making it clear that additional charges may be payable, if that is the case;

**IB(8.10)** using a name or description of your *firm* or *in-house practice* that includes the word '*solicitor(s)*' if none of the *managers* are *solicitors;*

**IB(8.11)** advertising your *firm* or *in-house practice* in a way that suggests that services provided by another business are provided by your *firm* or *in-house practice*;

**IB(8.12)** producing misleading information concerning the professional status of any *manager* or *employee* of your *firm* or *in-house practice*.

### In-house practice

Outcomes 8.1 to 8.4 apply to your *in-house practice* unless it is clear from the context that the outcome is not relevant in your particular circumstances.

### Overseas practice

Outcomes 8.1 and 8.4 apply to your *overseas practice*. In addition you must comply with the following outcome:

**OP(8.1)** *publicity* intended for a jurisdiction outside England and Wales must comply with any applicable law or rules regarding *lawyers' publicity* in the jurisdiction in which your office is based and the jurisdiction for which the *publicity* is intended.

### NOTES

This chapter should be read in conjunction with Chapters 1 and 9.

## CHAPTER 9 – FEE SHARING AND REFERRALS

This chapter is about protecting *clients'* interests where you have *arrangements* with third parties who introduce business to you and/or with whom you share your fees. The relationship between *clients* and *firms* should be built on trust, and any such *arrangement* should not jeopardise that trust by, for example, compromising your independence or professional judgement.

The outcomes in this chapter show how the *Principles* apply in the context of fee sharing and *referrals*.

### Outcomes

You must achieve these outcomes:

**O(9.1)**    your independence and your professional judgement are not prejudiced by virtue of any *arrangement* with another *person*;

**O(9.2)**    your *clients'* interests are protected regardless of the interests of an *introducer* or *fee sharer* or your interest in receiving *referrals*;

**O(9.3)**    *clients* are in a position to make informed decisions about how to pursue their matter;

**O(9.4)**    *clients* are informed of any financial or other interest which an *introducer* has in referring the *client* to you;

**O(9.5)**    *clients* are informed of any fee sharing *arrangement* that is relevant to their matter;

**O(9.6)**    you do not make payments to an *introducer* in respect of *clients* who are the subject of criminal proceedings or who have the benefit of public funding;

**O(9.7)**    where you enter into a financial *arrangement* with an *introducer* you ensure that the agreement is in writing.

### Indicative behaviours

Acting in the following way(s) may tend to show that you have achieved these outcomes and therefore complied with the *Principles*:

**IB(9.1)**    only entering into *arrangements* with reputable third parties and monitoring the outcome of those *arrangements* to ensure that *clients* are treated fairly;

**IB(9.2)**    in any case where a *client* has entered into, or is proposing to enter into, an *arrangement* with an *introducer* in connection with their matter, which is not in their best interests, advising the *client* that this is the case;

**IB(9.3)**    terminating any *arrangement* with an *introducer* or *fee sharer* which is causing you to breach the *Principles* or any requirements of the Code;

**IB(9.4)**    being satisfied that any *client* referred by an *introducer* has not been acquired as a result of marketing or other activities which, if done by a *person* regulated by the *SRA*, would be contrary to the *Principles* or any requirements of the Code;

**IB(9.5)**    drawing the *client's* attention to any payments you make, or other consideration you provide, in connection with any *referral*;

**IB(9.6)**    where information needs to be given to a *client*, ensuring the information is clear and in writing or in a form appropriate to the *client's* needs.

Acting in the following way(s) may tend to show that you have not achieved these outcomes and therefore not complied with the *Principles*:

**IB(9.7)**    entering into any type of business relationship with a third party, such as an unauthorised *partnership*, which places you in breach of the *SRA Authorisation Rules* or any other regulatory requirements in the Handbook;

**IB(9.8)**    allowing an *introducer* or *fee sharer* to influence the advice you give to *clients*;

**IB(9.9)** accepting *referrals* where you have reason to believe that *clients* have been pressurised or misled into instructing you.

### In-house practice

Outcomes 9.1 to 9.3 apply to your *in-house practice*.

Outcomes 9.4 to 9.7 apply unless it is clear from the context that the outcome is not relevant to your particular circumstances.

### Overseas practice

The outcomes in this chapter apply to your *overseas practice*, except where they conflict with the SRA European Cross-Border Practice Rules which will prevail in any conflict.

### NOTES

1. This chapter should be read in conjunction with:
   - Chapter 1 (Client care)
   - Chapter 4 (Confidentiality and disclosure)
   - Chapter 8 (Publicity)
   - The *SRA Authorisation Rules*
   - The SRA European Cross-Border Practice Rules

### 3rd Section – You and your regulator

### CHAPTER 10 – YOU AND YOUR REGULATOR

This chapter is about co-operation with your regulators and ombudsmen, primarily the *SRA* and the *Legal Ombudsman*.

The information which we request from you will help us understand any risks to *clients*, and the public interest more generally.

The outcomes in this chapter show how the *Principles* apply in the context of you and your regulator.

### Outcomes

You must achieve these outcomes:

**O(10.1)** you ensure that you comply with all the reporting and notification requirements in the Handbook that apply to you;

**O(10.2)** you provide the *SRA* with information to enable the *SRA* to decide upon any application you make, such as for a practising certificate, registration, recognition or a licence and whether any conditions should apply;

**O(10.3)** you notify the *SRA* promptly of any material changes to relevant information about you including serious financial difficulty, action taken against you by another regulator and serious failure to comply with or achieve the *Principles*, rules, outcomes and other requirements of the Handbook;

**O(10.4)** you report to the *SRA* promptly, serious misconduct by any person or *firm* authorised by the *SRA*, or any *employee*, *manager* or *owner* of any such *firm* (taking into account, where necessary, your duty of confidentiality to your *client*);

**O(10.5)**    you ensure that the *SRA* is in a position to assess whether any persons requiring prior approval are fit and proper at the point of approval and remain so;

**O(10.6)**    you co-operate fully with the *SRA* and the *Legal Ombudsman* at all times including in relation to any investigation about a *claim for redress* against you;

**O(10.7)**    you do not attempt to prevent anyone from providing information to the *SRA* or the *Legal Ombudsman*;

**O(10.8)**    you comply promptly with any written notice from the *SRA*;

**O(10.9)**    pursuant to a notice under Outcome 10.8, you:

(a)    produce for inspection by the *SRA documents* held by you, or held under your control;

(b)    provide all information and explanations requested; and

(c)    comply with all requests from the *SRA* as to the form in which you produce any *documents* you hold electronically, and for photocopies of any *documents* to take away;

in connection with your *practice* or in connection with any trust of which you are, or formerly were, a trustee;

**O(10.10)**    you provide any necessary permissions for information to be given, so as to enable the *SRA* to:

(a)    prepare a report on any *documents* produced; and

(b)    seek verification from *clients*, staff and the banks, building societies or other financial institutions used by you;

**O(10.11)**    when required by the *SRA* in relation to a matter specified by the *SRA*, you:

a)    act promptly to investigate whether any *person* may have a *claim for redress* against you;

(b)    provide the *SRA* with a report on the outcome of such an investigation, identifying *persons* who may have such a claim;

(c)    notify *persons* that they may have a right of redress against you, providing them with information as to the nature of the possible claim, about the *firm's complaints* procedure and about the *Legal Ombudsman*; and

(d)    ensure, where you have identified a *person* who may have a *claim for redress*, that the matter is dealt with under the *firm's complaints* procedure as if that *person* had made a *complaint*;

**O(10.12)**    you do not attempt to abrogate to any third party your regulatory responsibilities in the Handbook, including the role of Compliance Officer for Legal Practice (*COLP*) or Compliance Officer for Finance and Administration (*COFA*);

**O(10.13)**    once you are aware that your *firm* will cease to *practise*, you effect the orderly and transparent wind-down of activities, including informing the *SRA* before the firm closes.

**Indicative behaviours**

Acting in the following way(s) may tend to show that you have achieved these outcomes and therefore complied with the *Principles*:

**IB(10.1)**    actively monitoring your achievement of the outcomes in order to improve standards and identify non-achievement of the outcomes;

**IB(10.2)**    actively monitoring your financial stability and viability in order to identify and mitigate any risks to the public;

**IB(10.3)**    notifying the *SRA* promptly of any indicators of serious financial difficulty, such as inability to pay your professional indemnity insurance premium, or rent or salaries, or breach of bank covenants;

**IB(10.4)** notifying the *SRA* promptly when you become aware that your business may not be financially viable to continue trading as a going concern, for example because of difficult trading conditions, poor cash flow, increasing overheads, loss of *managers* or *employees* and/or loss of sources of revenue;

**IB(10.5)** notifying the *SRA* of any serious issues identified as a result of monitoring referred to in IB10.1 and IB10.2 above, and producing a plan for remedying issues that have been identified;

**IB(10.6)** responding appropriately to any serious issues identified concerning competence and fitness and propriety of your *employees*, *managers* and *owners*;

**IB(10.7)** reporting disciplinary action taken against you by another regulator;

**IB(10.8)** informing the *SRA* promptly when you become aware of a significant change to your *firm*, for example:

- key personnel, such as a *manager*, *COLP* or *COFA*, joining or leaving the *firm*;
- a merger with, or an acquisition by or of, another *firm*;

**IB(10.9)** having appropriate arrangements for the orderly transfer of *clients*' property to another *authorised body* if your *firm* closes;

**IB(10.10)** having a 'whistle-blowing' policy.

Acting in the following way(s) may tend to show that you have not achieved these outcomes and therefore not complied with the *Principles*:

**IB(10.11)** entering into an agreement which would attempt to preclude the *SRA* or the *Legal Ombudsman* from investigating any actual or potential *complaint* or allegation of professional misconduct;

**IB(10.12)** unless you can properly allege malice, issuing defamation proceedings in respect of a *complaint* to the *SRA*.

**In-house practice**

The outcomes in this chapter apply to your *in-house practice*.

**Overseas practice**

The outcomes in this chapter apply to your *overseas practice*.

**NOTES**

1. A notice under this chapter is deemed to be duly served:

   (a) on the date on which it is delivered to or left at your last notified *practising* address;
   (b) on the date on which it is sent electronically to your e-mail or fax address; or
   (c) seven days after it has been sent by post or document exchange to your last notified *practising* address.

2. The outcomes in this chapter should be considered in conjunction with the following:

   - Chapter 7 (Management of your business) – requirements for risk management procedures; and
   - note (xv) to Rule 8 of the *SRA Authorisation Rules*.

**4th Section – You and others**

## CHAPTER 11 – RELATIONS WITH THIRD PARTIES

This chapter is about ensuring you do not take unfair advantage of those you deal with and that you act in a manner which promotes the proper operation of the legal system.

This includes your conduct in relation to *undertakings*; there is no obligation to give or receive an *undertaking* on behalf of a *client* but, if you do, you must ensure that you achieve the outcomes listed in this chapter.

The conduct requirements in this area extend beyond professional and business matters. They apply in any circumstances in which you may use your professional title to advance your personal interests.

The outcomes in this chapter show how the *Principles* apply in the context of your relations with third parties.

### Outcomes

You must achieve these outcomes:

**O(11.1)**  you do not take unfair advantage of third parties in either your professional or personal capacity;

**O(11.2)**  you perform all *undertakings* given by you within an agreed timescale or within a reasonable amount of time;

**O(11.3)**  where you act for a seller of land, you inform all buyers immediately of the seller's intention to deal with more than one buyer;

**O(11.4)**  you properly administer oaths, affirmations or declarations where you are authorised to do so.

### Indicative behaviours

Acting in the following way(s) may tend to show that you have achieved these outcomes and therefore complied with the *Principles*:

**IB(11.1)**  providing sufficient time and information to enable the costs in any matter to be agreed;

**IB(11.2)**  returning documents or money sent subject to an express condition if you are unable to comply with that condition;

**IB(11.3)**  returning documents or money on demand if they are sent on condition that they are held to the sender's order;

**IB(11.4)**  ensuring that you do not communicate with another party when you are aware that the other party has retained a *lawyer* in a matter, except:

- to request the name and address of the other party's *lawyer*; or
- the other party's *lawyer* consents to you communicating with the *client*; or
- where there are exceptional circumstances;

**IB(11.5)**  maintaining an effective system which records when *undertakings* have been given and when they have been discharged;

**IB(11.6)**  where an *undertaking* is given which is dependent upon the happening of a future event and it becomes apparent the future event will not occur, notifying the recipient of this.

Acting in the following way(s) may tend to show that you have not achieved these outcomes and therefore not complied with the *Principles*:

**IB(11.7)** taking unfair advantage of an opposing party's lack of legal knowledge where they have not instructed a *lawyer*;

**IB(11.8)** demanding anything for yourself or on behalf of your *client*, that is not legally recoverable, such as when you are instructed to collect a simple debt, demanding from the debtor the cost of the letter of claim since it cannot be said at that stage that such a cost is legally recoverable;

**IB(11.9)** using your professional status or qualification to take unfair advantage of another *person* in order to advance your personal interests;

**IB(11.10)** taking unfair advantage of a public office held by you, or a member of your family, or a member of your *firm* or their family.

### In-house practice

The outcomes in this chapter apply to your *in-house practice*.

### Overseas practice

The outcomes in this chapter apply to your *overseas practice*, except that Outcome 11.3 only applies if the land in question is situated in England and Wales.

### NOTES

1. This chapter should be read in conjunction with Chapter 7 (Management of your business) in relation to the system you will need to have in place to control *undertakings*.

### CHAPTER 12 – SEPARATE BUSINESSES

The purpose of this chapter is to ensure *clients* are protected when they obtain mainstream legal services from a *firm* regulated by the *SRA*. This is accomplished by restricting the services that can be provided through a *separate business* that is not authorised by the *SRA* or another *approved regulator*.

This chapter addresses two kinds of services:

(a) those which you cannot offer through a *separate business* (*'prohibited separate business activities'*). These are 'mainstream' legal services which members of the public would expect you to offer as a *lawyer* regulated by the SRA or another *approved regulator*; and

(b) those which you can offer either through a *separate business* ('a *permitted separate business'*), or through an *authorised body*. These are the kind of services a member of the public would not necessarily expect to be provided only by a *lawyer* regulated by the *SRA* or another *approved regulator*, but which are 'solicitor-like' services.

*Clients* of a *permitted separate business* will not have the same statutory protections as *clients* of an *authorised body* and it is important that this is clear to *clients* of the *separate business*, particularly where they are being referred from one business to the other.

The outcomes in this chapter show how the *Principles* apply in the context of *separate businesses*.

**Outcomes**

You must achieve these outcomes:

**O(12.1)**  you do not:

> (a)  *own*;
> (b)  have a significant interest in; or
> (c)  *actively participate in*,

> a *separate business* which conducts *prohibited separate business activities*;

**O(12.2)**  if you are a *firm*:

> (a)  you are not *owned by*; or
> (b)  *connected with*,

> a *separate business* which conducts *prohibited separate business activities*;

**O(12.3)**  where you:

> (a)  have a significant interest in;
> (b)  *actively participate in*;
> (c)  *own*; or
> (d)  are a *firm* and *owned by* or *connected with*,

> a *permitted separate business*, you have safeguards in place to ensure that *clients* are not misled about the extent to which the services that you and the *separate business* offer are regulated;

**O(12.4)**  you do not represent any *permitted separate business* as being regulated by the *SRA* or any of its activities as being provided by an individual who is regulated by the *SRA*;

**O(12.5)**  you are only *connected with* reputable *separate businesses*;

**O(12.6)**  you are only *connected with* a *permitted separate business* which is an *appointed representative* if it is an *appointed representative* of an independent financial adviser.

**Indicative behaviours**

Acting in the following way(s) may tend to show that you have achieved these outcomes and therefore complied with the *Principles*:

**IB(12.1)**  ensuring that *client* information and records are not disclosed to the *permitted separate business*, without the express consent of the *client*;

**IB(12.2)**  complying with the *SRA Accounts Rules* and not allowing the *client account* to be used to hold money for the *permitted separate business*;

**IB(12.3)**  where you are referring a *client* to a *permitted separate business*, informing the *client* of your interest in the *separate business*;

**IB(12.4)**  terminating any connection with a *permitted separate business* where you have reason to doubt the integrity or competence of that *separate business*.

**In-house practice**

Outcomes 12.1 and 12.3 to 12.6 in this chapter apply to your *in-house practice*.

**Overseas practice**

If you *practise* from an office outside England and Wales and you have a *separate business*, Outcomes 12.3 to 12.6 in this chapter apply to you.

165

**NOTES**

1.  It is important that *clients* are not misled or confused about the regulatory status of a *permitted separate business*, the services it provides and the people working within it. Particular care needs to be taken regarding:

    - the name or branding of the *separate business*;
    - misleading *publicity*; and
    - the proximity of the *permitted separate business* to your *firm*, particularly if you share premises.

2.  This chapter should be read in conjunction with:

    - Chapter 3 (Conflicts of interests)
    - Chapter 6 (Your client and introductions to third parties); and
    - Chapter 8 (Publicity).

**5th section – Application, waivers and interpretation**

**CHAPTER 13 – APPLICATION AND WAIVERS PROVISIONS**

The SRA Code of Conduct applies to you in the following circumstances (and 'you' must be construed accordingly):

**Application of the SRA Code of Conduct in England and Wales**

1.  Subject to paragraphs 2 to 10 below and any other provisions in this Code, this Code applies to you, in relation to your activities carried out from an office in England and Wales, if you are:

    (a)  a *solicitor*, *REL* or *RFL*, and you are *practising* as such, whether or not the entity through which you *practise* is subject to this Code;
    (b)  a *solicitor*, *REL* or *RFL* who is:

        (i)   a *manager*, *employee* or *owner* of a body which should be a *recognised body*, but has not been recognised by the *SRA*;
        (ii)  a *manager*, *employee* or *owner* of a body that is a *manager* or *owner* of a body that should be a *recognised body*, but has not been recognised by the *SRA*;
        (iii) an *employee* of a *sole practitioner* who should be a *recognised sole practitioner*, but has not been recognised by the *SRA*;
        (iv)  an *owner* of an *authorised body* or a body which should be a *recognised body* but has not been recognised by the *SRA*, even if you undertake no work for the body's *clients*; or
        (v)   a *manager* or *employee* of an *authorised non-SRA firm*, or a *manager* of a body which is a *manager* of an *authorised non-SRA firm*, when doing work of a sort authorised by the *SRA*, for that firm;

    (c)  an *authorised body*, or a body which should be a *recognised body* but has not been recognised by the *SRA*;
    (d)  any other person who is a *manager* or *employee* of an *authorised body*, or of a body which should be a *recognised body* but has not been recognised by the *SRA*;
    (e)  any other person who is an *employee* of a *recognised sole practitioner*, or of a *sole*

*practitioner* who should be a *recognised sole practitioner* but has not been recognised by the *SRA*;

and 'you' includes 'your' as appropriate.

2. Chapters 10, 12, 13, 14 and 15 of the Code apply to you if you are a *solicitor*, *REL* or *RFL* and you are:

(a) *practising* as a *manager* or *employee* of an *authorised non-SRA firm* when doing work of a sort authorised by the *authorised non-SRA firm's approved regulator*; or

(b) an *owner* of an *authorised non-SRA firm* even if you undertake no work for the body's *clients*.

## Application of the SRA Code of Conduct in relation to practice from an office outside England and Wales

3. Subject to 5 and 6 below, the Code applies to you, in relation to *practice from an office* in Scotland or Northern Ireland, if you are:

(a) a *solicitor* or an *REL practising* as such, whether or not your *firm* or *employer* is subject to this Code;

(b) a *lawyer-controlled body*;

(c) an *REL-controlled body*;

(d) any other person who is a *manager* of an *authorised body*; or

(e) a *solicitor* who was formerly an *REL*, when *practising* as a *lawyer* of an *Establishment Directive profession*.

4. Subject to 5 and 6 below, the Code applies to you, in relation to *practice from an office* outside the UK, if you are:

(a) a *solicitor practising* as such, whether or not your *firm* or *employer* is subject to this Code;

(b) a *lawyer-controlled body*; or

(c) any other person who is a *manager* of an *authorised body*.

5. If any outcome in the Code does not apply to your *overseas practice*, you may disregard that Outcome in relation to your *overseas practice*, but you must comply with any alternative provision substituted for *overseas practice*.

6. If compliance with any outcome in the Code would result in your breaching local law, you may disregard that outcome to the extent necessary to comply with that local law.

## Application of the SRA Code of Conduct outside practice

7. In relation to activities which fall outside *practice*, whether undertaken as a *lawyer* or in some other business or private capacity, the following apply to you if you are a *solicitor*, or *REL*:

(a) Outcome 11.1; and

(b) Outcome 11.2.

## General Provisions

8. The extent to which you are expected to implement the requirements of the Code will depend on your role in the *firm*, or your way of *practising*. For example, those who are managing the business will be expected to have more influence on how the *firm* or business is run than those *practising* in-house but not managing a legal department, or those *practising* as *employees* of a *firm*.

9.  You must deliver all outcomes which are relevant to you and your situation.
10. Where in accordance with this chapter, the requirements of the Code apply to a *licensed body*, this extends to the *reserved legal activities*, and other activities regulated by the *SRA*, carried on by the body.

### Waivers

In any particular case or cases the *SRA* Board shall have the power, in exceptional circumstances, to waive in writing the provisions of these outcomes for a particular purpose or purposes expressed in such waiver, to place conditions on and to revoke such a waiver.

### CHAPTER 14 – INTERPRETATION

'*AJA*' means the Administration of Justice Act 1985;

'*actively participate in*' means, in relation to a *separate business*, having any active involvement in the *separate business*, and includes:

(a) any direct control over the business, and any indirect control through another person such as a spouse; and

(b) any active participation in the business or the provision of its services to customers;

'*appointed representative*' has the meaning given in *FSMA*;

'*approved regulator*' means any body listed as an approved regulator in paragraph 1 of Schedule 4 to the *LSA* or designated as an approved regulator by an order under paragraph 17 of that Schedule;

'*arrangement*' in relation to financial services, fee sharing and *referrals*, in chapters 1, 6 and 9 of the *SRA Code of Conduct*, means any express or tacit agreement between you and another *person*, whether contractually binding or not;

'*assets*' includes money, documents, wills, deeds, investments and other property;

'*authorised body*' means a body that has been authorised by the *SRA*, to *practise* as a *licensed body* or a *recognised body*;

'*authorised non-SRA firm*' means a firm which is authorised to carry on *legal activities* by an *approved regulator* other than the *SRA*;

'*body corporate*' means a *company*, an *LLP*, or a *partnership* which is a legal *person* in its own right;

'*claim for redress*' has the meaning given in section 158 of the *LSA*;

'*client*' means the *person* for whom you act and, where the context permits, includes prospective and former *clients*;

'*client account*' has the meaning given in Rule 13(2) of the *SRA Accounts Rules*, save that for the purposes of Part G (Overseas Practice) of the *SRA Accounts Rules*, '*client account*' means an account at a bank or similar institution, subject to supervision by a public authority, which is used only for the purpose of holding *client money* and/or *trust* money, and the title or designation of which indicates that the funds in the account belong to the *client* or *clients* of a *solicitor* or *REL* or are held subject to a trust;

'*client conflict*' for the purposes of Chapter 3 of the *SRA Code of Conduct* means any situation where you owe separate duties to act in the best interests of two or more *clients* in relation to the same or related matters, and those duties conflict, or there is a significant risk that those duties may conflict;

'*client money*' has the meaning given in Rule 12 of the *SRA Accounts Rules*, save that for the purposes of Part G (Overseas Practice) of the *SRA Accounts Rules*, means money received or held for or on behalf of a *client* or *trust* (but excluding money which is held or received by a MDP – a *licensed body* providing a range of different services – in relation to those activities for which it is not regulated by the SRA);

'*COFA*' means compliance officer for finance and administration in accordance with rule 8.5 of the *SRA Authorisation Rules* and in relation to a *licensable body* is a reference to its Head of Finance and Administration within the meaning of the *LSA*;

'*COLP*' means compliance officer for legal practice in accordance with rule 8.5 of the *SRA Authorisation Rules* and in relation to a *licensable body* is a reference to its Head of Legal Practice within the meaning of the *LSA*;

'*Companies Acts*' means the Companies Act 1985 and the Companies Act 2006;

'*company*' means a *company* registered under the *Companies Acts*, an overseas company incorporated in an *Establishment Directive state* and registered under the Companies Act 1985 and/or the Companies Act 2006 or a *societas Europaea*;

'*competing for the same objective*' for the purposes of Chapter 3 of the *SRA Code of Conduct* means any situation in which two or more *clients* are competing for an 'objective' which, if attained by one *client* will make that 'objective' unattainable to the other *client* or *clients* and '*objective*' means, for the purposes of Chapter 3, an asset, contract or business opportunity which one or more *clients* are seeking to acquire or recover through a liquidation (or some other form of insolvency process) or by means of an auction or tender process or a bid or offer which is not public;

'*complaint*' means an oral or written expression of dissatisfaction which alleges that the complainant has suffered (or may suffer) financial loss, distress, inconvenience or other detriment;

'*compulsory professional indemnity insurance*' means the insurance you are required to have in place under the *SIIR*;

'*conflict of interests*' means any situation where:
   (a)  you owe separate duties to act in the best interests of two or more *clients* in relation to the same or related matters, and those duties conflict, or there is a significant risk that those duties may conflict (a '*client conflict*'); or
   (b)  your duty to act in the best interests of any *client* in relation to a matter conflicts, or there is a significant risk that it may conflict, with your own interests in relation to that or a related matter (an '*own interest conflict*');

'*connected with*' means in relation to a *separate business* for the purpose of Chapter 12 of the *SRA Code of Conduct*:
   (a)  having one or more *partner(s)*, *owner(s)*, *director(s)* or *member(s)* in common with the separate business;
   (b)  being a *subsidiary company* of the same *holding company* as the *separate business*; or
   (c)  being a *subsidiary company* of the separate business;

'*court*' means any court, tribunal or enquiry of England and Wales, or a British court martial, or any court of another jurisdiction;

'*director*' means a director of a *company*; and in relation to a *societas Europaea* includes:
   (a)  in a two-tier system, a member of the management organ and a member of the supervisory organ; and
   (b)  in a one-tier system, a member of the administrative organ;

169

'*disbursement*' means, in respect of those activities for which the practice is regulated by the *SRA*, any sum spent or to be spent on behalf of a *client* or *trust* (including any VAT element);

'*document*' in Chapter 10 of the *SRA Code of Conduct*, includes documents, whether written or electronic, relating to the *firm*'s *client accounts* and *office accounts*;

'*employee*' for the purposes of the *SRA Code of Conduct*, includes an individual who is:

    (a)   employed as a *director* of a *company*;

    (b)   engaged under a contract of service (for example, as an assistant *solicitor*) by a *firm* or its wholly owned service company; or

    (c)   engaged under a contract for services (for example, as a consultant or a locum), made between a *firm* or organisation and:

        (i)   that individual;

        (ii)   an employment agency; or

        (iii)   a *company* which is not held out to the public as providing legal services and is wholly owned and directed by that individual,

under which the *firm* or organisation has exclusive control over the individual's time for all or part of the individual's working week; or in relation to which the *firm* or organisation has designated the individual as a fee earner in accordance with arrangements between the *firm* or organisation and the Legal Services Commission pursuant to the Access to Justice Act 1999;

and '*employer*' is to be construed accordingly;

'*Establishment Directive*' means the Establishment of Lawyers Directive 98/5/EC;

'*Establishment Directive profession*' means any profession listed in Article 1.2(a) of the *Establishment Directive*, including a *solicitor*, *barrister* or advocate of the *UK*;

'*Establishment Directive state*' means a state to which the *Establishment Directive* applies;

'*fee sharer*' means another *person* or business who or which shares your fees;

'*financial benefit*' includes, for example, any commission, discount or rebate, but does not include your fees or interest earned on any *client account*;

'*firm*' means an *authorised body*, a *recognised sole practitioner* or a body or person which should be authorised by the *SRA* as a *recognised body* or *recognised sole practitioner* (but which could not be authorised by another *approved regulator*);

'*general insurance contract*' means any contract of insurance within Part I of Schedule 1 to the *Regulated Activities Order*;

'*holding company*' has the meaning given in the Companies Act 2006;

'*immigration work*' means the provision of immigration advice and immigration services, as defined in section 82 of the Immigration and Asylum Act 1999;

'*independent intermediary*' in chapter 6 of the *SRA Code of Conduct*, means an independent financial adviser who is able to advise on investment products from across the whole of the market and offers consumers the option of paying fees rather than receiving payment through commission;

'*introducer*' means any *person*, business or organisation who or that introduces or refers potential *clients* to your business, or recommends your business to *clients* or otherwise puts you and *clients* in touch with each other;

'*investment*' for the purposes of chapter 6 of the *SRA Code of Conduct*, has the meaning given in the SRA Financial Services (Scope) Rules 2001;

'*in-house practice*' means *practice* as a *solicitor*, *REL* or *RFL* (as appropriate) in accordance with Rules 1.1(c)(B), 1.1(d)(B), 1.1(e), 1.2(f), 2.1(c)(B), 2.1(d)(B), 2.1(e), 2.2(f), 3.1(b)(B) or 3.1(c)(B) of the *SRA Practice Framework Rules*;

'*lawyer*' means a member of one of the following professions, entitled to practise as such:
    (a)  the profession of *solicitor*, *barrister* or advocate of the *UK*;
    (b)  a profession whose members are authorised to carry on *legal activities* by an *approved regulator* other than the *SRA*;
    (c)  an *Establishment Directive profession* other than a *UK* profession;
    (d)  a legal profession which has been approved by the *SRA* for the purpose of *recognised bodies* in England and Wales; and
    (e)  any other regulated legal profession specified by the *SRA* for the purpose of this definition;

'*lawyer-controlled body*' means an *authorised body* in which *lawyers of England and Wales* constitute the national group of *lawyers* with the largest (or equal largest) share of control of the body either as individual *managers* or by their share in the control of bodies which are *managers*;

'*lawyer of England and Wales*' means:
    (a)  a *solicitor*; or
    (b)  an individual who is authorised to carry on *legal activities* in England and Wales by an *approved regulator* other than the *SRA*, but excludes a member of an *Establishment Directive profession* registered with the *BSB* under the *Establishment Directive*;

'*Legal Ombudsman*' means the scheme administered by the Office for Legal Complaints under Part 6 of the *LSA*;

'*licensable body*' means a body which meets the criteria in rule 14 (eligibility criteria for licensable bodies) of the *SRA Practice Framework Rules*;

'*licensed body*' means a body licensed by the *SRA* under Part 5 of the *LSA*;

'*LLP*' means a limited liability partnership incorporated under the Limited Liability Partnerships Act 2000;

'*LSA*' means the Legal Services Act 2007;

'*manager*' means:
    (a)  a *member* of an *LLP*;
    (b)  a *director* of a *company*;
    (c)  a *partner* in a *partnership*; or
    (d)  in relation to any other body, a member of its governing body; save that for the purposes of Part G (Overseas Practice) of the *SRA Accounts Rules* 'a manager' includes the director of any company, and is not limited to the director of a *company* as defined herein;

'*member*' means:
    (a)  in relation to a *company*, a person who has agreed to be a *member* of the *company* and whose name is entered in the *company's* register of members; and
    (b)  in relation to an *LLP*, a member of that *LLP*;

'*members of the public*' for the purposes of Chapter 8 of the *SRA Code of Conduct* does not include:
    (a)  a current or former *client*;

(b) another *firm* or its *manager*;

(c) an existing or potential professional or business connection; or

(d) a commercial organisation or public body;

'*office account*' means an account of the *firm* for holding *office money* and/or *out-of-scope money*, or other means of holding *office money* or *out-of-scope money* (for example, the office cash box or an account holding money regulated by a regulator other than the *SRA*);

'*office money*' has the meaning given in Rule 12 of the *SRA Accounts Rules*;

'*out-of-scope money*' means money held or received by a MDP in relation to those activities for which it is not regulated by the *SRA*;

'*overseas practice*' means *practice from an office* outside England and Wales, except in the case of an *REL*, where it means *practice from an office* in Scotland or Northern Ireland;

'*owner*' for the purposes of Chapter 12 of the *SRA Code of Conduct* means a person having a *substantial ownership interest* in and '*own*' and '*owned by*' shall be construed accordingly;

'*own interest conflict*' for the purpose of Chapter 3 of the *SRA Code of Conduct*, means any situation where your duty to act in the best interests of any *client* in relation to a matter conflicts, or there is a significant risk that it may conflict, with your own interests in relation to that or a related matter;

'*partner*' means a *person* who is or is held out as a partner in a *partnership*;

'*partnership*' means an unincorporated body in which *persons* are or are held out as *partners* and does not include a body incorporated as an *LLP*;

'*permitted separate business*' means, for the purpose of Chapter 12 of the *SRA Code of Conduct*, a *separate business* offering any of the following services:

(a) alternative dispute resolution;

(b) financial services;

(c) estate agency;

(d) management consultancy;

(e) company secretarial services;

(f) acting as a parliamentary agent;

(g) practising as a lawyer of another jurisdiction;

(h) acting as a bailiff;

(i) acting as nominee, *trustee* or executor outside England and Wales;

(j) acting as a nominee, *trustee* or executor in England and Wales where such activity is provided as a subsidiary but necessary part of a *separate business* providing financial services;

(k) providing legal advice or drafting legal documents not included in (a) to (j) above, where such activity is provided as a subsidiary but necessary part of some other service which is one of the main services of the *separate business*; and

(l) providing any other business, advisory or agency service which could be provided through a *firm* or *in-house practice* but is not a *prohibited separate business activity*;

'*person*' includes a *body corporate*, *partnership* and other unincorporated association or body of persons;

'*practice*' means the activities, in that capacity, of:

(a) a *solicitor*;

(b) an *REL*, from an office or offices within the *UK*;

(c)   a member of an *Establishment Directive profession* registered with the *BSB* under the *Establishment Directive*, carried out from an office or offices in England and Wales;

(d)   an *RFL*, from an office or offices in England and Wales as:

    (i)   an *employee* of a *recognised sole practitioner*;

    (ii)   a *manager*, *employee* or *owner* of an *authorised body* or of an *authorised non-SRA firm*; or

    (iii)   a *manager*, *employee* or *owner* of a body which is a *manager* or *owner* of an *authorised body* or of an *authorised non-SRA firm*;

(e)   an *authorised body*;

(f)   a *manager* of an *authorised body*;

(g)   a *person employed* in England and Wales by an *authorised body* or *recognised sole practitioner*;

(h)   a *lawyer of England and Wales*; or

(i)   an *authorised non-SRA firm*;

'*practice from an office*' includes practice carried on:

(a)   from an office at which you are based; or

(b)   from an office of a *firm* in which you are the sole principal, or a *manager*, or in which you have an ownership interest, even if you are not based there;

and '*practising from an office*' should be construed accordingly;

'*Principles*' means the Principles in the SRA Handbook;

'*prohibited separate business activities*' means for the purpose of Chapter 12 of the *SRA Code of Conduct*:

(a)   the conduct of any matter which could come before a *court*, whether or not proceedings are started;

(b)   advocacy before a court, tribunal or enquiry;

(c)   instructing counsel in any part of the *UK*;

(d)   *immigration work*;

(e)   any activity in relation to conveyancing, applications for probate or letters of administration, or drawing trust deeds or *court* documents, which is reserved to *solicitors* and others under the *LSA*;

(f)   drafting wills;

(g)   acting as nominee, trustee or executor in England and Wales, where such activity is not provided as a subsidiary but necessary part of a *separate business* providing financial services; and

(h)   providing legal advice or drafting legal documents not included in (a) to (g) above where such activity is not provided as a subsidiary but necessary part of some other service which is one of the main services of the *separate business*;

'*publicity*' includes all promotional material and activity, including the name or description of your *firm*, stationery, advertisements, brochures, websites, directory entries, media appearances, promotional press releases, and direct approaches to potential *clients* and other *persons*, whether conducted in person, in writing, or in electronic form, but does not include press releases prepared on behalf of a *client*;

'*pure protection contract*' has the meaning given in rule 8(1) of the SRA Financial Services (Scope) Rules 2001;

'*recognised body*' means a body recognised by the *SRA* under section 9 of the *AJA*;

'*recognised sole practitioner*' means a *solicitor* or *REL* authorised by the *SRA* under section 1B of the Solicitors Act 1974 to *practise* as a *sole practitioner*;

'*referrals*' includes any situation in which another *person*, business or organisation introduces or refers a *client* to your business, recommends your business to a *client* or otherwise puts you and a *client* in touch with each other;

'*REL*' means registered European lawyer, namely, an individual registered with the *SRA* under regulation 17 of the European Communities (Lawyer's Practice) Regulations 2000 (SI 2000/1119);

'*REL-controlled body*' means an *authorised body* in which *RELs* or *RELs* together with *lawyers of England and Wales* and/or European *lawyers* registered with the *BSB*, constitute the national group of *lawyers* with the largest (or equal largest) share of control of the body, either as individual *managers* or by their share in the control of bodies which are *managers*, and for this purpose *RELs* and European *lawyers* registered with the BSB belong to the national group of England and Wales;

'*Regulated Activities Order*' means the Financial Services and Markets Act 2000 (Regulated Activities) Order 2001;

'*regulated mortgage contract*' has the meaning given by article 61(3) of the *Regulated Activities Order*;

'*reserved legal activity*' has the meaning given in section 12 of the *LSA*, and includes the exercise of a right of audience, the conduct of litigation, reserved instrument activities, probate activities, notarial activities and the administration of oaths, as defined in Schedule 2 of the *LSA*;

'*RFL*' means registered foreign lawyer, namely, an individual registered with the *SRA* under section 89 of the Courts and Legal Services Act 1990;

'*SA*' means the Solicitors Act 1974;

'*separate business*' means a business which is not an *authorised body*, a *recognised sole practitioner*, an *authorised non-SRA firm* or an *in-house practice* and includes businesses situated overseas;

'*societas Europaea*' means a European public limited liability *company* within the meaning of article 1 of Council Regulation 2157/2001/EC;

'*Society*' means the Law Society, in accordance with section 87 of the *SA*;

'*sole practitioner*' means a *solicitor* or *REL* practising as a sole principal, and does not include a *solicitor* or *REL practising* in-house;

'*solicitor*' means a person who has been admitted as a solicitor of the Senior Courts of England and Wales and whose name is on the roll kept by the *Society* under section 6 of the *SA*, save that in the *SIIR* includes a person who practises as a solicitor whether he or she has in force a practising certificate and also includes practice under home title of a former *REL* who has become a solicitor;

'*SRA*' means the Solicitors Regulation Authority, and reference to the SRA as an *approved regulator* or *licensing authority* means the SRA carrying out regulatory functions assigned to the *Society* as an *approved regulator* or *licensing authority*;

'*SRA Authorisation Rules*' means the SRA Authorisation Rules for Legal Services Bodies and Licensable Bodies 2011;

'*subsidiary company*' has the meaning given in the Companies Act 2006;

'*substantial ownership interest*' in a *firm* ('A') means:
    (a) owning at least 10% of the shares in A;
    (b) owning at least 10% of the shares in a parent undertaking of A;

(c) being entitled to exercise, or control the exercise of, at least 10% of the *voting rights* in A; or

(d) being entitled to exercise, or control the exercise of, at least 10% of the *voting rights* of a parent undertaking of A;

and for the purpose of this definition, 'parent undertaking' has the meaning given in the Companies Act 2006;

*'substantially common interest'* for the purposes of Chapter 3 of the *SRA Code of Conduct*, means a situation where there is a clear common purpose in relation to any matter or a particular aspect of it between the *clients* and a strong consensus on how it is to be achieved and the *client conflict* is peripheral to this common purpose;

*'UK'* means United Kingdom;

*'undertaking'* means a statement, given orally or in writing, whether or not it includes the word 'undertake' or 'undertaking', made by or on behalf of you or your *firm*, in the course of practice, or by you outside the course of practice but as a *solicitor* or *REL*, to someone who reasonably places reliance on it, that you or your *firm* will do something or cause something to be done, or refrain from doing something;

*'voting rights'* in relation to a body which does not have general meetings at which matters are decided by the exercise of *voting rights*, means the right under the constitution of the body to direct the overall policy of the body or alter the terms of its constitution.

## CHAPTER 15 – TRANSITIONAL PROVISIONS

1. For the avoidance of doubt, where a breach of any provision of the Solicitors' Code of Conduct 2007 comes to the attention of the *SRA* after 6 October 2011, this shall be subject to action by the *SRA* notwithstanding any repeal of the relevant provision.

2. From 31 March 2012, Chapter 13 shall have effect subject to the following amendment:

   (a) paragraphs 1(b)(iii) and 1(e) shall be omitted.

3. From 31 March 2012, Chapter 14 shall have effect subject to the following amendments:

   (a) in the definition of *authorised body*, the words ', and include a sole practitioner authorised by the SRA' shall be inserted after '*recognised body*';

   (b) in the definition of '*manager*' the words '(ai) a *sole practitioner*;' shall be inserted before the words '(a) a *member* of an *LLP*;';

   (c) in the definition of *practice*, sub-paragraph (d)(i) and, in sub-paragraph (g) the words 'or *recognised sole practitioner*' shall be omitted;

   (d) in the definition of *separate business*, the words '*recognised sole practitioner*' shall be omitted;

   (e) the following shall be substituted for the definition of *recognised body*:

   'means a legal services body recognised by the *SRA* under section 9 of the *AJA*, and includes a *sole practitioner* authorised by the *SRA*;';

   (f) the definition of *recognised sole practitioner* shall be omitted and the following definition inserted after the definition of '*sole practitioner*':

   '*sole practitioner authorised by the SRA*' means a *solicitor* or *REL* authorised by the *SRA* under section 1B of the *SA* or section 9 of the *AJA* to practise as a *sole practitioner*;'.

# Draft SRA Handbook Glossary

## GLOSSARY

**Important: The Glossary is currently a draft.** The final version of the Glossary, which we will publish in the summer, will comprise all the terms used throughout the Handbook, and set out their definitions. Terms which are defined, and which are being used in their defined sense, will appear in the text in italics. The Glossary will be central to all the rules and regulations within the Handbook. When we publish the final version of the Glossary, we will have removed all the individual interpretation clauses which currently appear within these rules and regulations.

### INTRODUCTION

This section of the Handbook contains:

* the SRA Handbook Glossary.

The Glossary comprises all the terms which are used throughout the Handbook and sets out their definitions.

Terms which are defined, and which are being used in their defined sense, appear in the text in italics.

We believe that the Glossary provides a unifying element to the Handbook and, for this reason, the individual sets of provisions which comprise the Handbook do not contain their own interpretation clauses. We consider that the unified Glossary will assist users and provide cohesion to the Handbook.]

*academic stage of training* means that stage of the training of an entrant to the *solicitors'* profession which is completed by satisfying regulation 3 of the *SRA Training Regulations* Part 1 – Qualification Regulations.

*accounting period* has the meaning given in rule 33 of the *SRA Accounts Rules*.

*actively participate in* means, in relation to a *separate business*, having any active involvement in the *separate business*, and includes:

    (a) any direct control over the business, and any indirect control through another person such as a spouse; and

    (b) any active participation in the business or the provision of its services to customers.

*adequate training* under a training contract means:

    (a) gaining at least three months' experience in each of at least three different areas of English law;

(b) developing skills in both contentious and non-contentious areas; and

(c) being given the opportunity to practise and/or observe the activities set out in the *Practice Skills Standards*.

*adjudicator* in the *SRA Cost of Investigations Regulations* means a person not involved in the investigation or preparation of a case who is authorised by the SRA to make an *SRA finding*; and in the *SRA Disciplinary Procedure Rules* means a person not involved in the investigation or preparation of a case who is authorised by the SRA to take *disciplinary decisions*.

*agreed fee* has the meaning given in rule 17(5) of the *SRA Accounts Rules*.

*agreement provider* has the meaning given by article 63J(3) of the *Regulated Activities Order* read with paragraphs (6) and (7) of that article.

*agreement seller* has the meaning given by article 63J(3) of the *Regulated Activities Order*.

AJA means the Administration of Justice Act 1985.

*appellate body* means the body designated as such in accordance with section 80(1) of the LSA.

*applicant* means a person or persons applying for a grant out of the Compensation Fund under rule 3 of the *SRA Compensation Fund Rules*.

*applicant body* means a *licensable body* or a *legal services body* which makes an application to the SRA for *authorisation* in accordance with the *SRA Authorisation Rules*.

*application for admission* means application to *us* for a *certificate of satisfaction* under section 3(1) of the SA and for admission as a *solicitor* under section 3(2) of the SA.

*appointed person* in the SIIR, means any person who is designated as a fee-earner in accordance with any arrangements made from time to time between the *firm* and the Legal Services Commission pursuant to the provisions of the Access to Justice Act 1999, regardless of whether the services performed for the *firm* by that person in accordance with Rule 4.1 of those Rules are performed pursuant to such arrangements or otherwise, and who is engaged by the *firm* under a contract for services in the course of the *private practice* of the *firm*.

*appointed representative* has the meaning given in FSMA.

*approved regulator* means any body listed as an approved regulator in paragraph 1 of Schedule 4 to the LSA or designated as an approved regulator by an order under paragraph 17 of that Schedule.

ARP means the Assigned Risks Pool, namely, the arrangements by which an *eligible firm* may obtain professional indemnity insurance against civil liability by means of an *ARP policy* on the terms set out in Part 3 of the SIIR.

*ARP default premium* means the premium calculated in accordance with Part 2 of Appendix 2 to the SIIR.

*ARP manager* means the manager of the ARP being any person from time to time appointed by the SRA to carry out all or any particular functions of the manager of the ARP or the SRA and any such person.

*ARP policy* means a contract of professional indemnity insurance issued by the *ARP manager* on behalf of *qualifying insurers* to an *eligible firm* in the ARP including where the context permits a *policy* provided to a *firm in default*.

*ARP premium* means the premium calculated in accordance with Part 1 of Appendix 2 to the SIIR.

*ARP run-off policy* means a contract of professional indemnity insurance issued by the *ARP manager* on behalf of *qualifying insurers* to a *run-off firm* in the ARP.

*ARP run-off premium* means the premium calculated in accordance with Part 3 of Appendix 2 to the SIIR.

*arrangement* in relation to financial services, fee sharing and *referrals* in chapters 1, 6 and 9 of the *SRA Code of Conduct*, means any express or tacit agreement between you and another person, whether contractually binding or not.

*assessment organisation* in the QLTSR, means the organisation awarded the initial three year contract to provide the *QLTS assessments*, together with any other organisations subsequently authorised to provide the *QLTS assessments* after the initial three year period has expired.

*assets* includes money, documents, wills, deeds, investments and other property.

*associate* has the meaning given in paragraph 5 to Schedule 13 of the LSA, namely:

    (1)  'associate', in relation to a *person* ('A') and –

          (a)  a shareholding in a body ('S'), or

          (b)  an entitlement to exercise or control the exercise of voting power in a body ('V'),

    means a *person* listed in sub-paragraph (2).

    (2)  The *persons* are–

          (a)  the spouse or civil partner of A,

          (b)  a child or stepchild of A (if under 18),

          (c)  the *trustee* of any settlement under which A has a life interest in possession (in Scotland a life interest),

          (d)  an undertaking of which A is a *director*,

          (e)  an *employee* of A,

          (f)  a *partner* of A (except, where S or V is a *partnership* in which A is a *partner*, another *partner* in S or V),

          (g)  if A is an undertaking–

              (i)  a *director* of A,

              (ii)  a subsidiary undertaking of A, or

              (iii)  a *director* or *employee* of such a subsidiary undertaking,

          (h)  if A has with any other *person* an agreement or arrangement with respect to the acquisition, holding or disposal of shares or other interests in S or V (whether or not they are interests within the meaning of section 72(3) of the LSA), that other *person*, or

          (i)  if A has with any other *person* an agreement or arrangement under which they undertake to act together in exercising their voting power in relation to S or V, that *person*.

*associated firm* means:

    (a)  a *partnership* with whom you have one *partner* in common;

    (b)  a LLP or a *company* without shares with whom you have one *member* in common; or

    (c)  a *company* with shares with whom you have one *owner* in common.

*authorisation* granted to a body under Rule 6 of the *SRA Authorisation Rules* means:

(a)   recognition under section 9 of the AJA, if it is granted to a *legal services body*; and

(b)   a licence under Part 5 of the LSA, if it is granted to a *licensable body*;

   and the term '*certificate of authorisation*' shall be construed accordingly.

*authorised activities* means:

(a)   any *reserved legal activity* in respect of which the body is authorised;

(b)   any other *legal activity*;

(c)   any other activity in respect of which a *licensed body* is regulated pursuant to Part 5 of the LSA; and

(d)   any other activity a *recognised body* carries out in connection with its *practice*.

*authorised body* means a body that has been authorised by the SRA to practise as a *licensed body* or a *recognised body*.

*authorised CPD course providers* means those providers authorised by *us* to provide training that attracts CPD hours as a result of attendance.

*authorised distance learning provider* means those providers authorised by *us* to provide distance learning courses delivered by methods including correspondence, webinar, webcast, podcast, DVD, video and audio cassettes, television or radio broadcasts and computer based learning programmes.

*authorised insurer* means:

(a)   a person who has permission under Part IV of FSMA to effect or carry out contracts of insurance of a relevant class;

(b)   a person who carries on an insurance market activity, within the meaning of section 316(3) of FSMA;

(c)   an EEA Firm of the kind mentioned in paragraph 5(d) of Schedule 3 to FSMA, which has permission under paragraph 15 of that Schedule (as a result of qualifying for authorisation under paragraph 12 of that Schedule) to effect or carry out contracts of insurance of a relevant class; or

(d)   a person who does not fall within paragraph (a), (b) or (c) and who may lawfully effect or carry out contracts of insurance of a relevant class in a member state other than the UK,

where relevant 'class' has the meaning set out in section 87(1B) of the SA provided that this definition must be read with section 22 of FSMA, any relevant order under that section, and Schedule 2 to FSMA.

*authorised non-SRA firm* means a firm which is authorised to carry on *legal activities* by an *approved regulator* other than the SRA.

*authorised person(s)*

(1)   subject to sub-paragraph (2) below, means a person who is authorised by the SRA or another *approved regulator* to carry on a *legal activity* and for the purposes of the *SRA Authorisation Rules*, the *SRA Practice Framework Rules* and the SRA Recognised Bodies Regulations 2011 includes a *solicitor*, a *sole practitioner*, an REL, an EEL, an RFL, an *authorised body*, an *authorised non-SRA firm* and a *European corporate practice* and the terms '*authorised individual*' and '*non-authorised person*' shall be construed accordingly.

(2)   in the *SRA Financial Services (Scope) Rules*, has the meaning given in section 31 of FSMA.

*authorised role holder* means COLP, COFA *owner* or *manager* under rules 8.5 and 8.6 of the *SRA Authorisation Rules* and '*authorised role*' should be construed accordingly.

*bank* has the meaning given in section 87(1) of the SA.

*barrister* in the *SRA Higher Rights of Audience Regulations*, means a person called to the bar by one of the Inns of Court and who has completed pupillage and is authorised by the General Council of the Bar to practise as a barrister.

*beneficiary* means a person with a beneficial entitlement to funds held by the *Society* on *statutory trust*.

*best list* means a list of potential beneficial entitlements to *statutory trust monies* which, in cases where it is not possible to create a *reconciled list*, is, in the view of the SRA, the most reliable that can be achieved with a reasonable and proportionate level of work taking into account the circumstances of the *intervention* and the nature of the evidence available.

*body* where the context permits includes a *sole practitioner*, and a special body within the meaning of section 106 of the LSA.

*body corporate* means a company, an LLP, or a *partnership* which is a legal person in its own right.

*broker funds arrangement* means an arrangement between a *firm* and a *life office* (or operator of a *regulated collective investment scheme*) under which the *life office* (or operator of the *regulated collective investment scheme*) agrees to establish a separate fund whose composition may be determined by instructions from the *firm* and in which it is possible for more than one *client* to invest.

*BSB* means the Bar Standards Board.

*building society* means a building society within the meaning of the Building Societies Act 1986.

*buyer* includes a prospective buyer.

*candidate* means a *person* who is assessed by the SRA for approval as an *owner*, *manager* or *compliance officer* under Part 4 of the *SRA Authorisation Rules*.

CCBE means the Council of the Bars and Law Societies of Europe.

*CCBE Code* means the CCBE's Code of Conduct for European lawyers.

*CCBE state* means any state whose legal profession is a full member, an associate member or an observer member of the CCBE.

*certificate of eligibility* means a certificate issued by *us* confirming eligibility to take assessments under QLTSR, or the QLTT under QLTR, or an authorisation under those regulations to apply for admission as a *solicitor* without taking any test or assessment.

*certificate of enrolment* should be construed as evidence of *student enrolment* within the *SRA Training Regulations* Part 1 – Qualifying Regulations.

*certificate of satisfaction* means a certificate or certifying letter from *us* confirming that *you* have received adequate training and are of the proper *character and suitability* to be a *solicitor* as required by the *SRA Training Regulations*.

*certificate of training* means the certification by a *training principal* that a *trainee* has received training in accordance with the *SRA Training Regulations* Part 2 – Training Providers Regulations.

*character and suitability* satisfies the requirement of section 3 of the SA in order that an individual shall be admitted as a *solicitor*.

*charity* has the meaning given in section 96(1) of the Charities Act 1993.

*circumstances* means an incident, occurrence, fact, matter, act or omission which may give rise to a *claim* in respect of civil liability.

*claim* means a demand for, or an assertion of a right to, civil compensation or civil damages or an intimation of an intention to seek such compensation or damages. For these purposes, an obligation on an *insured firm* and/or any *insured* to remedy a breach of the Solicitors' Accounts Rules 1998 (as amended from time to time), or any rules (including, without limitation, the *SRA Accounts Rules*) which replace the Solicitors' Accounts Rules 1998 in whole or in part, shall be treated as a claim, and the obligation to remedy such breach shall be treated as a civil liability for the purposes of clause 1, whether or not any person makes a demand for, or an assertion of a right to, civil compensation or civil damages or an intimation of an intention to seek such compensation or damages as a result of such breach, except where any such obligation may arise as a result of the insolvency of a bank (as defined in section 87 of the SA) or a building society (within the meaning of the Building Societies Act 1986) which holds *client money* in a *client account* of the *insured firm* or the failure of such bank or building society generally to repay monies on demand.

*claimant* means:
  (a) in the SRA Statutory Trust Rules, a person making a claim to statutory trust monies; and
  (b) in the SIIR and MTC, a person or entity which has made or may make a claim including a claim for contribution or indemnity.

*claim for redress* has the meaning given in section 158 of the LSA.

*client* means:
  (a) in the *SRA Code of Conduct*, the person for whom you act and where the context permits, includes prospective and former clients;
  (b) in Parts A-F of the *SRA Accounts Rules*, the person for whom *you* act; and
  (c) in the *SRA Financial Services (Scope) Rules*, in relation to any *regulated activities* carried on by a *firm* for a *trust* or the estate of a deceased person (including a controlled *trust*), the *trustees* or personal representatives in their capacity as such and not any person who is a beneficiary under the *trust* or interested in the estate.

*client account* has the meaning given in Rule 13(2) of the *SRA Accounts Rules*, save that for the purposes of Part G (Overseas practice) of the *SRA Accounts Rules*, 'client account' means an account at a bank or similar institution, subject to supervision by a public authority, which is used only for the purpose of holding *client money* and/or *trust* money, and the title or designation of which indicates that the funds in the account belong to the client or clients of a *solicitor* or REL or are held subject to a *trust*.

*client conflict* for the purposes of Chapter 3 of the *SRA Code of Conduct*, means any situation where you owe separate duties to act in the best interests of two or more *clients* in relation to the same or related matters, and those duties conflict, or there is a significant risk that those duties may conflict.

*client money* has the meaning given in Rule 12 of the *SRA Accounts Rules*, save that for the purposes of Part G (Overseas practice) of the *SRA Accounts Rules*, means money received or held for or on behalf of a client or *trust* (but excluding money which is held or received by a multi-disciplinary practice—a *licensed body* providing a range of different services—in relation to those activities for which it is not regulated by the SRA).

COFA means compliance officer for finance and administration in accordance with rule 8.5 of the *SRA Authorisation Rules*, and in relation to a *licensable body* is a reference to its HOFA.

*collective investment scheme* means (in accordance with section 235 of FSMA (Collective Investment Schemes)) any arrangements with respect to property of any description, including money, the purpose or effect of which is to enable persons taking part in the arrangements (whether by becoming owners of the property or any part of it or otherwise) to participate in or receive profits or income arising from the acquisition, holding, management or disposal of the property or sums paid out of such profits or income, which are not excluded by the Financial Services and Markets Act (Collective Investment Schemes) Order 2001 (SI 2001/1062).

COLP means compliance officer for legal practice in accordance with rule 8.5 of the *SRA Authorisation Rules* and in relation to a *licensable body* is a reference to its HOLP.

*comparable jurisdiction* means:
- (a)  for lawyers qualified through the QLTR, those jurisdictions listed in paragraphs 1 and 2 of the Schedule to the QLTR; or
- (b)  for lawyers qualified through the QLTSR, *recognised jurisdictions* as defined in the QLTSR.

*Companies Acts* means the Companies Act 1985 and the Companies Act 2006.

*company* means a company registered under the *Companies Acts*, an *overseas* company incorporated in an *Establishment Directive state* and registered under the Companies Act 1985 and/or the Companies Act 2006 or a *societas Europaea*.

*competing for the same objective* for the purposes of Chapter 3 of the *SRA Code of Conduct* means any situation in which one or more *clients* are competing for an 'objective' which, if attained by one *client* will make that 'objective' unattainable to the other *client* or *clients* and 'objective' means, for the purposes of Chapter 3, an asset, contract or business opportunity which one or more *clients* are seeking to acquire or recover through a liquidation (or some other form of insolvency process) or by means of an auction or tender process or a bid or offer which is not public.

*complaint* means an oral or written expression of dissatisfaction which alleges that the complainant has suffered (or may suffer) financial loss, distress, inconvenience or other detriment.

*compliance officer* is a reference to a body's COLP or its COFA.

*compulsory professional indemnity insurance* means the insurance you are required to have in place under the SIIR.

*conflict of interests* means any situation where:
- (a)  you owe separate duties to act in the best interests of two or more *clients* in relation to the same or related matters, and those duties conflict, or there is a significant risk that those duties may conflict (a '*client conflict*'); or
- (b)  your duty to act in the best interests of any *client* in relation to a matter conflicts, or there is a significant risk that it may conflict, with your own interests in relation to that or a related matter (an '*own interest conflict*').

*connected with* means in relation to a *separate business* for the purpose of Chapter 12 of the *SRA Code of Conduct*:
- (a)  having one or more partner(s), owner(s), director(s) or member(s) in common with the separate business;
- (b)  being a subsidiary company of the same holding company as the separate business; or
- (c)  being a subsidiary company of the separate business.

*contract of insurance* means (in accordance with article 3(1) of the Regulated Activities Order) any contract of insurance which is a long-term insurance contract or a general insurance contract.

*contractually based investment* has the meaning given by article 3(1) of the Regulated Activities Order but does not include an investment which falls within the definition of a packaged product.

*contributions* means contributions previously made to the fund in accordance with Part III of the Solicitors' Indemnity Rules 2007 (or any earlier corresponding provisions), and any additional sums paid in accordance with Rule 16 of the SRA Indemnity Rules.

*controller* has the meaning given in the section 422 of FSMA.

*CPD* means continuing professional development, namely, the training requirement(s) set by us to ensure solicitors and RELs maintain competence.

*costs* means your fees and disbursements.

*Council* has the meaning given in section 87 of the SA.

*court* means any court, tribunal or enquiry of England and Wales, or a British court martial, or any court of another jurisdiction.

*Court of Protection deputy*
    (a)  For the purposes of the SRA Accounts Rules includes a deputy who was appointed by the Court of Protection as a receiver under the Mental Health Act 1983 before the commencement date of the Mental Capacity Act 2005; and
    (b)  For the purposes of the *SRA Authorisation Rules* and *SRA Practice Framework Rules* also includes equivalents in other *Establishment Directive* states.

*CPD training record* means a record of all CPD undertaken to comply with the *SRA Training Regulations* Part 3 – CPD Regulations.

*CPD year* means each year commencing 1 November to 31 October.

CPE means the Common Professional Examination, namely, a course, including assessments and examinations, approved by the JASB for the purposes of completing the *academic stage of training* for those who have not *satisfactorily completed* a QLD.

*date of any notification or notice given* is deemed to be:
    (a)  the date on which the communication is delivered to or left at the recipient's address or is sent electronically to the recipient's e-mail or fax address;
    (b)  if the recipient is *practising*, seven days after the communication has been sent by post or document exchange to the recipient's last notified *practising address*; or
    (c)  if the recipient is not *practising*, seven days after the communication has been sent by post or document exchange to the recipient's last notified contact address.

*defaulting practitioner* means:
    (a)  a *solicitor* in respect of whose act or default, or in respect of whose *employee's* act or default, an application for a grant is made;
    (b)  an REL in respect of whose act or default, or in respect of whose *employee's* act or default, an application for a grant is made;
    (c)  a *recognised body* in respect of whose act or default, or in respect of whose *manager's* or *employee's* act or default, an application for a grant is made;
    (d)  an RFL who is a *manager* of a *partnership*, LLP or *company* together with a *solicitor*, an REL or a *recognised body*, and in respect of whose act or default or in respect of whose *employee's* act or default, an application for a grant is made; or

(e)    a *licensed body* in respect of whose act or default, or in respect of whose *owner's*, or *manager's* or *employee's* act or default, an application for a grant is made;

and the expressions 'defaulting *solicitor*', 'defaulting REL', 'defaulting *recognised body*', 'defaulting RFL' and 'defaulting *licensed body*' shall be construed accordingly.

*decision period* is the period specified in Rule 5 of the *SRA Authorisation Rules*.

*defence costs*

(1)    means legal costs and disbursements and investigative and related expenses reasonably and necessarily incurred with the consent of the *insurer* in:

   (a)    defending any proceedings relating to a *claim*; or

   (b)    conducting any proceedings for indemnity, contribution or recovery relating to a *claim*; or

   (c)    investigating, reducing, avoiding or compromising any actual or potential *claim*; or

   (d)    acting for any *insured* in connection with any investigation, inquiry or disciplinary proceeding (save in respect of any disciplinary proceeding under the authority of the *Society* (including, without limitation, the SRA and *the Tribunal*)).

(2)    Defence costs do not include any internal or overhead expenses of the *insured firm* or the *insurer* or the cost of any *insured's* time.

*difference in conditions policy* means a contract of professional indemnity insurance, made between one or more *qualifying insurers* and a *firm*, which provides cover including the MTC as modified in accordance with paragraph 2 of Appendix 3 to the SIIR.

*Diploma in Law* means a graduate or postgraduate diploma in law or second degree awarded by a body authorised by the JASB for the purposes of completing the *academic stage of training* for those who have not *satisfactorily completed* a QLD.

*director* means a director of a *company*; and in relation to a *societas Europaea* includes:

   (a)    in a two-tier system, a member of the management organ and a member of the supervisory organ; and

   (b)    in a one-tier system, a member of the administrative organ.

*disbursement* means, in respect of those activities for which the practice is regulated by the SRA, any sum spent or to be spent on behalf of the *client* or *trust* (including any VAT element).

*disciplinary decision* means a decision, following an *SRA finding*, to exercise one or more of the powers provided by:

   (a)    section 44D(2) and (3) of the SA;

   (b)    paragraph 14B(2) and (3) of Schedule 2 to the AJA; or

   (c)    section 95 or section 99 of the LSA;

or to otherwise give a *regulated person* a written rebuke or to publish details of a written rebuke or a direction to pay a penalty in accordance with the *SRA Disciplinary Procedure Rules*.

*discipline investigation* means:

   (a)    subject to sub-paragraph (b), an investigation by the SRA to determine whether a person should be subject to an *SRA finding*, a *disciplinary decision* or an application to *the Tribunal* under rule 10 of the *SRA Disciplinary Procedure Rules*; and

   (b)    for the purposes of the *SRA Cost of Investigations Regulations*, an investigation by the SRA to determine whether a regulated person should be subject to an *SRA finding* or an application to *the Tribunal*.

*discrimination* has the meaning set out in the Equality Act 2010, being when person (A) discriminates against another (B) if, because of a protected characteristic, A treats B less favourably than A treats or would treat others.

*Disqualified* refers to a *person* who has been disqualified under section 99 of the LSA by the SRA or by any other *approved regulator*.

*Document* in Chapter 10 of the *SRA Code of Conduct*, includes documents, whether written or electronic, relating to the *firm's client accounts* and *office accounts*.

*EEL* means exempt European *lawyer*, namely, a member of an *Establishment Directive profession*:

    (a)  registered with the BSB; or

    (b)  based entirely at an office or offices outside England and Wales,

who is not a *lawyer of England and Wales* (whether entitled to *practise* as such or not).

*eligible firm* in the SIIR means any *firm* which is eligible to be in the ARP, being any *firm* other than:

    (a)  a *firm* that has been in the ARP or, in respect of a *licensed body*, any similar arrangement for the provision of professional indemnity insurance for six months or more in the four *indemnity periods* immediately prior to the date from which cover is sought, without the prior written approval of the *Council* unless:

        (i)    subject to sub-paragraph;

        (ii)   immediately prior to 1 October 2011 the *firm* was in the ARP and had been in the ARP, without the prior written approval of the *Council*, for less than twelve months in the four *indemnity periods* immediately prior to that date, in which case the *firm* is eligible to be in the ARP only for any unexpired part of the twelve month period; or

        (iii)  immediately prior to 1 October 2010 the *firm* was in the ARP and had been in the ARP, without the prior written approval of the *Council*, for less than twenty four months (or twenty five months in the case of a *firm* which was in the ARP for the whole of the *indemnity period* from 1 September 2003 to 30 September 2004) in the four *indemnity periods* immediately prior to that date, in which case the *firm* is eligible to be in the ARP only for any unexpired part of the twenty four or twenty five month period (as the case may be);

    (b)  a *firm* determined by the *Council* not to be an eligible firm by reason of its being treated as one single *firm* with one or more other *firms* already in the ARP for the purposes of Rule 12.5 or Rule 12.6; or

    (c)  subject to Rule 12.3, a *firm* that at the end of any *policy period* to which those Rules apply is in *policy default*; or

    (d)  a *firm* which applies to enter the ARP for any period in respect of which it already has in place a *policy* of *qualifying insurance* outside the ARP for all or part of that period except a *firm* that is required to obtain *qualifying insurance* pursuant to Rule 6; or

    (e)  a *firm* that has never had in place *qualifying insurance* except through the ARP, unless:

        (i)    subject to sub-paragraph

        (ii)   immediately prior to 1 October 2011 the *firm* was in the ARP and had been in the ARP, without the prior written approval of the *Council*, for less than twelve months in the four *indemnity periods* immediately prior to that date; or

        (iii)  immediately prior to 1 October 2010 the *firm* was in the ARP and had been in the ARP, without the prior written approval of the *Council*, for less than twenty four months (or twenty five months in the case of a *firm* which was in the ARP for the whole of the *indemnity period* from 1 September 2003 to 30 September 2004) in the four *indemnity period*s immediately prior to that date, in which case the *firm* is eligible to be in the ARP only for any unexpired part of the twenty four or twenty five month period (as the case may be).

*employee*

(1) for the purposes of the *SRA Code of Conduct*, includes an individual who is:

    (a)    employed as a *director* of a *company*;

    (b)    engaged under a contract of service (for example, as an assistant *solicitor*) by a *firm* or its wholly owned service company; or

    (c)    engaged under a contract for services (for example, as a consultant or a locum), made between a *firm* or organisation and:

        (i)    that individual;

        (ii)    an employment agency; or

        (iii)    a *company* which is not held out to the public as providing legal services and is wholly owned and directed by that individual, under which the *firm* or organisation has exclusive control over the individual's time for all or part of the individual's working week; or in relation to which the *firm* or organisation has designated the individual as a fee earner in accordance with arrangements between the *firm* or organisation and the Legal Services Commission pursuant to the Access to Justice Act 1999; and 'employer' is to be construed accordingly.

(2) means, for the purposes of the *SRA Financial Services (Scope) Rules*, an individual who is employed in connection with the *firm's regulated activities* under a contract of service or under a contract for services such that he or she is held out as an employee or consultant of the *firm*.

(3) means, for the purposes of the MTC, any person other than a *principal*:

    (a)    employed or otherwise engaged in the *insured firm's practice* (including under a contract for services) including, without limitation, as a *solicitor*, *lawyer*, *trainee solicitor* or *lawyer*, consultant, *associate*, locum tenens, agent, appointed person (as defined in the *SRA Indemnity Insurance Rules*), office or clerical staff member or otherwise;

    (b)    seconded to work in the *insured firm's practice*; or

    (c)    seconded by the *insured firm* to work elsewhere; but does not include any person who is engaged by the *insured firm* under a contract for services in respect of any work where that person is required, whether under the *SRA Indemnity Insurance Rules* or under the rules of any other professional body, to take out or to be insured under separate professional indemnity insurance in respect of that work.

*entitled to practise* means having the right to practise without restrictions or conditions as a *qualified lawyer* of the *recognised jurisdiction*.

*Establishment Directive* means the Establishment of Lawyers Directive 98/5/EC.

*Establishment Directive profession* means any profession listed in Article 1.2(a) of the *Establishment Directive*, including a solicitor, barrister or advocate of the UK.

*Establishment Directive state* means a state to which the *Establishment Directive* applies.

*European corporate practice* means a *lawyers'* practice which is a body incorporated in an *Establishment Directive state*, or a *partnership* with separate legal identity formed under the law of an *Establishment Directive state*:

(a) which has an office in an *Establishment Directive state* but does not have an office in England and Wales;

(b) whose ultimate beneficial owners include at least one individual who is not a *lawyer of England and Wales* but is, and is entitled to practise as, a *lawyer* of an *Establishment Directive profession*; and

(c) whose *managers* include at least one such individual, or at least one *body corporate* whose *managers* include at least one such individual.

*European cross-border practice* has the meaning set out in rule 2.1 of the SRA European Cross-border Rules.

*excess* means the first amount of a claim which is not covered by the insurance.

*execution-only* means a transaction which is effected by a firm for a client where the firm assumes on reasonable grounds that the client is not relying on the firm as to the merits or suitability of that transaction.

*exempt person* in the SRA Financial Services (Scope) Rules: means a person who is exempt from the general prohibition as a result of an exemption order made under section 38(1) or as a result of section 39(1) or 285(2) or (3) of FSMA and who, in engaging in the activity in question, is acting in the course of business in respect of which that person is exempt.

*exempting law degree* means a QLD incorporating an LPC, approved by us.

*expired run-off claim* means any claim made against the fund for indemnity under the SIIR in respect of which no preceding qualifying insurance remains in force to cover such claim, by reason only of:

(a) the run-off cover provided or required to be provided under the policy having been activated; and

(b) the sixth anniversary of the date on which cover under such *qualifying insurance* would have ended but for the activation of such run-off cover having passed; or

(c) (in the case of a *firm in default* or a *run-off firm*) the period of run-off cover provided or required to be provided under arrangements made to cover such claim through the ARP having expired.

*expired run-off cover* means either:

(a) (unless (b) below applies) the terms of the ARP *policy* in force at the time immediately prior to the date on which run-off cover was triggered under the *preceding qualifying insurance*, excluding clause 5 (Run-off cover) of the MTC, as if it were a contract between Solicitors Indemnity Fund Limited and the firm or person making an *expired run-off claim*; or

(b) where they are provided to Solicitors Indemnity Fund Limited prior to payment of the *claim*, the terms of the *preceding qualifying insurance*, provided that:

    (i) references in the *preceding qualifying insurance* to the *qualifying insurer* that issued such insurance shall be read as references to Solicitors Indemnity Fund Limited;

    (ii) any obligation owed by any insured under the *preceding qualifying insurance* to the *qualifying insurer* which issued such insurance shall be deemed to be owed to Solicitors Indemnity Fund Limited in place of such *qualifying insurer*, unless and to the extent that Solicitors Indemnity Fund Limited in its absolute discretion otherwise agrees;

    (iii) the obligations of the *fund* and/or any *insured* in respect of an *expired run-off claim* shall neither exceed nor be less than the requirements of the MTC which, in accordance with the applicable SIIR, such *preceding qualifying insurance* included or was required to include.

Solicitors Indemnity Fund Limited shall be under no obligation to take any steps to obtain the terms of any such *preceding qualifying insurance*, which for these purposes includes the terms on which it was written in respect of the *insured firm* or *person* in question, and not merely a standard policy wording.

*fees* in the *SRA Accounts Rules*, means *your* own charges or profit costs (including any VAT element).

*fee sharer* means another person or business who or which shares *your* fees.

FILEX means a Fellow of the Institute of Legal Executives.

*financial benefit* includes, for example, any commission, discount or rebate but does not include your fees or interest earned on any *client account*.

*financial institution* means any undertaking or unincorporated association which carries on a business of lending money (which may include mortgage lending) or otherwise providing or issuing credit including, without limitation, any bank or building society.

*firm* means:

(a) subject to sub-paragraph (b) and (e) below, an *authorised body*, a *recognised sole practitioner* or a body or individual which should be authorised by the SRA as a *recognised body* or *recognised sole practitioner* (but which could not be author-ised by another *approved regulator*);

(b) for the purposes of the *SRA Accounts Rules*, 'firm' has the same meaning as at sub-paragraph (a) above but can also include in-house practice;

(c) in Part G (Overseas practice) of the *SRA Accounts Rules*, any business through which a *solicitor* or REL carries on practice other than in-house practice;

(d) in the *SIIR:*

(i) any recognised sole practitioner; or

(ii) any recognised body (as constituted from time to time); or

(iii) any solicitor or REL who is a sole practitioner, unless that sole practi-tioner is a non-SRA firm; or

(iv) any partnership (as constituted from time to time) which is eligible to become a recognised body and which meets the requirements applica-ble to recognised bodies set out in the SRA Practice Framework Rules, SRA Recognised Bodies Regulations 2011 (until [31 March 2012]), and the SRA Authorisation Rules (from [31 March 2012]), unless that partnership is a non-SRA firm; or

(v) any licensed body in respect of its regulated activities, whether before or during any relevant indemnity period;

(e) In the *SRA European Cross-border Rules*, means any business through which a *solicitor* or REL carries on *practice* other than *in-house practice*.

*firm in default* in the SIIR, means a *firm* that has failed to obtain *qualifying insurance* outside the ARP and which:

(a) in the case of an *eligible firm*, has failed to apply in accordance with the SIIR to be admitted into the ARP before either the expiry (or earlier termination) of any *qualifying insurance* obtained outside the ARP or the start of its *practice*, which-ever is the later; or

(b)  in the case of a *firm* which is not an *eligible firm*, is a *firm* which is carrying on or continuing to carry on a *practice* without *qualifying insurance* outside the ARP; or

(c)  in the case of a *run-off firm*, is a *run-off firm* which has failed to make an application in the manner prescribed by the SIIR to be issued with an *ARP run-off policy*; or

(d)  is a *firm* which is a 'firm in default' by virtue of Rule 10.4 of the SIIR,

or a *firm* which, having previously obtained *qualifying insurance*, has failed to obtain alternative *qualifying insurance* when required to do so in accordance with Rule 6 of the SIIR.

*fit and proper* satisfies the requirement of Schedule 13 of the LSA in order that an individual may be an *authorised role holder*.

*foreign lawyer* means an individual who is not a solicitor or barrister of England and Wales, but who is a member, and entitled to practise as such, of a legal profession regulated within a jurisdiction outside England and Wales.

*foundations of legal knowledge* means those foundations of law the study of which is prescribed by *us* and the BSB through the JASB for the purpose of completing the *academic stage of training* by undertaking a QLD or CPE and passing the assessments and examinations set during that course.

FSA means the Financial Services Authority.

*FSA Register* means the record maintained by the FSA as required by section 347 of FSMA and including those persons that carry on, or are proposing to carry on, *insurance mediation activities*.

FSMA means the Financial Services and Markets Act 2000.

*full route to qualification* means that the applicant has not completed a shortened or fast-track route to qualification, which would be evidenced if non-domestic lawyers are not assessed on all the same outcomes/subjects/practices in the law of that jurisdiction as domestic candidates, prior to qualification.

*fund* means the fund maintained in accordance with the *SRA Indemnity Rules*.

*funeral plan contract* has the meaning given in article 59 of the *Regulated Activities Order*.

*general client account* has the meaning given in rule 13(5)(b) of the *SRA Accounts Rules* .

*general insurance contract* means any contract of insurance within Part I of Schedule 1 to the *Regulated Activities Order*.

*general prohibition* has the meaning given in section 19(2) of FSMA.

*higher courts* means the Crown Court, High Court, Court of Appeal and Supreme Court in England and Wales.

*higher courts advocacy qualification* means, subject to regulation 6 of the SRA Higher Rights of Audience Regulations, one of the qualifications referred to in regulation 3 of those regulations to exercise extended rights of audience in the *higher courts*.

HOFA means a Head of Finance and Administration within the meaning of paragraph 13(2) of Schedule 11 to the LSA.

*holding company* has the meaning given in the Companies Act 2006.

HOLP means a Head of Legal Practice within the meaning of paragraph 11(2) of Schedule 11 to the LSA.

*home purchaser* has the meaning given by article 63F(3) of the *Regulated Activities Order*.

*immigration work* means the provision of immigration advice and immigration services, as defined in section 82 of the Immigration and Asylum Act 1999.

*indemnity period* means:

    (a)  in the SIIR, the period of one year starting on 1 September 2000, 2001 or 2002, the period of 13 calendar months starting on 1 September 2003, or the period of one year starting on 1 October in any subsequent calendar year; and

    (b)  in the *SRA Indemnity Rules*, the period of one year commencing on 1 September in any calendar year from 1987 to 2002 inclusive, the period of 13 calendar months commencing on 1 September 2003, and the period of one year commencing on 1 October in any subsequent calendar year.

*independent intermediary* in chapter 6 of the *SRA Code of Conduct*, means an independent financial adviser who is able to advise on investment products from across the whole of the market and offers consumers the option of paying fees.

*individual pension contract* means a *pension policy* or *pension contract* under which contributions are paid to:

    (a)  a *personal pension scheme* approved under section 630 of the Income and Corporation Taxes Act 1988, whose sole purpose is the provision of annuities or lump sums under arrangements made by individuals in accordance with the scheme; or

    (b)  a retirement benefits scheme approved under section 591(2)(g) of the Income and Corporation Taxes Act 1988, for the provision of relevant benefits by means of an annuity contract made with an insurance company of the *employee's* choice.

*Insolvency event* means in relation to a qualifying insurer:

    (a)  the appointment of a provisional liquidator, administrator, receiver or an administrative receiver; or

    (b)  the approval of a voluntary arrangement under Part I of the Insolvency Act 1986 or the making of any other form of arrangement, composition or compounding with its creditors generally; or

    (c)  the passing of a resolution for voluntary winding up where the winding up is or becomes a creditors' voluntary winding up under Part IV of the Insolvency Act 1986; or

    (d)  the making of a winding up order by the court; or

    (e)  the making of an order by the court reducing the value of one or more of the *qualifying insurer's* contracts under section 377 of FSMA; or

    (f)  the occurrence of any event analogous to any of the foregoing insolvency events in any jurisdiction outside England and Wales.

*insurance mediation activity* means any of the following activities specified in the *Regulated Activities Order* which is carried on in relation to a *contract of insurance* or rights to or interests in a *life policy*:

    (a)  dealing in *investments* as agent;

    (b)  arranging (bringing about) deals in *investments*;

    (c)  making arrangements with a view to *transactions* in *investments*;

    (d)  assisting in the administration and performance of a *contract of insurance*;

    (e)  advising on *investments*;

    (f)  agreeing to carry on a regulated activity in (a) to (e) above.

*insurance mediation officer* means the individual within the management structure of the *firm* who is responsible for an *insurance mediation activity*.

*insurance undertaking* means an undertaking, whether or not an *insurer*, which carries on insurance business.

*insured* in the SIIR and MTC means each person and entity named or described as a person to whom the insurance extends and includes, without limitation, those referred to in clause 1.3 and, in relation to *prior practices* and *successor practices* respectively, those referred to in clauses 1.5 and 1.7.

*insured firm* means the *firm* (as defined for the purposes of the *SRA Indemnity Insurance Rules*) which contracted with the *insurer* to provide the insurance.

*insured firm's practice* means:
> (a)  the legal *practice* carried on by the *insured firm* as at the commencement of the *period of insurance*; and
> (b)  the continuous legal *practice* preceding and succeeding the *practice* referred to in paragraph (a) (irrespective of changes in ownership of the *practice* or in the composition of any *partnership* which owns or owned the *practice*).

*insurer* means:
> (a)  for the purposes of the *SRA Financial Services (Scope) Rules* a *firm* with permission to effect or carry out *contracts of insurance* (other than a bank); and
> (b)  for the purposes of the MTC the underwriter(s) of the insurance.

*integrated course* means a *Diploma in Law*/CPE incorporating an LPC, approved by *us*.

*interest* in the *SRA Accounts Rules* includes a sum in lieu of interest.

*interest holder* means a *person* who has an interest or an indirect interest, or holds a *material interest*, in a body (and 'indirect interest' and 'interest' have the same meaning as in the LSA), and references to '*holds an interest*' shall be construed accordingly.

*international lawyers* means lawyers who are not basing their application on a professional qualification as a *qualified lawyer* gained within the UK or within the EEA or Switzerland.

*intervened practitioner* means the *solicitor*, *recognised body*, *licensed body*, REL or RFL whose *practice* or *practices* are the subject of an *intervention*.

*intervention* means the exercise of the powers specified in section 35 and Schedule 1 of the SA, or section 9 and paragraphs 32 to 35 of Schedule 2 to the AJA, or section 89 and paragraph 5 of Schedule 14 to the Courts and Legal Services Act 1990, or section 102 and Schedule 14 of the LSA.

*introducer* means any person, business or organisation who or that introduces or refers *clients* to *your* business, or recommends *your* business to *clients* or otherwise puts *you* and *clients* in touch with each other.

*Investment*
> (1)  for the purposes of the *Financial Services (Scope) Rules*, any of the *investments* specified in Part III of the *Regulated Activities Order*.
> (2)  for the purposes of chapter 6 of the *SRA Code of Conduct* has the meaning given in the SRA Financial Services (Scope) Rules 2001.

*investment trust* means a closed-ended *company* which is listed in the UK or another member state and:
> (a)  is approved by the Inland Revenue under section 842 of the Income and Corporation Taxes Act 1988 (or, in the case of a newly formed *company*, has declared its intention to conduct its affairs so as to obtain approval); or
> (b)  s resident in another member state and would qualify for approval if resident and listed in the UK.

*investment trust savings scheme* means a dedicated service for investment in the securities of one or more *investment trust*s within a particular marketing group (and references to an *investment trust savings scheme* include references to securities to be acquired through that scheme).

*in-house practice* means *practice* as a *solicitor*, REL or RFL (as appropriate) in accordance with Rules 1.1(c)(B), 1.1(d)(B), 1.1(e), 1.2(f), 2.1(c)(B), 2.1(d)(B), 2.1(e), 2.2(f), 3.1(b)(B) or 3.1(c)(B) of the *SRA Practice Framework Rules*.

ISA means an *Individual Savers Account*, namely, an account which is a scheme of investment satisfying the conditions prescribed in the Individual Savings Account Regulations 1998 (S.I. 998/1870).

JASB means the Joint Academic Stage Board, namely, the joint committee of the BSB and the SRA responsible for the setting and implementation of policies in respect of the *academic stage of training*, and validation and review of *QLDs* and *CPEs*.

*Justice's Clerks Assistant* bears the meaning contained in the Assistants to Justice's Clerks Regulations 2006.

*lawyer* means a member of one of the following professions, entitled to practise as such:
- (a) the profession of solicitor, barrister or advocate of the UK;
- (b) a profession whose members are authorised to carry on *legal activities* by an *approved regulator* other than the SRA;
- (c) an *Establishment Directive profession* other than a UK profession;
- (d) a legal profession which has been approved by the SRA for the purpose of *recognised bodies* in England and Wales; and
- (e) any other regulated legal profession specified by the SRA for the purpose of this definition.

*lawyer-controlled body* means:
- (a) an *authorised body* in which *lawyers of England and Wales* constitute the national group of *lawyers* with the largest (or equal largest) share of control of the body either as individual *managers* or by their share in the control of bodies which are *managers*;
- (b) for the purposes of Part G (Overseas practice) of the *SRA Accounts Rules* the definition at sub-paragraph (a) above applies save that the second reference to 'lawyers' is to be given its natural meaning.

*lawyer of England & Wales* means:
- (a) a *solicitor*; or
- (b) an individual who is authorised to carry on *legal activities* in England and Wales by an *approved regulator* other than the SRA, but excludes a member of an *Establishment Directive profession* registered with the BSB under the *Establishment Directive*.

*lead insurer* means the insurer named as such in the *contract of insurance*, or, if no lead insurer is named as such, the first-named insurer on the relevant certificate of insurance.

*legal activity* has the meaning given in section 12 of the LSA and includes any *reserved legal activity* and any other activity which consists of the provision of legal advice or assistance, or representation in connection with the application of the law or resolution of legal disputes.

*Legal Ombudsman* means the scheme administered by the Office for Legal Complaints under Part 6 of the LSA.

*legally qualified* means any of the following:

(a)  a *lawyer*;

(b)  a *recognised body*;

(c)  an *authorised non-SRA firm* of which all the *managers* and *interest holders* are *lawyers* save that where another body ('A') is a *manager* of or has an interest in the firm, *non-authorised persons* are entitled to exercise, or control the exercise of, less than 10% of the *voting rights* in A;

(d)  *European corporate practice* of which all the *managers* and *interest holders* are *lawyers*;

and references to a '*legally qualified body*' shall be construed accordingly.

*legal services body* means a body which meets the criteria in Rule 13 (Eligibility criteria and fundamental requirements for recognised bodies) of the *SRA Practice Framework Rules*.

*licensable body* means a body which meets the criteria in rule 14 (Eligibility criteria and fundamental requirements for licensed bodies) of the *SRA Practice Framework Rules*.

*licensed body* means a body licensed by the SRA under Part 5 of the LSA.

*licensing authority* means an *approved regulator* which is designated as a licensing authority under Part 1 of Schedule 10 to the LSA, and whose licensing rules have been approved for the purposes of the LSA.

*life office* means a person with permission to effect or carry out *long-term insurance contracts*.

*life policy* means a *long-term insurance contract* other than a *pure protection contract* or a *reinsurance contract*, but including a *pension policy*.

LLP means a limited liability partnership incorporated under the Limited Liability Partnerships Act 2000.

*local authority* means any of those bodies which are listed in section 270 of the Local Government Act 1972 or in section 21(1) of the Local Government and Housing Act 1989.

*long-term care insurance contract* has the meaning given in the *Regulated Activities Order*.

*long-term insurance contract* has the meaning given in Part II of Schedule 1 to the *Regulated Activities Order*.

LPC means a Legal Practice Course, namely, a course the *satisfactory completion* of which is recognised by *us* as satisfying, in part, the *vocational stage of training* .

*LPC outcomes* means *our* minimum educational standards that LPC students must meet in order to *satisfactorily complete* the course.

LSA means the Legal Services Act 2007.

*manager* means:

(a)  a member of an LLP;

(b)  a *director* of a *company*;

(c)  a *partner* in a *partnership*; or

(d)  in relation to any other body, a member of its governing body,

save that for the purposes of:

(a)  Part G (Overseas practice) of the *SRA Accounts Rules* 'a manager' includes the director of any company, and is not limited to the director of a *company* as defined herein; and

(b)  the *SRA Cost of Investigations Regulations* and the *SRA Disciplinary Procedure Rules* where in (c) above terms partner and partnership are to be given their natural meaning.

*market making* means where a *firm* holds itself out as willing, as principal, to buy, sell or subscribe for *investments* of the kind to which the *transaction* relates at prices determined by the *firm* generally and continuously rather than in respect of each particular *transaction*.

*master policies and master policy certificates* means the policies and certificates referred to in Rule 5 of the *SRA Indemnity Rules* and *master policy insurers* means the *insurers* thereunder.

*material interest* has the meaning given to it in Schedule 13 to the LSA; and a person holds a 'material interest' in a body ('B'), if that person:

  (a)  holds at least 10% of the shares in B;

  (b)  is able to exercise significant influence over the management of B by virtue of the person's shareholding in B;

  (c)  holds at least 10% of the shares in a parent undertaking ('P') of B;

  (d)  is able to exercise significant influence over the management of P by virtue of the person's shareholding in P;

  (e)  is entitled to exercise, or control the exercise of, voting power in B which, if it consists of *voting rights*, constitutes at least 10% of the *voting rights* in B;

  (f)  is able to exercise significant influence over the management of B by virtue of the person's entitlement to exercise, or control the exercise of, *voting rights* in B;

  (g)  is entitled to exercise, or control the exercise of, voting power in P which, if it consists of *voting rights*, constitutes at least 10% of the *voting rights* in P; or

  (h)  is able to exercise significant influence over the management of P by virtue of the person's entitlement to exercise, or control the exercise of, *voting rights* in P;

and for the purpose of this definition, 'person' means:

  (i)  the person

  (ii)  any of the person's associates, or

  (iii)  the person and any of the person's associates taken together, and 'parent undertaking' and 'voting power' are to be construed in accordance with paragraphs 3 and 5 of Schedule 13 to the LSA.

*mature student* means someone who intends to undertake the *Diploma in Law* or CPE and who has:

  (a)  considerable experience or shown exceptional ability in an academic, professional, business or administrative field; and

  (b)  attained such standard of general education as we may consider sufficient.

MDP means a *licensed body* which is a multi-disciplinary practice providing a range of different services, only some of which are regulated by the SRA.

*member* means:

  (a)  in relation to a *company* a *person* who has agreed to be a member of the *company* and whose name is entered in the *company's* register of members; and

  (b)  in relation to an LLP, a member of that LLP.

*a member of a practice* means, in the SRA Indemnity Rules:

  (a)  any principal (including any *principal*) therein;

  (b)  any *director* or officer thereof, in the case of a *recognised body* or a *licensed body* which is a *company*;

  (c)  any member thereof in the case of a *recognised body* or a *licensed body* which is a LLP;

  (d)  any *recognised body* or a *licensed body* which is a *partner* or held out to be a *partner* therein and any officer of such *recognised body* or a *licensed body* which is a *company*, or any member of such *recognised body* or a *licensed body* which is a LLP;

(e) any person employed in connection therewith (including any *trainee solicitor*);

(f) any *solicitor* or REL who is a consultant to or associate in the practice;

(g) any *foreign lawyer* who is not an REL and who is a consultant or associate in the practice; and

(h) any *solicitor* or *foreign lawyer* who is working in the practice as an agent or locum tenens, whether he or she is so working under a contract of service or contract for services; and

includes the estate and/or personal representative(s) of any such *persons*.

*members of the public* for the purposes of Chapter 8 of the *SRA Code of Conduct*, does not include:

(a) a current or former *client*;

(b) another *firm* or its *manager*;

(c) an existing or potential professional or business connection; or

(d) a commercial organisation or public body.

MILEX means a Member of the Institute of Legal Executives.

*mixed payment* has the meaning given in rule 18(1) of the *SRA Accounts Rules*.

*modular training contract* means a *training contract* in which employment and training is provided by a *training contract consortium*, each member of which has a defined contribution to training process and content.

MTC means the Minimum Terms and Conditions with which a *policy* of *qualifying insurance* is required by the SIIR to comply, a copy of which is annexed as Appendix 1 to those Rules.

*non-lawyer* means:

(a) an individual who is not a *lawyer* practising as such; or

(b) a *body corporate* or *partnership* which is not:

   (i) an authorised body;

   (ii) an authorised non-SRA firm; or

   (iii) a business, carrying on the practice of lawyers from an office or offices outside England and Wales, in which a controlling majority of the owners and managers are lawyers,

save in Part G (Overseas practice) of the *SRA Accounts Rules* where the term lawyer is to be given its natural meaning.

*non-mainstream regulated activity* means a *regulated activity* of a *firm* regulated by the FSA in relation to which the conditions in the Professional Firms Sourcebook (5.2.1R) are satisfied.

*a non-registered European lawyer* means:

(a) in the *SRA Indemnity Rules*, a member of a legal profession which is covered by the *Establishment Directive*, but who is not:

   (i) a *solicitor*, REL or RFL,

   (ii) a barrister of England and Wales, Northern Ireland or the Irish Republic, or

   (iii) a Scottish advocate; and

(b) in the *SRA Financial Services (Scope) Rules*, a member of a profession covered by the Establishment Directive who is based entirely at an office or offices outside England and Wales and who is not a solicitor, REL or RFL.

*non-solicitor employer* means any employer other than a recognised body, recognised sole practitioner, licensed body or authorised non-SRA firm.

*non-SRA firm* means a sole practitioner, partnership, LLP or company which is not authorised to practise by the SRA, and which is either:

(a) authorised or capable of being authorised to practise by another *approved regulator*; or

(b) not capable of being authorised to practise by any *approved regulator*.

*occupational pension scheme* means any scheme or arrangement which is comprised in one or more documents or agreements and which has, or is capable of having, effect in relation to one or more descriptions or categories of employment so as to provide benefits, in the form of pensions or otherwise, payable on termination of service, or on death or retirement, to or in respect of earners with qualifying service in an employment of any such description or category.

*office account* means an account of the *firm* for holding *office money* and/or *out-of-scope money*, or other means of holding *office money* or *out-of-scope money* (for example, the office cash box or an account holding money regulated by a regulator other than the SRA).

*office money* has the meaning given in rule 12 of the *SRA Accounts Rules*.

*opt-out* means a *transaction* resulting from a decision by an individual to opt-out of or decline to join a final salary or money-purchase *occupational pension scheme* of which he or she is a current member, or which he or she is, or at the end of a waiting period will become, eligible to join, in favour of an *individual pension contract* or contracts.

*out-of-scope money* means money held or received by an MDP in relation to those activities for which it is not regulated by the SRA.

*overseas* means outside England and Wales.

*overseas practice* means:

(a) subject to sub-paragraph (b), *practice from an office* outside England and Wales, except in the case of an REL, where it means *practice from an office* in Scotland or Northern Ireland; and

(b) in the *SRA Indemnity Rules* means a practice carried on wholly from an *overseas* office or offices, including a *practice* deemed to be a *separate practice* by virtue of paragraph (b) of the definition of *separate practice*.

*own interest conflict* for the purpose of Chapter 3 of the *SRA Code of Conduct*, means any situation where your duty to act in the best interests of any *client* in relation to a matter conflicts, or there is a significant risk that it may conflict, with your own interests in relation to that or a related matter.

*owner* means, in relation to a body, a person with any ownership interest in the body, save that

(a) in the *SRA Authorisation Rules* owner means any *person* who holds a *material interest* in an *authorised body*, and in the case of a *partnership*, any *partner* regardless of whether they hold a *material interest* in the *partnership*; and

(b) for the purposes of Chapter 12 of the *SRA Code of Conduct* means a person having a substantial ownership interest in a *separate business* and 'own' and 'owned by' shall be construed accordingly.

*packaged product* means a life policy, a unit or share in a regulated collective investment scheme, or an investment trust savings scheme whether or not held within an ISA or PEP, or a stakeholder pension scheme.

*panel solicitors* means any solicitors appointed by the Solicitors Indemnity Fund in accordance with clause 14.15 of the SRA Indemnity Rules.

*parent training establishment* means one member of a training contract consortium which is authorised to take trainees and which has appointed a training principal who is responsible for the training of the training contract consortium's trainees.

*partner* means a person who is or is held out as a partner in a partnership save for in the SRA Accounts Rules, in which it means an individual who is or is held out as a partner in a partnership.

*partnership* means an unincorporated body in which persons are or are held out as partners and does not include a body incorporated as an LLP save that in the MTC means an unincorporated insured firm in which persons are or are held out as partners and does not include a insured firm incorporated as an LLP.

*participation* for the purposes of regulation 8 of the SRA Training Regulations Part 3 – CPD Regulations includes preparing, delivering and/or attending accredited courses and 'participating' should be construed accordingly.

*part-time* means working fewer than 32 hours per week.

*pension contract* means a right to benefits obtained by the making of contributions to an occupational pension scheme or to a personal pension scheme, where the contributions are paid to a regulated collective investment scheme.

*pension policy* means a right to benefits obtained by the making of contributions to an occupational pension scheme or to a personal pension scheme, where the contributions are paid to a life office.

*pension transfer* means a transaction resulting from a decision by an individual to transfer deferred benefits from a final salary occupational pension scheme, or from a money-purchase occupational pension scheme, in favour of an individual pension contract or contracts.

PEP means a personal equity plan within the Personal Equity Plan Regulations 1989.

*period of default* means in relation to a firm in default the period starting with the date when such firm first became a firm in default and ending with the date when it ceased to be a firm in default.

*period of insurance* means the period for which the insurance operates.

*permitted separate business* means for the purpose of Chapter 12 of the SRA Code of Conduct, a separate business offering any of the following services:
  (a) alternative dispute resolution;
  (b) financial services;
  (c) estate agency;
  (d) management consultancy;
  (e) company secretarial services;
  (f) acting as a parliamentary agent;
  (g) practising as a *lawyer* of another jurisdiction;
  (h) acting as a bailiff;
  (i) acting as nominee, *trustee* or executor outside England and Wales;
  (j) acting as a nominee, *trustee* or executor in England and Wales where such activity is provided as a subsidiary but necessary part of a *separate business* providing financial services;
  (k) providing legal advice or drafting legal documents not included in (a) to (j) above, where such activity is provided as a subsidiary but necessary part of some other service which is one of the main services of the *separate business*; and

(l)   providing any other business, advisory or agency service which could be provided through a *firm* or *in-house practice* but is not a *prohibited separate business activity.*

*person* means an individual or a body of persons (corporate or unincorporated).

*person under investigation* means a *person* subject to a *discipline investigation.*

*person who has an interest in a licensed body* means a *person* who has an interest or an indirect interest in a *licensed body* as defined by sections 72(3) and (5) of the LSA.

references to a *person who lacks capacity under Part 1 of the Mental Capacity Act 2005* include a 'patient' as defined by section 94 of the Mental Health Act 1983 and a person made the subject of emergency powers under that Act, and equivalents in other *Establishment Directive states.*

*personal pension scheme* means any scheme or arrangement which is not an *occupational pension scheme* or a *stakeholder pension scheme* and which is comprised in one or more instruments or agreements, having or capable of having effect so as to provide benefits to or in respect of people on retirement, or on having reached a particular age, or on termination of service in an employment.

*plan provider* has the meaning given by article 63B(3) of the *Regulated Activities Order* read with paragraphs (7) and (8) of that article.

*policy* means a contract of professional indemnity insurance made between one or more *persons,* each of which is a *qualifying insurer,* and a *firm,* including where the context permits an *ARP policy* and an *ARP run-off policy.*

*policy default*
(1)   means in the SIIR a failure on the part of a *firm* or any *principal* of that *firm:*

(a)   to pay by the earlier to occur of:

(i)     two months after the due date for payment; and
(ii)    the end of the *policy period,*
all or any part of the premium or any other sum due in respect of a *policy* (including without limitation any payment due under Rule 14.1 of those Rules); or

(b)   to pay by the earlier to occur of:

(i)     two months after the due date for payment; and
(ii)    the end of the *policy period,*
all or any part of any *ARP premium,* any *ARP default premium,* or any *ARP run-off premium,* or any instalment payable in relation thereto whether payable to the *ARP manager* or otherwise; or

(c)   to reimburse within two months a *qualifying insurer* (including the *ARP manager* on behalf of *qualifying insurers*) in respect of any amount falling within a *firm's policy* excess which has been paid on an insured's behalf to a *claimant* by a *qualifying insurer* or by the *ARP manager.*

(2)   For the purposes of this definition, the due date for payment means, in respect of any *policy* or any payment to be made under any *policy:*

(i)     the date on which such payment fell due under the terms of the *policy* or any related agreement or arrangement; or
(ii)    if a *firm* was first required under those or any previous Rules to effect such a *policy* prior to the date on which it did so, the date if earlier on which such payment would have fallen due had such *policy* been

effected by the *firm* when it was first required to do so under those Rules or any previous rules.

*policy period* means the period of insurance in respect of which risks may attach under a *policy* of *qualifying insurance*.

*practice* means the activities, in that capacity, of:

- (a)  a solicitor;
- (b)  an REL, from an office or offices within the UK;
- (c)  a member of an Establishment Directive profession registered with the BSB under the Establishment Directive, carried out from an office or offices in England and Wales;
- (d)  an RFL, from an office or offices in England and Wales as:
    - (i)    an employee of a recognised sole practitioner;
    - (ii)   a manager, employee or owner of an authorised body or of an authorised non-SRA firm; or
    - (iii)  a manager, employee or owner of a body which is a manager or owner of an authorised body or of an authorised non-SRA firm;
- (e)  an authorised body;
- (f)  a manager of an authorised body;
- (g)  a person employed in England and Wales by an authorised body or recognised sole practitioner;
- (h)  a lawyer of England and Wales; or
- (i)  an authorised non-SRA firm;

and '*practise*' and '*practising*' should be construed accordingly; save for in:

- (i)    the SIIR where 'practice' means the whole or such part of the *private practice* of a *firm* as is carried on from one or more offices in England and Wales; and
- (ii)   the *SRA Indemnity Rules* where it means a practice to the extent that:
    - (aa)   in relation to a *licensed body*, it carries on *regulated activities*; and
    - (bb)   in all other cases, it carries on *private practice* providing professional services as a sole *solicitor* or REL or as a *partnership* of a type referred to in Rule 6.1(d) to 6.1(f) and consisting of or including one or more *solicitors* and/or *RELs*, and shall include the business or practice carried on by a *recognised body* in the providing of professional services such as are provided by individuals practising in *private practice* as *solicitors* and/or *RELs* or by such individuals in *partnership* with *RFLs*, whether such *practice* is carried on by the *recognised body* alone or in *partnership* with one or more *solicitors*, *RELs* and/or other *recognised bodies*.

*practice from an office* includes practice carried on:

- (a)  from an office at which you are based; or
- (b)  from an office of a *firm* in which you are the *sole practitioner*, or a *manager*, or in which you have an ownership interest, even if you are not based there,

save that for the purposes of Part G (Overseas practice) of the *SRA Accounts Rules* the term practice is to be given its natural meaning;

and '*practising from an office*' should be construed accordingly.

199

*practice of a lawyer of a CCBE state* means the activities of a *lawyer* of a *CCBE state* in that capacity.

*Practice Skills Standards* means the standards published by *us* which set out the practice skills *trainees* will develop during the *training contract* and use when qualified.

*practising address* means, in relation to an *authorised body*, an address from which the body provides services consisting of or including the carrying on of activities which it is authorised to carry on.

*preceding qualifying insurance* means, in the case of any *firm* or *person* who makes an *expired run-off claim*, the policy of *qualifying insurance* which previously provided run-off cover in respect of that *firm* or *person*, or which was required to provide such cover, or (in the case of a *firm in default* or a *run-off firm*) arrangements to provide such run-off cover through the ARP.

*pre-contract deposit* means the aggregate of all payments which constitute pre-contract deposits from a *buyer* in relation to the proposed sale of a *property*.

*prescribed* means prescribed by the SRA from time to time.

*previous practice* means any *practice* which shall have ceased to exist as such (for whatever reason, including by reason of (a) any death, retirement or addition of *principals* or (b) any split or cession of the whole or part of its practice to another without any change of *principals*).

*principal*
    (1)  subject to paragraph (2) means:

        (a)  a sole practitioner;
        (b)  a partner in a partnership;
        (c)  in the case of a recognised body which is an LLP or company, the recognised body itself;
        (d)  in the case of a licensed body which is an LLP or company, the licensed body itself; or
        (e)  the principal solicitor or REL (or any one of them) employed by a non-solicitor employer (for example, in a law centre or in commerce and industry).

    (2)  means:

        (a)  in the SRA Authorisation Rules, SRA Practice Framework Rules, SRA Practising Regulations and SRA Recognised Bodies Regulations 2011, a sole practitioner or a partner in a partnership;
        (b)  in the SIIR:

            (i)  where the *firm* is or was:
                (aa) a *sole practitioner* – that practitioner;
                (bb) a *partnership* – each *partner*;
                (cc) a *company* with a share capital – each *director* of that *company* and any *person* who:
                    (A)  is held out as a *director*; or
                    (B)  beneficially *owns* the whole or any part of a share in the *company*; or
                    (C)  is the ultimate beneficial *owner* of the whole or any part of a share in the *company*;
                (dd) a *company* without a share capital – each *director* of that *company* and any *person* who:

(A)  is held out as a *director*; or

(B)  is a *member* of the *company*; or

(C)  is the ultimate *owner* of the whole or any part of a *body corporate* or other legal person which is a *member* of the *company*;

(ee) an LLP – each *member* of that LLP, and any *person* who is the ultimate *owner* of the whole or any part of a *body corporate* or other legal person which is *member* of the LLP;

(ii)  where a *body corporate* or other legal person is a *partner* in the *firm*, any *person* who is within paragraph (i)(cc) of this definition (including sub-paragraphs (A) and (C) thereof), paragraph (i)(dd) of this definition (including sub-paragraphs (A) and (C) thereof), or paragraph (i)(ee) of this definition;

(c)  in the MTC:

(i)  where the *insured firm* is or was:

(aa)  a *sole practitioner* – that practitioner;

(bb)  a *partnership* – each *partner*;

(cc)  a *company* with a share capital – each *director* of that *company* and any *person* who:

(A)  is held out as a *director*; or

(B)  beneficially *owns* the whole or any part of a share in the *company*; or

(C)  is the ultimate beneficial *owner* of the whole or any part of a share in the *company*;

(dd)  a *company* without a share capital – each *director* of that *company* and any *person* who:

(A)  is held out as a *director*; or

(B)  is a *member* of the *company*; or

(C)  is the ultimate *owner* of the whole or any part of a *body corporate* or other legal person which is a *member* of the *company*;

(ee)  an LLP – each *member* of that LLP, and any *person* who is the ultimate *owner* of the whole or any part of a body corporate or other legal person which is *member* of the LLP;

(ii)  where a body corporate or other legal person is a *partner* in the *insured firm*, any *person* who is within paragraph (i)(cc) of this definition (including sub-paragraphs (A) and (C) thereof), paragraph (i)(dd) of this definition (including sub-paragraphs (A) and (C) thereof), or paragraph (i)(ee) of this definition;

(d)  in the SRA Indemnity Rules:

(i)  a *solicitor* who is a *partner* or a sole solicitor within the meaning of section 87 of the SA, or an REL who is a *partner*, a *recognised body* or who on or before [31 March 2012] was a sole practitioner, or an RFL or *non-registered European lawyer* who is a *partner*, and includes any *solicitor*, REL, RFL or *non-registered European lawyer* held out as a principal; and

(ii)  additionally in relation to a *practice* carried on by a *recognised body* or a *licensed body* alone, or a *practice* in which a *recognised body* or a *licensed body* is or is held out to be a *partner*:

(aa)  a *solicitor*, REL, RFL or *non-registered European lawyer* (and in the case of a *licensed body* any other person) who:

(A) beneficially owns the whole or any part of a share in such *recognised body* or *licensed body* (in each case, where it is a *company* with a share capital); or

(B) is a *member* of such *recognised body* or *licensed body* (in each case, where it is a *company* without a share capital or a LLP or a *partnership* with legal personality); or

(bb) a *solicitor*, REL, RFL or *non-registered European lawyer* (and in the case of a *licensed body* any other person) who is:

(A) the ultimate beneficial owner of the whole or any part of a share in such *recognised body* or *licensed body* (in each case, where the *recognised body* or *licensed body* is a *company* with a share capital); or

(B) the ultimate owner of a member or any part of a member of such *recognised body* or *licensed body* (in each case, where the *recognised body* or *licensed body* is a *company* without a share capital or a LLP or a *partnership* with legal personality).

*Principles* means the *Principles* in the SRA Handbook.

*prior practice* means each *practice* to which the *insured firm's practice* is ultimately a *successor practice* by way of one or more mergers, acquisitions, absorptions or other transitions, but does not include any such *practice* which has elected to be insured under run-off cover in accordance with clause 5.3(a) of the MTC.

*private legal practice* means the provision of services in *private practice* as a *solicitor* or REL including, without limitation:

(a) providing such services in England, Wales or anywhere in the world, whether alone or with other *lawyers* in a *partnership* permitted to practise in England and Wales by the *SRA Practice Framework Rules*; and

(b) the provision of such services as a secondee of the *insured firm*; and

(c) any *insured* acting as a personal representative, *trustee*, attorney, notary, insolvency practitioner or in any other role in conjunction with a *practice*; and

(d) the provision of such services by any *employee*; and

(e) the provision of such services pro bono publico;

but does not include:

(a) practising as an *employee* of an employer other than a *solicitor*, an REL, a *partnership* permitted to practise in England and Wales by the *SRA Practice Framework Rules*, a *recognised body* or a *licensed body* (in respect of its *regulated activities*); or

(b) discharging the functions of any of the following offices or appointments:

(i) judicial office;

(ii) Under Sheriffs;

(iii) members and clerks of such tribunals, committees, panels and boards as the *Council* may from time to time designate but including those subject to the Tribunals and Inquiries Act 1992, the Competition Commission, Legal Services Commission Review Panels and Parole Boards;

(iv) Justices' Clerks; or

(v) Superintendent Registrars and Deputy Superintendent Registrars of Births, Marriages and Deaths and Registrars of Local Crematoria.

*private loan* means a loan other than one provided by an institution which provides loans on standard terms in the normal course of its activities.

*private practice*

(1)  for the purposes of the SIIR:

    (a)    means in relation to a *firm* which is a *licensed body* its *regulated activities*; and

    (b)    subject to paragraph (a) of this definition, in relation to all *firms*, includes without limitation all the professional services provided by the *firm* including acting as a personal representative, trustee, attorney, notary, insolvency practitioner or in any other role in conjunction with a *practice*, and includes services provided pro bono publico, but does not include:

        (i)    *practice* carried on by a *solicitor* or REL in the course of employment with an employer other than a *firm*; or

        (ii)    *practice* carried on through a *non-SRA firm*; or

        (iii)    discharging the functions of any of the following offices or appointments:

            (aa) judicial office;

            (bb) Under Sheriffs;

            (cc) members and clerks of such tribunals, committees, panels and boards as the *Council* may from time to time designate but including those subject to the Tribunals and Inquiries Act 1992, the Competition Commission, Legal Services Commission Review Panels and Parole Boards;

            (dd) Justices' Clerks;

            (ee) Superintendent Registrars and Deputy Superintendent Registrars of Births, Marriages and Deaths and Registrars of Local Crematoria;

            (ff) such other offices as the *Council* may from time to time designate; or

        (iv)    *practice* consisting only of providing professional services without remuneration for friends, relatives, or to companies wholly owned by the *solicitor* or REL's family, or registered charities.

(2)  for the purposes of the *SRA Indemnity Rules* 'private practice' shall be deemed to include:

    (a)    the acceptance and performance of obligations as trustees;

    (b)    notarial practice where a solicitor notary operates such notarial practice in conjunction with a solicitor's practice, whether or not the notarial fees accrue to the benefit of the solicitor's practice;

but does not include:

    (c)    practice to the extent that any fees or other income accruing do not accrue to the benefit of the *practice* carrying on such practice (except as provided by paragraph (b) in this definition);

    (d)    practice by a *solicitor* or REL in the course of his or her employment with an employer other than a *solicitor*, REL, *recognised body*, *licensed body* or *partnership* such as is referred to in Rule 6.1(d) to 6.1(f); in which connection and for the avoidance of doubt:

        (i)    any such *solicitor* or REL does not carry on private practice when he or she acts in the course of his or her employment for persons other than his or her employer;

        (ii)    any such *solicitor* or REL does not carry on private practice merely because he or she uses in the course of his or her employment a style of stationery or description which appears to hold him or her out as a *principal* or *solicitor* or *foreign lawyer* in private practice;

  (iii) any practice carried on by such a *solicitor* outside the course of his or her employment will constitute private practice;

 (e) discharging the functions of the following offices:

  (i) judicial office;

  (ii) Under Sheriffs;

  (iii) members and clerks of such tribunals, committees, panels and boards as the *Council* may from time to time designate but including those subject to the Tribunals and Inquiries Act 1992, the Competition Commission, Legal Services Commission Review Panels and Parole Boards;

  (iv) Justices' Clerks;

  (v) Superintendent Registrars and Deputy Superintendent Registrars of Births, Marriages and Deaths and Registrars of Local Crematoria;

  (vi) such other offices as the *Council* may from time to time designate.

*professional activity* means a professional activity which is regulated by the SRA.

*professional contact* means professional contact which is regulated by the SRA.

*professional disbursement* means, in respect of those activities for which the practice is regulated by the SRA, the fees of counsel or other *lawyer*, or of a professional or other agent or expert instructed by *you*, including the fees of interpreters, translators, process servers, surveyors and estate agents but not travel agents' charges.

*professional principles* are as set out in section 1(3) of the LSA:

 (a) that authorised persons should act with independence and integrity;

 (b) that authorised persons should maintain proper standards of work;

 (c) that authorised persons should act in the best interests of their *clients*;

 (d) that persons who exercise before any *court* a right of audience, or conduct litigation in relation to proceedings in any *court*, by virtue of being authorised persons should comply with their duty to the *court* to act with independence in the interests of justice; and

 (e) that the affairs of *clients* should be kept confidential, and in this definition 'authorised persons' has the meaning set out in section 18 of the LSA.

*professional services* means services provided by a *firm* in the course of its *practice* and which do not constitute carrying on a *regulated activity*.

*prohibited separate business activities* means, for the purpose of Chapter 12 of the *SRA Code of Conduct*:

 (a) the conduct of any matter which could come before a *court*, whether or not proceedings are started;

 (b) advocacy before a *court*;

 (c) instructing counsel in any part of the UK;

 (d) *immigration work*;

 (e) any activity in relation to conveyancing, applications for probate or letters of administration, or drawing *trust* deeds or *court* documents, which is reserved to *solicitors* and others under the LSA;

(f)  drafting wills;

(g)  acting as nominee, *trustee* or executor in England and Wales, where such activity is not provided as a subsidiary but necessary part of a *separate business* providing financial services; and

(h)  providing legal advice or drafting legal documents not included in (a) to (g) above where such activity is not provided as a subsidiary but necessary part of some other service which is one of the main services of the *separate business*.

*property* includes an interest in property.

*property selling* means things done by any person in the course of a business (including a business in which they are *employed*) pursuant to instructions received from another person (in this definition referred to as the '*client*') who wishes to dispose of or acquire an interest in land:

(a)  for the purpose of, or with a view to, effecting the introduction to the *client* of a third person who wishes to acquire or, as the case may be, dispose of such an interest; and

(b)  after such an introduction has been effected in the course of that business, for the purpose of securing the disposal or, as the case may be, the acquisition of that interest.

PSC means the Professional Skills Course, namely, a course normally completed during the *training contract*, building upon the LPC, providing training in Financial and Business Skills, Advocacy and Communication Skills, and Client Care and Professional Standards. *Satisfactory completion* of the PSC is recognised by *us* as satisfying, in part, the *vocational stage of training*.

*PSC provider* means an organisation authorised by *us* to provide the PSC under the *SRA Training Regulations* Part 2 – Training Provider Regulations.

*PSC standards* means the standards which set out the content of, and level of achievement required from individuals studying, the PSC.

*publicity* includes all promotional material and activity, including the name or description of your *firm*, stationery, advertisements, brochures, websites, directory entries, media appearances, promotional press releases, and direct approaches to potential *clients* and other persons, whether conducted in person, in writing, or in electronic form, but does not include press releases prepared on behalf of a *client*.

*pure protection contract* means:

(a)  a long-term insurance contract:

(i)  under which the benefits are payable only in respect of death or of incapacity due to injury, sickness or infirmity;

(ii)  which has no surrender value or the consideration consists of a single premium and the surrender value does not exceed that premium; and

(iii)  which makes no provision for its conversion or extension in a manner which would result in its ceasing to comply with (a) or (b); or

(b)  a *reinsurance contract* covering all or part of a risk to which a person is exposed under a *long-term insurance contract*.

QLD means a qualifying law degree, namely, a degree or qualification awarded by a body approved by the JASB for the purposes of completing the *academic stage of training*, following a course of study which includes:

(a)  the study of the foundations of legal knowledge; and

(b)  the passing of appropriate assessments set in those foundations.

QLTR means the Qualified Lawyers Transfer Regulations 1990 and 2009.

*QLTR certificate of eligibility* means a certificate issued under the QLTR.

QLTSR means the SRA Qualified Lawyers Transfer Scheme Regulations 2010 and 2011.

QLTT means the Qualified Lawyers Transfer Test, namely, the test which some lawyers are required to pass under the QLTR.

*QLTS assessments* means the suite of assessments approved by *us* and provided by the *assessment organisation*.

*QLTS certificate of eligibility* means a certificate of eligibility to take the *QLTS assessments* under the QLTSR, or an authorisation under the QLTSR to apply for admission as a *solicitor* without taking any of the *QLTS assessments*.

*qualified lawyer*
> (a)   a lawyer whose qualification *we* have determined:
>> (i)   gives the lawyer rights of audience;
>> (ii)  makes the lawyer an officer of the court in the *recognised jurisdiction*; and
>> (iii) has been awarded as a result of a generalist (non-specialist) legal education and training; or
>
> (b)   any other lawyer to whom *we* determine Directive 2005/36 applies.

*qualified to supervise* means a person complying with the requirements of Rule 12.2 of the *SRA Practice Framework Rules*.

*qualifying employment* in the *SRA Training Regulations* Part 1 – Qualification Regulations means employment to do legal duties under the supervision of a *solicitor*.

*qualifying insurance* means a single *policy* which includes the MTC, or more than one *policy* which, taken together, include the MTC, and each of which includes the MTC except only in relation to the *sum insured* (as defined in the MTC).

*qualifying insurer* means an *authorised insurer* which has entered into a *qualified insurer's agreement* with the *Society* which remains in force for the purposes of underwriting new business at the date on which the relevant contract of *qualifying insurance* is made.

*qualifying insurer's agreement* means an agreement in such terms as the *Society* may prescribe setting out the terms and conditions on which a *qualifying insurer* may provide professional indemnity insurance to *solicitors* and others in *private practice* in England and Wales.

*recognised body* means a body recognised by the SRA under section 9 of the AJA.

*recognised jurisdiction* means a jurisdiction where we have determined that:
> (a)   to become a *qualified lawyer* applicants have completed specific education and training at a level that is at least equivalent to that of an English/Welsh H – Level (e.g. Bachelor's) degree;
> (b)   members of the *qualified lawyer's* profession are bound by an ethical code that requires them to act without conflicts of interest and to respect their *client's* interests and confidentiality;
> (c)   members of the *qualified lawyer's* profession are subject to disciplinary sanctions for breach of their ethical code, including the removal of the right to practise.

*recognised sole practitioner* means a *solicitor* or REL authorised by the SRA under section 1B of the SA to practise as a *sole practitioner*; or in the *SRA Indemnity Insurance Rules*, with effect on and from 31 March 2012, means a sole *solicitor* or REL which is a 'legal services body' pursuant to section 9(A)(1) of the AJA.

*reconciled accounts* means that all elements of the accounting records of an *intervened practitioner's practice* are consistent with each other.

*reconciled list* means a list of beneficial entitlements to *statutory trust monies* created from a set of *reconciled accounts*.

*referrals* includes any situation in which another person, business or organisation introduces or refers a *client* to your business, recommends your business to a *client* or otherwise puts you and a *client* in touch with each other.

*register of European lawyers* means the register of European lawyers maintained by the SRA under regulation 15 of the European Communities (Lawyer's Practice) Regulations 2000 (SI 2000/1119).

*register of foreign lawyers* means the register of foreign lawyers maintained by the SRA under the Courts and Legal Services Act 1990.

*registered European Lawyer* means an individual registered by the SRA under regulation 17 of the European Communities (Lawyer's Practice) Regulations 2000 (SI 2000/1119).

*registered foreign lawyer* means an individual registered by the SRA under section 89 of the Courts and Legal Services Act 1990.

*regular payment* has the meaning given in rule 19 of the *SRA Accounts Rules*.

*Regulated Activities Order* means the Financial Services and Markets Act 2000 (Regulated Activities) Order 2001.

*regulated activity* means:
    (a)  subject to sub-paragraph (b) below:
          (i)    any reserved legal activity;
          (ii)   any other legal activity; and
          (iii)  any other activity in respect of which a licensed body is regulated pursuant to Part 5 of the LSA; and

    (b)  in the SRA Financial Services (Scope) Rules, an activity which is specified in the Regulated Activities Order.

*regulated collective investment scheme* means:
    (a)  an investment *company* with variable capital;
    (b)  an authorised unit trust scheme as defined in section 237(3) of FSMA; or
    (c)  a scheme recognised under sections 264, 270 or 272 of FSMA.

*regulated home purchase plan* has the meaning given by article 63F(3) of the Regulated Activities Order.

*regulated home reversion plan* has the meaning given by article 63B(3) of the Regulated Activities Order.

*regulated mortgage contract* has the meaning given by article 61(3) of the Regulated Activities Order.

*regulated person*
    (1)  in the *SRA Indemnity Rules* has the meaning given in section 21 of the LSA.
    (2)  means, in the *SRA Disciplinary Procedure Rules*:
          (a)    a solicitor;
          (b)    an REL;

       (c)    an RFL;

       (d)    a recognised body;

       (e)    a manager of a recognised body;

       (f)    a licensed body;

       (g)    a manager of a licensed body;

       (h)    an employee of a recognised body, a licensed body, a solicitor, or an REL; or

       (i)    to the extent permitted by law, any person who has previously held a position or role described in (a) to (h) above.

(3)   for the purposes of the *SRA Cost of Investigations Regulations* means the persons at paragraph (2) (a) to (i) above and also includes a person who has an interest in a *licensed body* and, to the extent permitted by law, any person who has previously held an interest in a *licensed body*.

*regulated sale and rent back agreement* has the meaning given by article 63J(3) of the Regulated Activities Order.

*regulatory arrangements* has the meaning given to it by section 21 of the LSA, and includes all rules and regulations of the SRA in relation to the authorisation, practice, conduct, discipline and qualification of persons carrying on legal activities and the accounts rules and indemnification and compensation arrangements in relation to their practice.

*regulatory objectives* has the meaning given to it by section 1 of the LSA and includes the objectives of protecting and promoting the public interest, supporting the constitutional principle of the rule of law, improving access to justice, protecting and promoting the interests of consumers, promoting competition in the provision of legal activities by authorised persons, encouraging an independent, strong, diverse and effective legal profession, increasing public understanding of the citizen's legal rights and duties, and promoting and maintaining adherence to the professional principles; and for the purpose of this definition, 'authorised person' has the meaning given in section 1(4) and 18 of the LSA.

*reinsurance contract* means a contract of insurance covering all or part of a risk to which a person is exposed under a contract of insurance.

REL means registered European lawyer, namely, an individual registered with the SRA under regulation 17 of the European Communities (Lawyer's Practice) Regulations 2000 (SI 2000 no. 1119).

*REL-controlled body* means an authorised body in which RELs, or RELs together with lawyers of England and Wales and/or European lawyers registered with the BSB, constitute the national group of lawyers with the largest (or equal largest) share of control of the body, either as individual managers or by their share in the control of bodies which are managers, and for this purpose RELs and European lawyers registered with the BSB belong to the national group of England and Wales.

*related body* in relation to in-house practice means a body standing in relation to your employer as specified in Rule 4.7(a) to (d) or 4.15(c) of the SRA Practice Framework Rules.

*relevant claim* means a claim made on or after 1 September 2000 against a relevant successor practice.

*relevant indemnity period* in relation to contributions or indemnity means that indemnity period in respect of which such contributions are payable or such indemnity is to be provided in accordance with the SRA Indemnity Rules.

a *relevant insolvency event*

occurs in relation to a body if:

(a) a resolution for a voluntary winding-up of the body is passed without a declaration of solvency under section 89 of the Insolvency Act 1986;

(b) the body enters administration within the meaning of paragraph 1(2)(b) of Schedule B1 to that Act;

(c) an administrative receiver within the meaning of section 251 of that Act is appointed;

(d) a meeting of creditors is held in relation to the body under section 95 of that Act (creditors' meeting which has the effect of converting a *members'* voluntary winding up into a creditors' voluntary winding up);

(e) an order for the winding up of the body is made;

(f) all of the *managers* in a body which is unincorporated have been adjudicated bankrupt; or

(g) the body is an *overseas* company or a *societas Europaea* registered outside England, Wales, Scotland and Northern Ireland and the body is subject to an event in its country of incorporation analogous to an event as set out in paragraphs (a) to (f) above.

*relevant recognised body* means a recognised body other than:

(a) an unlimited company, or an overseas company whose members' liability for the *company's* debts is not limited by its constitution or by the law of its country of incorporation; or

(b) a nominee company only, holding *assets* for *clients* of another *practice*; and

      (i) it can act only as agent for the other *practice*; and

      (ii) all the individuals who are *principals* of the *recognised body* are also *principals* of the other *practice*; and

      (iii) any fee or other income arising out of the *recognised body* accrues to the benefit of the other *practice*; or

(c) a *partnership* in which none of the *partners* is a limited company, a LLP or a legal person whose *members* have limited liability.

*relevant successor practice* means in respect of a *previous practice*, a *successor practice* or a 'successor practice' (as defined in Appendix 1 to the SIIR) (as may be applicable) against which a *relevant claim* is made.

*representative* in the *SRA Compensation Fund Rules*, means the personal representative of a deceased *defaulting practitioner*; the *trustee* of a bankrupt *defaulting practitioner*; the administrator of an insolvent *defaulting practitioner*, or other duly appointed representative of a *defaulting practitioner*.

*reserved legal activity* has the meaning given in section 12 of the LSA, and includes the exercise of a right of audience, the conduct of litigation, reserved instrument activities, probate activities, notarial activities and the administration of oaths, as defined in Schedule 2 to the LSA.

*reserved work* means activities which *persons* are authorised by the SRA to carry out, or prohibited from carrying out, under the *SRA Practice Framework Rules*.

*reversion seller* has the meaning given by article 63B(3) of the *Regulated Activities Order*.

*revocation* in relation to a practising certificate or registration under the *SRA Practising Regulations*, includes withdrawal of a practising certificate or registration for the purposes of the SA and cancellation of registration for the purposes of Schedule 14 to the Courts and Legal Services Act 1990.

RFL means registered foreign lawyer, namely, an individual registered with the SRA under section 89 of the Courts and Legal Services Act 1990.

*run-off firm* means a *firm* or former *firm* which has ceased to practise in circumstances where, in accordance with paragraph 5.1 of the MTC, run-off cover is not required to be provided by any *qualifying insurer*.

SA means *the Solicitors Act 1974*.

*satisfactory completion*

of a course or courses means:

(a) passing all the examinations and assessments required; and/or

(b) where appropriate having part or parts awarded through condonation, deemed pass, or exemption;

in order to graduate from or pass an assessable course of study, and being awarded a certificate from the course provider confirming this; and '*satisfactorily completed*' should be construed accordingly.

*seats* means an arrangement where a *trainee* works in different departments of, or in different roles within, a *training establishment* in order to gain exposure to different areas of law.

*secondment* means an arrangement between a *training establishment* and another employer for a part of the period of a *training contract*.

*section 43 investigation* means an investigation by the SRA as to whether there are grounds for the SRA:

(a) to make an order under section 43(2) of the SA; or

(b) to make an application to *the Tribunal* for it to make such an order.

*security* has the meaning given by article 3(1) of the *Regulated Activities Order* but does not include an *investment* which falls within the definition of a *packaged product*.

*separate business* means a business which is not an *authorised body*, a *recognised sole practitioner*, an *authorised non-SRA firm* or an *in-house practice* and includes businesses situated *overseas*.

*separate designated client account* has the meaning given in rule 13(5)(a) of the *SRA Accounts Rules*.

*separate practice* means:

(a) a *practice* in which the number and identity of the *principals* is not the same as the number and identity of the *principals* in any other *practice*. When the same *principals* in number and identity carry on practice under more than one name or style, there is only one *practice*;

(b) in the case of a *practice* of which more than 25% of the *principals* are *foreign lawyers*, any *overseas* offices shall be deemed to form a separate practice from the offices in England and Wales;

(c) in the case of an *overseas* office of a *practice*, the fact that a *principal* or a limited number of *principals* represent all the *principals* in the *practice* on a local basis shall not of itself cause that *overseas* office to be a separate practice provided that any fee or other income arising out of that office accrues to the benefit of the *practice*; and

(d) in the case of a *recognised body* or *licensed body* the fact that all of the shares in the *recognised body* or *licensed body* (as the case may be) are beneficially owned by only some of the *principals* in another *practice*, shall not, of itself, cause such a *recognised body* or *licensed body* (as the case may be) to be a separate practice provided that any fee or other income arising out of the *recognised body* or *licensed body* accrues to the benefit of that other *practice*.

*shareowner* means:
    (a)  a *member* of a *company* with a share capital, who owns a share in the body; or
    (b)  a *person* who is not a *member* of a *company* with a share capital, but owns a share in the body, which is held by a *member* as nominee.

SIIR means the Solicitors' Indemnity Insurance Rules 2000 to 2010 or the *SRA Indemnity Insurance Rules* or any rules subsequent thereto.

*societas Europaea* means a European public limited liability *company* within the meaning of article 1 of Council Regulation 2157/2001/EC.

*Society* means the Law Society, in accordance with section 87 of the SA.

*sole practitioner* means a *solicitor* or an REL *practising* as a sole *principal* and does not include a *solicitor* or an REL *practising* in-house save for the purposes of the *SRA Accounts Rules* where references to 'practising' are to be given their natural meaning.

*solicitor* means a person who has been admitted as a solicitor of the Senior Courts of England and Wales and whose name is on the roll kept by the *Society* under section 6 of the SA, save that in the SIIR includes a person who practises as a solicitor whether or not he or she has in force a practising certificate and also includes practice under home title of a former REL who has become a solicitor.

*special measures* means such measures as the *Council* may from time to time require with a view to reducing the risk of claims being made against a *firm* in the future or with a view to enabling a *firm* in the future to obtain *qualifying insurance* outside the ARP including, without limitation, requiring a *firm* to establish, agree with the SRA and implement either:
    (a)  a rehabilitation plan; or
    (b)  a plan for the orderly closure of the *firm* in a manner which fully protects its *clients'* interests,

in either case on such terms, in such format and with such content as the SRA may require.

SRA means the Solicitors Regulation Authority, and reference to the SRA as an *approved regulator* or *licensing authority* means the SRA carrying out regulatory functions assigned to the *Society* as an *approved regulator* or *licensing authority*.

*SRA Accounts Rules* means the SRA Accounts Rules 2011.

*SRA Admission Regulations* means the SRA Admission Regulations 2011.

*SRA Authorisation Rules* means the SRA Authorisation Rules for Legal Services Bodies and Licensable Bodies 2011.

*SRA Code of Conduct* means the SRA Code of Conduct 2011.

*SRA Compensation Fund Rules* means the SRA Compensation Fund Rules 2011.

*SRA Cost of Investigations Regulations* means the SRA Cost of Investigations Regulations 2011.

*SRA Disciplinary Procedure Rules* means the SRA Disciplinary Procedure Rules 2011.

*SRA European Cross-border Rules* means the SRA European Cross-border Practice Rules 2011.

*SRA Financial Services (Scope) Rules* means the SRA Financial Services (Scope) Rules 2001.

*SRA finding* means:

    (a)  for the purposes of the *SRA Disciplinary Procedure Rules*, a decision that the SRA is satisfied:

        (i)    that a *regulated person* (which for the avoidance of doubt, shall include a *solicitor*) has failed to comply with a requirement imposed by or made under the SA, AJA or the LSA;

        (ii)   in relation to a *solicitor*, that there has been professional misconduct; or

        (iii)  that a HOLP, HOFA, *manager, employee, person who has an interest in a licensed body*, or any other person has (intentionally or through neglect) caused or substantially contributed to a significant breach of the terms of the *licensed body's* licence, or has failed to comply with duties imposed by section 90, 91, 92 or 176 of the LSA as appropriate,

    and for the avoidance of doubt does not include:

    (aa)  investigatory decisions such as to require the production of information or *documents*;

    (bb)  directions as to the provision or obtaining of further information or explanation;

    (cc)  decisions to stay or adjourn;

    (dd)  authorisation of the making of an application to *the Tribunal*;

    (ee)  authorisation of an *intervention* pursuant to the SA, AJA, the Courts and Legal Services Act 1990 or Schedule 14 of the LSA;

    (ff)  a letter of advice from the SRA; and

    (b)  for the purposes of the *SRA Cost of Investigations Regulations*, a decision that the SRA is satisfied:

        (i)    that a *regulated person* has failed to comply with a requirement imposed by or made under the SA, AJA or the LSA;

        (ii)   in relation to a *solicitor*, that there has been professional misconduct.

*SRA Indemnity Insurance Rules* means the SRA Indemnity Insurance Rules 2011.

*SRA Indemnity Rules* means the SRA Indemnity Rules 2011.

*SRA Practice Framework Rules* means the SRA Practice Framework Rules 2011.

*SRA Practising Regulations* means the SRA Practising Regulations 2011.

*SRA Suitability Test* means the SRA Suitability Test 2011.

*SRA Training Regulations* means the SRA Training Regulations 2011.

*stakeholder pension scheme* means a scheme established in accordance with Part I of the Welfare and Pensions Reform Act 1999 and the Stakeholder Pension Scheme Regulations 2000.

*statement of standards* means the 'statement of standards for solicitor higher court advocates' issued by the SRA.

*statutory trust* means the trust created by Schedule 1 of the SA, or Schedule 14 of the LSA, over monies vesting in the *Society* following an *intervention*.

*statutory trust account* means an account in which *statutory trust monies* are held by the *Society*.

*statutory trust monies* means the monies vested in the *Society* under the *statutory trust*.

*statutory undertakers* means:

(a) any persons authorised by any enactment to carry on any railway, light railway, tramway, road transport, water transport, canal, inland navigation, dock, harbour, pier or lighthouse undertaking or any undertaking for the supply of hydraulic power; and

(b) any licence holder within the meaning of the Electricity Act 1989, any public gas supplier, any water or sewerage undertaker, the Environment Agency, any public telecommunications operator, the Post Office, the Civil Aviation Authority and any relevant airport operator within the meaning of Part V of the Airports Act 1986.

*student enrolment*
(1) means the process where *we* satisfy *ourselves* that a student who intends to proceed to the *vocational stage of training* has *satisfactorily completed* the *academic stage of training* and is of the appropriate *character and suitability*.

(2) *'enrolment'* should be construed accordingly, and *certificate of enrolment* should be construed as evidence of 'student enrolment'.

*subsidiary company* has the meaning given in the Companies Act 2006.

*substantial ownership interest* in a *firm* ('A') means:
(a) owning at least 10% of the shares in A;
(b) owning at least 10% of the shares in a parent undertaking of A;
(c) being entitled to exercise, or control the exercise of, at least 10% of the *voting rights* in A; or
(d) being entitled to exercise, or control the exercise of, at least 10% of the *voting rights* of a *parent undertaking* of A;

and for the purpose of this definition, 'parent undertaking' has the meaning given in the Companies Act 2006.

*substantially common interest* for the purposes of Chapter 3 of the *SRA Code of Conduct*, means a situation where there is a clear common purpose in relation to any matter or a particular aspect of it between the *clients* and a strong consensus on how it is to be achieved and the *client conflict* is peripheral to this common purpose.

*successor firm* means for the purpose of Rule 12 of the SIIR any *firm* or *firms* resulting from:
(a) a split in the *practice* of a *firm* that has at any time been in the ARP; or
(b) the merger, acquisition, absorption or any other form of takeover of a *firm* that has at any time been in the ARP;

*successor practice*
(1) means a *practice* identified in this definition as 'B', where:
(a) 'A' is the *practice* to which B succeeds; and
(b) 'A's owner' is the owner of A immediately prior to transition; and
(c) 'B's owner' is the owner of B immediately following transition; and
(d) 'transition' means merger, acquisition, absorption or other transition which results in A no longer being carried on as a discrete legal *practice*.

(2) B is a successor practice to A where:
(a) B is or was held out, expressly or by implication, by B's owner as being the successor of A or as incorporating A, whether such holding out is contained in notepaper, business cards, form of electronic communications, publications, promotional material or otherwise, or is contained in any statement or declaration by B's owner to any regulatory or taxation authority; and/or

(b)  (where A's owner was a *sole practitioner* and the transition occurred on or before 31 August 2000) – the *sole practitioner* is a *principal* of B's owner; and/or

(c)  (where A's owner was a *sole practitioner* and the transition occurred on or after 1 September 2000) – the *sole practitioner* is a *principal* or *employee* of B's owner; and/or

(d)  (where A's owner was a *recognised body*) – that body is a *principal* of B's owner; and/or

(e)  (where A's owner was a *partnership*) – the majority of the *principals* of A's owner have become *principals* of B's owner; and/or

(f)  (where A's owner was a *partnership* and the majority of *principals* of A's owner did not become *principals* of the owner of another legal practice as a result of the transition) – one or more of the *principals* of A's owner have become *principals* of B's owner and:

(i)  B is carried on under the same name as A or a name which substantially incorporates the name of A (or a substantial part of the name of A); and/or

(ii)  B is carried on from the same premises as A; and/or

(iii)  the owner of B acquired the goodwill and/or *assets* of A; and/or

(iv)  the owner of B assumed the liabilities of A; and/or

(v)  the majority of staff employed by A's owner became *employees* of B's owner.

(3)  Notwithstanding the foregoing, B is not a successor practice to A under paragraph (2) (b), (c), (d), (e) or (f) if another *practice* is or was held out by the owner of that other *practice* as the successor of A or as incorporating A, provided that there is insurance complying with these MTC in relation to that other *practice*.

*sum insured* means the aggregate limit of liability of each *insurer* under the insurance.

*supplementary run-off cover* means run-off cover provided by the Solicitors Indemnity Fund following the expiry of run-off cover provided to a *firm* in accordance with the SIIR or otherwise under a *policy* (but subject to compliance with the MTC).

*take a trainee* means the entering into a *training contract* with an individual by a *training establishment*, and *'take trainees'* and *'taking trainees'* should be construed accordingly.

*the singular* the singular includes the plural and vice versa, and references to the masculine or feminine include the neuter.

*the Tribunal* means the Solicitors Disciplinary Tribunal which is an independent statutory tribunal constituted under section 46 of the SA.

*trainee solicitor* means any person receiving workplace training with the express purpose of qualification as a *solicitor*, at an authorised *training establishment*, under a *training contract*; and *'trainee'* should be construed accordingly.

*training contract* means a written contract, complying with the *SRA Training Regulations*, between one or more *training establishments* and a *trainee solicitor*, setting out the terms and conditions of the workplace training that the *trainee solicitor* will receive.

*training contract consortium* means an arrangement between more than one employer, one of which is authorised to *take trainees*, to provide a *training contract* (referred to in the *SRA Training Regulations* Part 2 – Training Provider Regulations as a *modular training contract*).

*training contract record* means an adequate record maintained by a *trainee* recording the experience that the *trainee* is getting and the skills that the *trainee* is developing within a *training contract*.

*training establishment* means an organisation, body, *firm, company, in-house practice* or individual authorised by *us* under the *SRA Training Regulations* Part 2 – Trainer Provider Regulations to *take* and train a *trainee solicitor*.

*training principal* means any *solicitor* who:
    (a)  holds a current practising certificate;
    (b)  has held immediately prior to a current practising certificate four consecutive practising certificates;
    (c)  is nominated by a *training establishment* as such;
    (d)  is a *partner, manager, director, owner*, or has equivalent seniority and/or managerial status; and
    (e)  has undertaken such training as we may prescribe;

and for the purposes of (b) above a *solicitor* who has been an REL for a continuous period before their admission as a *solicitor* can use each complete year of registration as the equivalent of having held one practising certificate.

**Guidance note:**

A Government Legal Service *solicitor* with appropriate seniority, experience and training will be exempt from the practising certificate requirements for training principals.

*transaction* in the *SRA Financial Services (Scope) Rules* means the purchase, sale, subscription or underwriting of a particular *investment*.

*trustee* includes a personal representative (i.e. an executor or an administrator), and 'trust' includes the duties of a personal representative.

UK means United Kingdom.

*UK qualified lawyer* in the QLTSR, means solicitors and barristers qualified in Northern Ireland, solicitors and advocates qualified in Scotland and *barristers* qualified in England and Wales.

*unadmitted person* means a person who:
    (a)  holds a current *certificate of enrolment*;
    (b)  is serving under a *training contract*; or
    (c)  has completed any part or all of the *vocational stage of training*, in accordance with regulations 16 to 32 of the *SRA Training Regulations* Part 1 – Qualification Regulations but does not hold a current *certificate of enrolment*

but who has not been admitted as a *solicitor*;

*undertaking* means a statement, given orally or in writing, whether or not it includes the word 'undertake' or 'undertaking', made by or on behalf of you or your *firm*, in the course of *practice*, or by you outside the course of *practice* but as a *solicitor* or REL, to someone who reasonably places reliance on it, that you or your *firm* will do something or cause something to be done, or refrain from doing something.

*us and we* means the SRA, and *'our'* and *'ourselves'* should be construed accordingly.

*vocational stage of training* means that stage of the training of an entrant to the *solicitors'* profession which is completed by:
    (a)  satisfactory completion of an LPC, or satisfactory completion of an exempting law degree or integrated course; and

(b) subject to regulations 31, 32 and 33 of the SRA Training Regulations Part 1 – Qualification Regulations, serving under a training contract; and

(c) satisfactory completion of a PSC and such other course or courses as we may from time to time prescribe.

*Voluntary Code of Good Practice* means a code agreed by the Association of Graduate Careers Advisory Services, the Association of Graduate Recruiters, the Junior Lawyers Division and *us* to assist all concerned with the recruitment of law degree students and non-law degree students as *trainee solicitors*.

*voting rights* in relation to a body which does not have general meetings at which matters are decided by the exercise of voting rights, means the right under the constitution of the body to direct the overall policy of the body or alter the terms of its constitution.

*without delay* means, in normal circumstances, either on the day of receipt or on the next working day.

*you* means:

(a) for the purposes of the *SRA Training Regulations* Part 1 any person intending to be a *solicitor*, other than those seeking admission under the QLTSR;

(b) for the purposes of the *SRA Training Regulations* Part 3 a *solicitor* or an REL;

(c) for the purposes of the *SRA Admission Regulations* any person intending to be a *solicitor*;

(d) for the purpose of the QLTSR a person seeking admission as a *solicitor* via transfer in accordance with those regulations;

(e) for the purpose of the SRA Suitability Test any individual intending to be a *solicitor*, and any person seeking authorisation as an *authorised role holder* under the *SRA Authorisation Rules*;

(f) for the purposes of the *SRA Accounts Rules* (save for Part G (Overseas practice)):

(i) a *solicitor*; or

(ii) an REL;

in either case who is:

(aa) a sole practitioner;

(bb) a partner in a partnership which is a recognised body, licensed body, or authorised non-SRA firm or in a partnership which should be a recognised body but has not been recognised by the SRA;

(cc) an assistant, associate, professional support lawyer, consultant, locum or person otherwise employed in the practice of a recognised body, licensed body, recognised sole practitioner or authorised non-SRA firm; or of a partnership which should be a recognised body but has not been recognised by the SRA, or of a sole practitioner who should be a recognised sole practitioner but has not been authorised by the SRA; and 'employed' in this context shall be interpreted in accordance with the definition of 'employee' for the purposes of the SRA Code of Conduct;

(dd) employed as an in-house lawyer by a non-solicitor employer (for example, in a law centre or in commerce and industry);

(ee) a director of a company which is a recognised body, licensed body, authorised non-SRA firm, or of a company which is a manager of a recognised body, licensed body or authorised non-SRA firm;

(ff) a member of an LLP which is a recognised body, licensed body, authorised non-SRA firm, or of an LLP which is a manager of a recognised body, licensed body or authorised non-SRA firm; or

(gg) a partner in a partnership with separate legal personality which is a manager of a recognised body, licensed body or authorised non-SRA firm;

(iii) an RFL practising:

(aa) as a *partner* in a *partnership* which is a *recognised body*, *licensed body* or *authorised non-SRA firm*, or in a *partnership* which should be a *recognised body* but has not been recognised by the SRA;

(bb) as the *director* of a *company* which is a *recognised body*, *licensed body* or *authorised non-SRA firm*, or as the *director* of a *company* which is a *manager* of a *recognised body*, *licensed body* or *authorised non-SRA firm*;

(cc) as a member of an LLP which is a *recognised body*, *licensed body* or *authorised non-SRA firm*, or as a member of an LLP which is a *manager* of a *recognised body*, *licensed body* or *authorised non-SRA firm*;

(dd) as a *partner* in a *partnership* with separate legal personality which is a *manager* of a *recognised body*, *licensed body* or *authorised non-SRA firm*;

(ee) as an employee of a *recognised body*, *licensed body* or *recognised sole practitioner*; or

(ff) as an employee of a *partnership* which should be a *recognised body* but has not been authorised by the SRA, or of a *sole practitioner* who should be a *recognised sole practitioner* but has not been authorised by the SRA;

(iv) a recognised body;

(v) a licensed body;

(vi) a manager or employee of a recognised body or licensed body, or of a partnership which should be a recognised body but has not been authorised by the SRA; or

(vii) an employee of a recognised sole practitioner, or of a sole practitioner who should be a recognised sole practitioner but has not been authorised by the SRA; and

(g) for the purposes of the SRA Higher Rights of Audience Regulations means a solicitor or an REL;

and references to '*your*' and '*yourself*' should be construed accordingly.

# SRA: Outcomes-focused regulation at a glance

**Your quick guide to getting started with OFR and the new Handbook**

### 1. ABOUT THIS GUIDE

We have designed this guide to help you get used to the SRA's new approach to regulation, outcomes-focused regulation or 'OFR' and the new SRA Handbook.

In this guide we will:

- Explain OFR and how it differs from the current approach to regulation
- Show how it will work in practice, with examples of common ethical dilemmas and how these are affected by the changes
- Provide you with a quick overview of the Handbook

This guide is relevant to all individuals and firms regulated by the SRA, including solicitors practising in-house. However, some aspects are less relevant to those practising in-house, e.g. the requirements for compliance officers for legal practice and finance and administration (COLP and COFA).

This guide does not form part of the Handbook, but where we refer to specific parts of the Handbook we have provided links.

### 2. OVERVIEW OF THE NEW SRA HANDBOOK

The new SRA Handbook brings together, in one place, all of the regulatory requirements that apply to everyone we regulate – not just solicitors in traditional firms and in-house practice but also new entrants to the legal services market such as non-lawyer managers of alternative business structures ('ABSs'). This format will enable you to navigate easily between the various sections.

The new Handbook 'goes live' in time for it to apply to both traditional forms of practice and ABSs, so that clients of all types of legal practice regulated by the SRA receive the same level of protection.

The following diagram provides a snapshot of what the Handbook contains.

Snapshot of the handbook

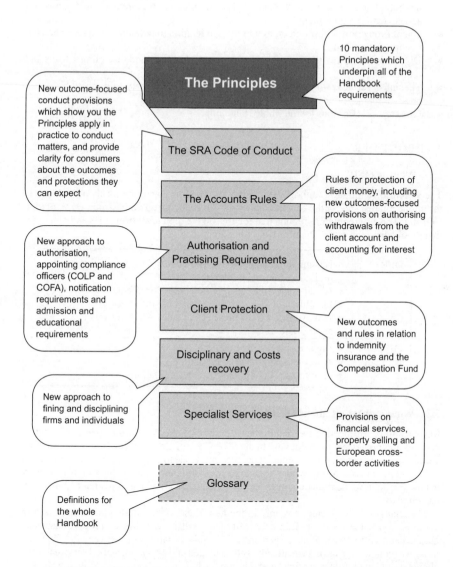

- The Principles – 10 mandatory Principles which underpin all of the Handbook requirements;
- The SRA Code of Conduct – New outcome focused conduct provisions, which show how the Principles apply in practice to conduct matters, and provide clarity for consumers about the outcomes and protections they can expect;
- The Accounts Rules – Rules for protection of client money, including new outcomes-focused provisions on authorising withdrawals from the client account and accounting for interest;

- Authorisation and Practising Requirements – New approach to authorisation, appointing compliance officers (COLP and COFA), notification requirements and admission and education requirements;
- Client Protection – New outcomes and rules in relation to indemnity insurance and the Compensation Fund;
- Disciplinary and Costs recovery – New approach to fining and disciplining firms and individuals;
- Specialist Services – Provisions on financial services, property selling and European cross-border activities;
- Glossary – Definitions for the whole Handbook.

## 3.  ABOUT OFR

### 3.1   What is OFR?

The Solicitors Regulation Authority (the 'SRA') is transforming its approach to regulation in the public interest and for the benefit of clients, by introducing outcomes-focused regulation ('OFR'). This is a regulatory regime that focuses on the high level Principles and outcomes that should drive the provision of services for clients.

| OFR is . . . | <ul><li>Designed to enable you to put clients first, where this doesn't prejudice the public interest</li><li>About achieving the right outcomes for clients</li><li>Flexible</li><li>A move away from prescriptive rules wherever this is appropriate</li></ul> |
|---|---|
| OFR isn't . . . | <ul><li>Light-touch regulation</li><li>A tick-box approach to regulation</li><li>A 'one-size-fits-all' approach to regulation</li></ul> |

### 3.2   What's different about OFR?

Responsibility for meeting the requirements in the Handbook, and for operating effective systems and processes, lies with you. In the SRA Code of Conduct (the Code) in particular, we have stripped out a lot of the detail of the previous Code to empower you to implement the right systems and controls for your clients and type of practice. You will have more flexibility in how you achieve the right outcomes for your clients, which will require greater judgement on your part.

The changes are reflected, not only in the new Handbook, but also in our approach to authorisation, supervision and enforcement. This will be risk based, proportionate and targeted and will involve a more open and constructive relationship between the SRA and those we regulate. Firms that are already well-managed and providing a good service to their clients should have nothing to fear from this approach.

### 3.3   The Principles

There are ten Principles. Most of these will be familiar to you as they are similar to the core duties contained in rule 1 of the current Code of Conduct, but there are some new ones. They now stand alone at the beginning of the Handbook and underpin all of the regulatory requirements. This is because we expect you to act in accordance with the Principles in everything you do; for example, when dealing with clients, or the SRA. Whenever you have to consider a regulatory issue, your first point of reference will always be the Principles.

## 4. OFR IN PRACTICE – A DIFFERENT WAY OF THINKING

### 4.1 The new Code of Conduct

The new Code looks very different from the current, 2007 Code. Rather than containing prescriptive rules, supported by guidance, it comprises mandatory outcomes and non-mandatory indicative behaviours.

- Outcomes – these describe what you are expected to achieve in order to comply with the Principles in specific contexts, as set out in the different chapters in the Code. The outcomes are mandatory.
- Indicative behaviours – these provide non-mandatory examples of the kind of behaviours which may establish whether you have achieved the relevant outcomes and complied with the Principles.

### 4.2 Table comparing old and new approaches

| | | |
|---|---|---|
| Client care | Rule 2 – sets out a detailed and prescriptive list of the type of information that you must give to clients. | Chapter 1 – general outcomes e.g. clients are in a position to make informed decisions about their matter. Indicative behaviours set out how you might go about this e.g. agreeing an appropriate level of service with the client. Allows greater flexibility, according to the needs of the client and the type of work you do, but there is also greater emphasis on the needs of the individual client, particularly those who are vulnerable. |
| Equality and diversity | Rule 6 reflects legal requirements. A written policy is mandatory. | Now elevated to the status of a Principle with outcomes in the Code focusing on creating a culture in which equality of opportunity and respect for diversity are encouraged. |
| Conflict of interests | Detailed rules, particularly in respect of conveyancing. | Greater emphasis on identifying and dealing with conflicts in all types of matters, and having systems and controls to enable you to do so. |
| Managing your business | Rule 5 provides detailed rules for effective management of your firm in limited areas | Now elevated to the status of a Principle with outcomes which focus on identification of risks and effective system and controls for mitigating these risks |

| Reporting requirements | Rule 20 contains reporting requirements on limited areas | New Principle on co-operating with regulators and ombudsmen. Outcomes on reporting require you to engage with the SRA in an open and constructive manner to enable the SRA to respond proportionately |
|---|---|---|

### 4.3 Q&As and case studies Issue Old approach – 2007 Code New approach – new Code

At the end of this guide you'll find some Q&As and case studies on particular issues, to help illustrate an outcomes-focused way of addressing them.

Q&As:

- client care
- complaints handling
- acting for a buyer and seller
- acting for lender and borrower
- referral arrangements
- outsourcing

Case studies:

- complaints
- conflict of interests
- Compliance Officer for Finance and Administration

### 4.4 Accounts Rules

The principal purpose of the Accounts Rules is to protect client money. To achieve this end, they have to be clear, specific and detailed.

Large parts of the existing rules have been retained in what is accepted to be a high-risk area. Nevertheless, some operational flexibility has been introduced, for example in relation to the payment of interest and signing on client account. These are areas where firms can exercise appropriate judgment without unnecessary prescription.

However, external owners of firms who are neither managers nor employees of an ABS are prohibited from signing on client account as there needs to be some element of proximity to client matters when determining appropriate client account signatories.

## 5. OFR IN PRACTICE – A DIFFERENT WAY OF OPERATING

### 5.1 Managing risk and ensuring compliance

Our approach to supervision will encourage you to identify, manage and mitigate risks to your ability to meet the requirements of the Handbook. This will allow us to concentrate on those who can't or don't manage these risks. We expect you to be straightforward in your dealings with us, forward-looking and able to identify emerging risks, for example, risks associated with changes in the legal services market and the economic climate. We may discuss with you what risks you foresee.

Your approach to dealing with risk will vary depending on the way in which you practise. If you are employed in-house you will still need to manage the risks associated with the work you undertake. This will generally form part of your employer's existing risk management arrangements.

*Effective compliance arrangements*

When considering the issues of risk and compliance, it would be helpful to think about all aspects of your firm, including:

| Your work | <ul><li>What type of work do you do?</li><li>Does this pose particular risks to meeting the Handbook requirements?</li><li>Is it subject to specific/additional regulatory requirements? (e.g. financial services, property selling.)</li></ul> |
| --- | --- |
| Your governance and culture | <ul><li>Is compliance with the Handbook a priority?</li><li>Is there effective communication throughout the firm on regulatory issues?</li><li>Is there effective oversight of regulatory matters by your managing body?</li></ul> |
| Your infrastructure | <ul><li>Do you have clear reporting lines?</li><li>How are risks identified, managed and mitigated?</li><li>How are regulatory issues identified and escalated?</li></ul> |
| Your people | <ul><li>Have you appointed a COLP and COFA, with the necessary skills and experience?</li><li>Do they understand their role, responsibilities and accountabilities?</li><li>Do they have sufficient resources and authority to do their job properly?</li><li>Do your management structure and reporting lines facilitate their roles?</li><li>Is their performance reviewed regularly by management?</li><li>Are other staff appropriately trained in compliance issues, including the role of the COLP and COFA?</li></ul> |
| Your Policies | <ul><li>Are your systems, controls and policies effective?</li><li>Do they meet all of the Handbook requirements and any relevant legal requirements?</li><li>Are they appropriate to your type of firm, client base and the type of work you do?</li><li>Are they appropriately documented, consistently applied and updated?</li><li>Are your policies clearly communicated throughout the firm?</li></ul> |

| Monitoring and reporting | • Is compliance with the firm's policies and procedures regularly monitored?<br>• Is there regular reporting to the managing body on regulatory issues and risks?<br>• Are there procedures for resolving issues identified through monitoring? |
|---|---|

*Identifying and managing risks*

The new Code requires firms to have effective systems and controls to enable them to meet the requirements of the Code. The nature of those systems and controls will vary according to the size of the firm or form of practice (e.g. in-house), its complexity, the activities that it conducts and its client base. For this reason, it is for you to decide on the form that your systems and controls take, bearing in mind:

• the application of the Handbook to your work;
• your assessment of the risks that you are running;
• your determination of the most effective means of mitigating those risks.

This is illustrated below:

Managing risks

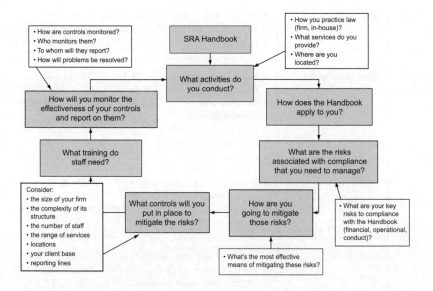

## 5.2 Thinking about your COLP and COFA

The SRA Authorisation Rules contain requirements that mean that ultimately all firms which we authorise (but not in-house legal teams) will need to appoint compliance officers for legal practice and for finance and administration (COLPs and COFAs). Risk management and proper governance is at the heart of these requirements.

Your quick guide to the key issues

|  | COLP | COFA |
|---|---|---|
| What do they do? | • Take all reasonable steps:<br>– to ensure that the authorised body complies with all terms and conditions of its authorisation (except any obligations imposed under the SRA Accounts Rules);<br>– to ensure that the authorised body complies with relevant statutory obligations (see guidance notes to rule 8 of the SRA Authorisation Rules);<br>– to record any failure to comply with authorisation or statutory obligations and make such records<br>• Record any material failure (either taken on its own or as part of a pattern of failures) to the SRA as soon as reasonably practical. | • Take all reasonable steps to ensure that the authorised body, its employees and managers, comply with any obligations imposed under the SRA Accounts Rules;<br>• Keep a record of any failure to comply and make this record available to the SRA.<br>• Report any material failure (either taken on its own or as part of a pattern of failures) to the SRA as soon as reasonably practical. |
| Who can be appointed? | A lawyer of England and Wales, a Registered European lawyer or an individual registered with the Bar Standards Board under regulation 17 of the European Communities (Lawyer's Practice) Regulations 2000; and who is<br>• a manager or employee of the authorised body;<br>• is designated as its COLP and whose designation is approved by the SRA; and<br>• is of sufficient seniority and in a position of sufficient responsibility to fulfil the role. | A manager or employee of the authorised body; and who is<br>• designated as its COFA and whose designation is approved by the SRA; and<br>• is of sufficient seniority and in a position of sufficient responsibility to fulfil the role. |
| Can the same person fulfil both roles? | Yes, providing they have the necessary skills to fulfil both roles. | Yes, providing they have the necessary skills to fulfil both roles. |

|  | COLP | COFA |
|---|---|---|
| Will the COLP and COFA have sole responsibility for compliance with the Handbook requirements? | No, definitely not. All individuals in the firm have a role to play in complying with the requirements of the Handbook. Ultimately compliance is the responsibility of the firm. The COLP and COFA have a key role in ensuring that systems and controls are in place and in reporting material issues to the SRA. See guidance note (viii) to rule 8 of the SRA Authorisation Rules and Chapter 10 of the SRA Code of Conduct | The responsibilities are the same as those of the COLP. See guidance note (ix) to rule 8 of the SRA Authorisation Rules and Chapter 10 of the SRA Code of Conduct. |
| Will the COLP and COFA have responsibility for systems and controls? | Yes, the COLP is responsible for ensuring that the firm has systems and controls in place to enable the firm to comply with the Handbook requirements on them. The type of systems etc needed is not prescribed and very much depends on what is appropriate for the type and size of the firm, its areas of risk, and the type of work and client base. See guidance note (iii) to rule 8 of the SRA Authorisation Rules. | Yes, as for the COLP, but again the type of systems and controls is not prescribed. See Guidance note (iii) to rule 8 of the SRA Authorisation Rules |

*Planning for these changes – what do you need to do?*

You will need to decide:

- who are you going to appoint?
- how will the COLP and COFA operate within your business structure?
- what systems are needed to support those roles?
- do you need to change your governance and reporting lines to empower the COLP and COFA?
- how will management review the effectiveness of the COLP and COFA?

*Timelines for appointing a COLP and COFA*

If you are an existing recognised body (including a sole practitioner, as these will become recognised bodies on 31 March 2012), and are not planning to convert to be an ABS, you will need to nominate your COLP and COFA for approval by 31 March 2012 and they will be authorised from 31 October 2012.

New recognised bodies will apply as from 28 February 2012 under the new Authorisation Rules and will need to nominate a COLP and COFA for approval as part of the authorisation process. Again, the COLP and COFA will be authorised as from 31 October 2012.

All LDPs with non-lawyer managers are ABSs and have a grace period but will need to become licensed as such by 31 October 2012 at the latest. This will be dealt with by the SRA as a passporting exercise. However such firms could elect to be passported at any time from 6 October 2011. They will need to apply for approval of their designated COLP and COFA which can be done from 10 August 2011. For firms wanting to take advantage of the grace period they will be asked to designate COLPs and COFAs by 31 March 2012.

New ABSs will have to nominate a COLP and COFA for approval as part of the authorisation process and they will take up their responsibilities at the point when the firm is authorised.

*Where will you find the key notification and information requirements in the Handbook?*

You will find the key notification and information requirements in the following places:

- SRA Authorisation Rules – rules 3, 8, 18, 23, 24 and 25;
- SRA Practice Framework Rules – rule 18;
- SRA Practising Regulations – regulations 1.2, 4.3, 4.5 and 14;
- SRA Code of Conduct – Chapter 10;
- SRA Accounts Rules – rules 23 and 32

Relevant statutory requirements include s84 of the Solicitors Act 1974 and paragraph 21 of Schedule 13 to the Legal Services Act 2007.

## 6. KEY DATES (SUBJECT TO PARLIAMENTARY APPROVAL)

Note: We will shortly be publishing on our website more information on what you need on each of these dates.

| Type of firm | Authorisation | COLP and COFA |
|---|---|---|
| If you are intending to be a new ABS . . . | 10 August 2011 – the earliest date on which you can submit an application to be a licensed body. | You must provide details of the individual(s) who will be the firm's COLP and COFA and seek approval of that designation from the SRA. |

| Type of firm | Authorisation | COLP and COFA |
|---|---|---|
| If you are an existing Legal Disciplinary Practice ('LDP') . . . | Existing LDPs with non-lawyer managers will continue to be treated as recognised bodies until 31 October 2012. However, they can choose to 'passport' to ABS status from 6 October 2011. | If you choose to 'passport', you will need to designate a COLP and COFA and seek approval of that designation from the SRA. The earliest date on which you can submit your application for your COLP and COFA to be approved is 10 August 2011. If you decide not to be passported early, then you must consider the requirements below which apply to existing recognised sole practitioners and existing recognised bodies. |
| If you are an existing recognised sole practitioner or an existing recognised body . . . | 31 March 2012 – recognised sole practitioners will be 'passported' to become recognised bodies. All recognised bodies, (including those with non-lawyer managers who have not chosen to 'passport' by this date and recognised sole practitioners), will become subject to the Authorisation Rules. 31 October 2012 -remaining LDPs with non-lawyer managers will be 'passported' to become ABSs and the first round of annual reporting commences for all firms. | All these types of firms must provide details of their prospective COLP and COFA to the SRA prior to 31 March 2012 (together with details of their managers and owners) in order that their designation can be approved. 31 October 2012 – COLPs and COFAs in existing recognised bodies must start to fulfil their obligations. |

| Type of firm | Authorisation | COLP and COFA |
|---|---|---|
| If you are intending to be a new recognised sole practitioner or recognised body . . . | 28 February 2012 – applications for authorisation as new recognised bodies (including recognised sole practitioners) will be dealt with under the SRA Authorisation Rules from this date. | SRA must be provided with details of the prospective COLP and COFA in order that their designation can be approved in readiness for 31 October 2012. |

## Q&AS – ACTING FOR A BUYER AND SELLER OF LAND

### Q1. Why are there no specific outcomes in relation to acting for buyers and sellers of land?

Whilst the 2007 Code contained provisions in relation to conveyancing, the aim of these provisions was to prevent firms from acting for buyers and sellers of land in a conflict of interests. Although there were some exceptions which enabled firms to act for a buyer and seller, these provisions were still subject to a proviso that there was no conflict of interests.

The new Code retains this approach: you cannot act for a buyer and seller of land in a conflict of interests. What is new and in keeping with OFR is that the decision as to whether or not a conflict of interests arises now rests with you.

### Q2. What is a conflict of interests?

When acting for a buyer and seller a conflict of interests arises 'where you owe separate duties to act in the best interests of two or more clients in relation to the same or related matters and those duties conflict or there is a significant risk that those duties may conflict'. (See Handbook glossary.)

The outcomes in chapter 3 of the Code support Principle 4 which requires you to act in the best interests of clients. The outcomes require you to have effective systems and controls to help you identify and assess conflicts of interests.

### Q3. How do I assess if there is a conflict of interests?

Using your systems and controls for assessing and identifying conflicts of interests you need to consider all the factors which might result in your independence or your ability to act in the best interests of the buyer and the seller being compromised. Outcome 3.3 of the Code requires you to consider such factors as: difference in the clients' interests, whether there is a need to negotiate, whether there is an imbalance in bargaining power or if any of the clients are vulnerable.

### Q4. Won't there always be a significant risk of a conflict of interests between a buyer and seller?

Acting for a buyer and seller is an area which carries a high risk of conflict of interests and we would not expect firms routinely to act for a buyer and seller. (See IB 3.14) This is because acting for a buyer and seller often involves some form of negotiation over matters of substance, and there may also be inequality of bargaining power. However there may be rare instances when it is possible to conclude that there is no conflict of interests. It will be for you to justify acting in these circumstances.

### Q5. What if I conclude there is no conflict of interests?

If you are satisfied there is no conflict of interests you should also satisfy yourself, that if you were to act, there is no other risk to the Principles. In particular your decision to act for a buyer and seller should be of benefit to both clients, rather than in your own commercial interests. You should monitor the issue of conflicts, particularly when the impact on a conveyancing chain could be considerable, should you have to pull out due to a conflict.

### Q6. Should I keep a record?

You may be asked to demonstrate compliance with the Principles and it will be easier to demonstrate compliance if you have kept a record of your decision. If you cannot demonstrate compliance we may take regulatory action.

### Q7. What other Principles and outcomes may become relevant if I am considering acting for a seller and buyer?

The other key Principles to consider are that you must:

- act with integrity (Principle 2)
- not allow your independence to be compromised (Principle 3)
- provide a proper standard of service to your clients (Principle 5)

Also, the outcomes in Chapter 4 (Confidentiality) may become relevant. For example, the buyer may want you to keep certain information confidential, but this information may also be material to the seller. In order to achieve Outcome 4.3 (which requires your duty of confidentiality to take precedence) you would have to consider ceasing to act for the seller.

### Q8. Do the above questions and answers apply to a lessor and lessee?

Yes the above responses do apply to a lessor and lessee.

### Q&AS – LENDER AND BORROWER

### Q 1. Can I act for a lender and borrower on the mortgage of land?

Yes you can act for a lender and borrower providing you can comply with the Principles in the Handbook and the Outcomes in the SRA Code of Conduct (the Code). The key Principle is Principle 4 which requires you to act in the best interests of clients. The key Outcomes which support Principle 4 are:

- 3.4 – you do not act if there is an own interest conflict;
- 3.5 – you do not act if there is a client conflict;
- 1.4 – you must have the resources, skills and procedures to carry out your clients' instructions.

There may be other Principles and outcomes which become key but this will depend on the circumstances (see Q.9).

**Q2. Why are these Principles and outcomes of particular relevance?**

The lender's instructions will often require you to undertake a number of tasks which could lead to an increased risk of a conflict of interests or require you to report on matters which fall outside your remit as a legal adviser.

**Q3. Are there any specific provisions for standard mortgages or transactions which are not at arms length?**

No there are no specific provisions for standard mortgages[1] or individual mortgages[2] The Principles and outcomes will apply to standard mortgages, individual mortgages, where the property is commercial or residential and whether or not the transaction is at arm's length. (See also Question 8)

**Q4. What is a conflict of interests?**

A conflict of interests is defined in the glossary to the Handbook and can arise in two ways:

- where you owe separate duties to act in the best interests of two or more clients in relation to the same or related matters, and those duties conflict or there is a significant risk that those duties may conflict ('client conflict'),
- where your duty to act in the best interests of any client in relation to a matter conflicts, or there is a significant risk that it may conflict, with your own interests in relation to that or a related matter ('own interest conflict').

Outcomes 3.1 and 3.3 require you to have effective systems and controls to help you identify and assess both types of conflict of interests.

**Q5. How do I assess if there is a conflict of interests?**

Using your systems and controls you will need to consider all factors which might result in your independence or your ability to act in the best interests of the lender and the borrower being compromised. Outcome 3.3 requires you to consider such factors as: differences in the clients interests, whether there is a need to negotiate, whether there is an imbalance in bargaining power or if any of the clients are vulnerable.

**Q6. Are there particular issues which I need to consider in relation to own interests conflicts?**

If the firm in which you work is an ABS, it is likely that there will be a high risk of an own interest conflict if you are considering acting for a borrower and the lender has a significant interest in the ABS.

**Q7. Are there particular issues which I need to consider in relation to conflicts between a lender and borrower?**

There is likely to be an increased risk of a conflict of interests if the mortgage is an individual mortgage of land at arm's length as the terms may be prejudicial or may involve negotiation.

---

[1] Standard mortgage definition- a mortgage which is provided in the normal course of the lender's activities which forms a significant part of the lender's activities and the mortgage is on standard terms.

[2] Individual mortgage definition-any other mortgage.

### Q8. Are there any situations where I can automatically act for a lender and borrower?

IB 3.7 provides an example of when it may be possible to act for a lender and borrower and reflects situations where the mortgage is a standard mortgage and the property is residential. However you should never automatically assume in these circumstances that there is no conflict of interests and that it is permissible to act.

### Q9. What other Principles and outcomes may become relevant to a lender and borrower?

You may find there are circumstances when a borrower discloses information to you, which you have an obligation to keep confidential.

You will need to bear in mind that you also have obligations to disclose information to the lender if it is material to them. Where these duties conflict, outcome 4.3 requires that your duty of confidentiality prevails and you may not be able to continue acting for the lender.

### Q&AS – REFERRALS

### Q1. I am thinking of entering into a referral arrangement with an estate agent. Where do I need to look in the Handbook?

Your starting point, as always, will be the Principles. You must keep these in mind both when entering into any referral arrangement and when acting for clients referred under these arrangements. The most relevant principles in relation to referral arrangements will be:

- Acting with integrity
- Acting in the best interests of your clients
- Not allowing your independence to be compromised
- Providing a proper standard of service to your clients

You should then look at chapter 9 (fee sharing and referrals) which sets out the outcomes you must achieve in relation to your fee sharing and referral arrangements. These include:

- ensuring your independence and professional judgement are not prejudiced by the arrangement,
- ensuring that your clients' interests are protected regardless of the interests of the introducer or your interest in receiving referrals,
- clients are in a position to make informed decisions about how to pursue their matter,
- clients are informed of any financial or other interest which an introducer has in referring the client to you,
- not making payments to introducers in respect of clients who are the subject of criminal proceedings or who have the benefit of public funding,
- ensuring that that all financial arrangements is in writing.

The indicative behaviours set out examples of behaviour that may indicate whether you have achieved (or not achieved) the outcomes.

You also need to bear in mind the outcomes in chapter 1, including the need to treat clients fairly and to tell the client about any arrangement that are relevant to the client's instructions.

**Q2. What information do I need to give to clients about the arrangement?**

The outcomes require that clients are in a position to make informed decisions about how to pursue their matter and that clients are informed of any financial or other interest which an introducer has in referring the client to you.

The information you give to clients will depend on the nature of the arrangement and any payments you are making to the introducer.

Simply telling the client that you have a financial arrangement may not be sufficient to enable the client to make an informed decision.

**Q3. When do I have to give this information to clients?**

The outcomes do not specify when the information should be provided. However, in order to achieve outcome 9.3, you will need to consider whether you need to give the information before the client has committed themselves to instructing your firm i.e. at the outset of the matter. The nature of the referral arrangement may affect the client's decision to instruct your firm.

**Q4. How do I decide whether a proposed arrangement meets the SRA's requirements? Can I have it approved by the SRA?**

The SRA does not approve any referral arrangements. It is up to you to satisfy yourself that the arrangements you enter into are appropriate for your firm, the type of work you do and your client base and enable you to meet all the requirements in the Handbook.

**Q5. Do I need to review my existing referral arrangements or can I assume that if they complied with the 2007 Code they will comply with the new one?**

You should always keep your referral arrangements under review to ensure that they are not causing you to breach the Principles or any other regulatory requirements. In particular you may need to think about whether:

- the arrangements continue to operate in the interests of your clients
- you continue to be confident that your independence or professional judgement is not being compromised by the arrangement
- any clients have complained about the nature of the arrangement, the conduct of the introducer, or the work you have carried out under the arrangement,
- you are satisfied that the quality of the work or the level of client care is not affected by the arrangement or the interests of the introducer

The new code does not impose any new requirements, nor does it prevent any arrangements that were permitted under the 2007 Code.

However, you do need to bear in mind that the referrals provisions now apply to referrals between lawyers, so you will have to ensure that any such arrangements are disclosed to client and, if they involve the payment of a referral fee, are put in writing. You will also need to be satisfied that they comply with the Principles and meet the outcomes.

**Q6. It's not my responsibility to ensure the introducer is behaving properly is it?**

Yes. You should not enter into, or continue with, any arrangement which prejudices the interests of the clients referred under that arrangement, for example if the introducer's publicity is misleading or if the client is being treated unfairly. If you have any reason to doubt the integrity of the introducer, or have concerns about the way clients are being treated, you should investigate further and if necessary terminate the arrangement.

## Q&AS – CLIENT CARE

### Q1. Rule 2 of the 2007 Code clearly sets out the information I need to give to clients. How will I know what to put in my client care letters under OFR?

Client care issues are dealt with in Chapter 1 of the Code. Apart from information about complaints, the outcomes in Chapter 1 do not specify the information that must be given to clients, or the form that it should take. This is because OFR requires you to focus on the Principles and achieving the right outcomes for your clients, and gives you flexibility in how you meet these outcomes. The indicative behaviours provide some examples of the information you may provide in order to meet the outcomes, but these are not mandatory and you will need to work out what is appropriate for your clients, taking into account their particular needs and circumstances.

You will also need to consider whether other rules etc. require you to give particular information to clients e.g. in relation to financial services and the interest provisions in the Accounts Rules.

The most relevant Principles in the context of client care will be:

- Providing a proper standard of service (Principle 5)
- Acting in the best interests of each client (Principle 4)

### Q2. Which outcomes do I need to achieve?

The outcomes you will need to achieve include:

- you treat clients fairly;
- clients are in a position to make informed decisions about the services they need, how their matter will be handled and the options available to them;
- clients receive the best possible information, both at the time of engagement, and when appropriate as their matter progresses, about the likely overall cost of their matter; and
- you inform clients whether and how the services you provide are regulated; and how this affects the protections available to the client.

### Q3. How will I know whether I am achieving these outcomes?

You will need to consider the needs and circumstances of your clients when deciding the best way to meet these outcomes.

The indicative behaviours include: agreeing an appropriate level of service with the client; clearly explaining your fees and if and when they are likely to change; and explaining your responsibilities and those of the client. These are not mandatory and you may develop your own ways of meeting the outcomes, which are suited to the needs of your clients and the type of work you do. Also these are not an exhaustive list: there may be other information you need to give the client. You know your clients best.

This gives you the freedom to decide what information you give to your clients to ensure they understand the basis on which they are instructing you. Factors you should consider are:

- Whether your client is used to dealing with law firms – the way you deal with a sophisticated commercial client will be very different from the way you deal with a first-time property buyer. When formulating your systems and procedures you will need to consider the firm's client base and areas of work. You may need to adopt a different approach for different types of work and different types of client.

- Whether standard letters are appropriate for all clients and all types of work – if you provide a client with so much, or such complex, information that they are unable to understand the basis on which they are instructing you, you may not have met the outcomes that clients are in a position to make an informed decision.
- Whether the client is vulnerable e.g. if the client has a learning difficulty or other disability that may affect their ability to understand the information you are providing, or if English is not the client's first language. You will also need to bear in mind your duties under the Equalities Act, in particular the need to make reasonable adjustments in relation to clients with disabilities. (Chapter 2 Equality and diversity)

Providing clear information at the outset and as the matter progresses, is of benefit not only to clients but also to your firm. Some of the most common causes of complaints are lack of clear information about costs, failure to follow instructions, delay and failure to keep clients informed. It is important to monitor complaints to your firm, as these can indicate failure to provide good client care as well as other problems within the firm.

### Q4. What evidence do I need to show that I am meeting the outcomes on client care?

Individual client files will often provide the best evidence of good client care. Well maintained files will contain copies of letters to the client, attendance notes or some other record of the information and explanations to the client and the steps you have taken to protect the client's interests. For example:

- In a case where you were concerned about the client's mental capacity the file should clearly document the steps you took to establish that the client had the necessary capacity to instruct you on the matter.
- In a case where you were concerned about the client's ability to speak and/or understand English, the file should indicate whether an independent interpreter was used.
- In a matter involving significant delays, there should be evidence that you have explained the reasons for these delays to the client.
- Where you have acted for a large multi-national company on a number of matters under a general retainer, it should be clear that the matter is being dealt with on terms previously agreed with the client.

### Q&AS – COMPLAINTS HANDLING

### Q1. We are reviewing all our firm's policies and procedures in anticipation of the introduction of OFR, including our complaints handling policy. Which aspects of the handbook are relevant?

Your starting point, as with any regulatory issue, will be the Principles. The most relevant Principles will be:

- Acting with integrity (Principle 2)
- Acting in the best interests of each client (Principle 4)
- Providing a proper standard of service to your clients (Principle 5)
- Complying with your legal and regulatory obligations and dealing with your regulators and ombudsmen in an open, timely and cooperative manner (Principle 7)

You will need to keep these Principles in mind, not only when reviewing your policy but when dealing with each complaint.

The outcomes in chapter 1 require that client complaints are dealt with promptly, fairly, openly and effectively and that clients are given information about their right to complain to the firm and the Legal Ombudsman.

The new Code does not require you to have a written complaints handling procedure. Instead the focus is on ensuring that clients know about their right to complain and that complaints are dealt with properly at firm level. However, having a written policy is a good way of showing your commitment to dealing with complaints properly, ensuring that complaints are dealt with consistently and ensuring that everyone in your staff is familiar with the way complaints should be handled.

You will also need to consider:

- the outcomes relating to client care generally. It is often possible to avoid complaints by ensuring that clients are well informed about issues such as cost, funding options and the time it will take to deal with their matter; and
- how you will monitor complaints received to identify whether they are the result of any underlying problems – for example, in relation to a particular department, staff member or procedure – and what steps you can take to address any problems you identify. This is an important part of your risk assessment process.

### Q2. Does the SRA intend to publish a standard form of complaints handling procedure that we can adopt in order to ensure that we comply with the Handbook requirements?

No. The content of your policy is a matter for you and will depend on the nature of the firm, your client base and the type of work you do. The indicative behaviours describe certain issues your policy should aim to deal with, such as allowing complaints to be made by any reasonable means, providing for decisions to be based on a sufficient investigation of the facts and providing for appropriate redress.

You can find information about the Legal Ombudsman and how it handles complaints at www.legalombudsman.org.uk. The Ombudsman has also produced a 'Guide to good complaint handling', which sets out how it expects lawyers to deal with complaints.

### Q&AS – OUTSOURCING

### Q1. Outcomes 7.9 and 7.10 in the SRA Code of Conduct contain provisions on outsourcing. What is outsourcing?

Outsourcing is not defined in the Handbook, but Outcomes 7.9 and 7.10 are aimed at firms or in-house solicitors who use a third party to undertake work that the firm or in-house solicitor would normally do themselves and for which the firm or in-house solicitor remains responsible. It is important that when firms outsource work this does not affect our ability to regulate the firm's activities and that clients remain fully protected.

### Q2. I outsource a number of activities, what sort of activities are caught by outcome 7.10?

Outcome 7.10 refers to the outsourcing of 'legal activities or any operational functions that are critical to the delivery of any legal activities'. Legal activities are defined in the glossary to the Handbook and include the provision of legal advice or assistance, or representation in connection with the application of the law or resolution of legal disputes. Outcome 7.9

prohibits the outsourcing of reserved legal activities to a person who is not authorised to conduct such activities (since to conduct unauthorised reserved legal activities is unlawful).

**Q3. Can you provide examples of activities which would be caught by outcome 7.10?**

This list is not exhaustive, but the following are examples of the type of activities which, if outsourced, would be caught by Outcome 7.10:

- activities which would normally be conducted by a paralegal
- initial drafting of contracts
- legal secretarial services – digital dictation to an outsourced secretarial service for word-processing or typing
- proofreading
- research
- document review
- Companies House filing
- due diligence, for example in connection with the purchase of a company
- IT functions which support the delivery of legal activities
- business process outsourcing

**Q4. What about when I instruct counsel – is this not caught by the outsourcing provisions in the Handbook?**

The outsourcing provisions in the Code apply when you outsource work that you could have conducted and do not apply when you use a specialist service to assist with the provision of legal services to a client, for example instructing counsel, medical experts, tax experts or accountancy services.

**Q5. Outcome 7.10(b) requires me to ensure that my contractual arrangements with a third party allow the SRA to obtain information from that third party? When does this provision take effect?**

Outcome 7.10(b), like the rest of the Code, will come into force on 10 August 2011 in respect of ABSs and 6 October 2011 for all other purposes. We would therefore expect all new outsourcing agreements to contain provisions that meet this outcome by 6 October 2011. In relation to existing outsourcing agreements, we are unlikely to take action against firms before 6 April 2012 purely on the basis that an agreement does not include specific terms to meet this outcome. However, we would expect you to have taken reasonable steps to ensure that the SRA can obtain access to relevant information if necessary, bearing in mind that Principle 7 requires you to deal with your regulator in an open, timely and co-operative manner. This could mean, for example, ensuring that the party with whom you have the agreement is aware of your professional obligations and that you keep adequate records relating to outsourced matters.

**Q6. I am thinking of entering into an outsourcing arrangement. What should I consider?**

*(i) Your clients*

- Is it in your client's interests to outsource?
- Informing clients of your arrangements and the risks attached

- Obtaining clients consent and if necessary informed consent
- Billing appropriately
- Do not rubber stamp, take ownership of the outsourced work

## (ii) Assess the risks

Outsourcing carries specific risks which you need to consider before making the decision to outsource, and manage throughout the term of the outsourcing and not simply at the outset. This diagram should assist you to identify and manage these risks.

Outsourcing

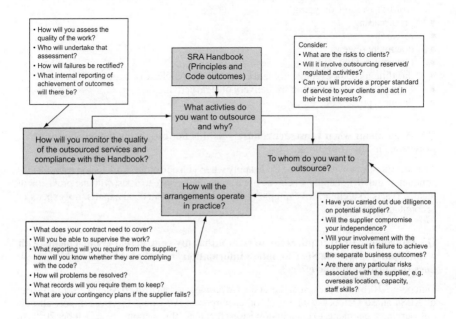

## (iii) The third party should be reputable so consider due diligence:

- investigate the background of the third party company
- review the ethical standards of those who perform the work
- obtain references of the company
- be aware of qualifications of the individuals carrying out the work
- what are their systems for conflict checking?
- what are their systems for protecting client confidentiality?
- Informing clients as to what activities are outsourced and the risks attached
- If the third party is based overseas, are there different laws or ethical standards which may be relevant?

## (iv) Your arrangements with the third party

- must not compromise your independence and integrity;
- must not breach the outcomes in chapter 12 (separate businesses) of the SRA Code of Conduct

## CASE STUDY 1 – COMPLAINTS

Your firm, which specialises in conveyancing, receives a complaint from a client concerning unexpected additional charges. The client feels that they were misled about the overall cost of the conveyance, both over the telephone and in the client care letter.

Having investigated the complaint you identify that:

- the property was leasehold and the client was quoted the cost for a freehold conveyance;
- the member of staff who provided the quote had not asked sufficient questions to understand that the transaction involved a leasehold property before giving the quote;
- it also appears that some charges are routinely being treated as disbursements when in fact they are additional fees.

### An outcomes-focused approach to looking at this issue:

Outcome 1.1 requires you to treat all your clients fairly. Where complaints have been received, an outcomes-focused approach would involve:

- treating the complainant fairly – making sure their complaint is properly investigated and that they are offered an appropriate remedy;
- treating current and former clients fairly – considering whether other clients may have been misled in the same way and proactively contacting them to rectify that situation;
- understanding the root cause of the complaint and making sure this situation does not arise again.

## CASE STUDY 2 – CONFLICT OF INTERESTS

Your firm has decided to act for two co-defendants charged with assault. To begin with, their stories are consistent. However, one of the defendants is particularly concerned about a custodial sentence in view of past convictions and changes his story to blame his co-defendant. This individual is a long-standing client of the firm. You are uncertain whether you can continue to represent both or either of them.

### An outcomes-focused approach to looking at this issue:

Key issues to bear in mind are:

- as the matter is the same, can you act in the best interests of both clients?
- if you decide that you can't, can you continue to act for either of them, bearing in mind confidentiality and the duty of disclosure of material information to clients?

These issues are to be considered in the light of the outcomes that you should be achieving:

- neither client's interests are prejudiced;
- each client's confidentiality is protected;
- you are in a position to disclose material information
- the court is not misled;
- your independence is not prejudiced by your own commercial interests.

239

**CASE STUDY 3 – COMPLIANCE OFFICER FOR FINANCE AND ADMINISTRATION**

You are the COFA for a small, three partner firm. You are an employee and not a manager of the firm. In accordance with reporting procedures that you have established, the cashier explains to you that they have been unable to pay the firm's invoices because the firm has exceeded its overdraft. Further investigation reveals that the overdraft facility has been extended on a number of occasions but the bank is now refusing to extend it further.

You approach the managing partner to discuss the matter, since you are concerned that the firm is in serious financial difficulties. The managing partner tells you that this is a temporary cash-flow problem and there is no necessity to report the matter to the SRA.

**An outcomes-focused approach to looking at this issue:**

As the COFA, you have specific reporting responsibilities. When deciding whether the matter is reportable, points to consider are:

- how prolonged is this issue?
- how severe is the problem?
- are clients' interests at risk?
- is there a risk to client money?
- can you still say that you are being open with the SRA if you keep this information to yourself?
- is the firm trying to prevent you from reporting, or is this a difference of opinion that can be resolved?

# Index